The American Pageant

Guidebook

The American Pageant

Guidebook
A Manual for Students
Volume I: To 1877
THIRTEENTH EDITION

Mel Piehl

Valparaiso University

HOUGHTON MIFFLIN COMPANY   BOSTON   NEW YORK

Sponsoring Editor: Sally Constable
Development Editor: Lisa Kalner Williams
Editorial Assistant: Arianne Vanni
Manufacturing Coordinator: Karmen Chong
Senior Marketing Manager: Sandra McGuire

Printed in the U.S.A.

ISBN: 0-618-57427-1

789 – EB – 09 08

Contents

Contents

Foreword

This revised *Guidebook* is intended to assist you in comprehending American history as presented in *The American Pageant*, Thirteenth Edition, by David M. Kennedy, Lizabeth Cohen, and Thomas A. Bailey. The *Guidebook* focuses attention on the central themes and major historical developments of each chapter while presenting a variety of exercises and other material designed to reinforce your comprehension of the text and reinforce the broad historical perspective that the *The American Pageant* aims to foster. Factual knowledge of history is important, and some of the exercises will help you to review facts and recall their significance. But the *Guidebook* attempts to demonstrate that facts are best learned when they are understood in relation to key historical events and issues.

The *Guidebook* is available in a complete edition as well as in splits by volume. All chapters of the *Guidebook* correspond with those of *The American Pageant* and are best used in close association with the text. Each chapter of the *Guidebook* contains the same sequence of material and exercises, except for the Map Discrimination section, which is omitted from some chapters.

The **Checklist of Learning Objectives** in Part I ("Reviewing the Chapter") of each *Guidebook* chapter provides a summary of the essential chapter themes and underscores the major historical developments to be learned. The **Glossary** defines basic social science terms and illustrates their usage in the text. Learning this vocabulary will not only reinforce your understanding of *The American Pageant* but also familiarize you with terms often encountered in the study of politics, economics, geography, military science, and law, as well as history.

The various exercises in Part II ("Checking Your Progress") will assist in your careful reading of the text as well as foster your comprehension and spotlight the essential facts and concepts. **True-False**, **Multiple Choice**, and **Identification** exercises stress reading for understanding of important ideas and terms. **Matching People, Places, and Events** checks your knowledge of key historical figures, locations, and events. **Putting Things in Order** (which is specifically tied to the Chronology section at the end of each chapter of *The American Pageant*) and **Matching Cause and Effect** develop two essential principles of historical understanding: chronological sequence, and the causal relation between events. **Developing Historical Skills** is designed to hone your ability to use the diverse techniques employed in the study of history, including the interpretation of charts, maps, and visual evidence. **Map Mastery** includes Map Discrimination—specific questions focused on map reading—and Map Challenge, which asks you to use maps to discuss a historical issue or problem in a brief essay.

Completion of the exercises in Part II should enable you to address successfully the crucial interpretive questions in Part III ("Applying What You Have Learned"). Your instructor may ask you to use these questions as guides to study and review, or may assign them as essay questions to be answered following your reading of the chapter. The last question is an especially challenging one that often draws on earlier chapters of *The American Pageant* and asks you to make historical comparisons, draw conclusions, or consider broad historical issues.

You and your instructor hence may utilize the *Guidebook* in a variety of ways, and to suit a variety of academic goals. It can be used for class preparation and assignments, for guidance in your reading of the text, or for independent review of course contents in preparation for comprehensive subject examinations. The answers to all the exercises may be found by your careful rereading of the pertinent sections of *The American Pageant*. May your exploration of American history be stimulating and enriching.

M. P.

CHAPTER 1

New World Beginnings, 33,000 B.C.–A.D. 1769

PART I: REVIEWING THE CHAPTER

A. CHECKLIST OF LEARNING OBJECTIVES

After mastering this chapter, you should be able to

1. describe the geological and geographical conditions that set the stage for North American history.

2. describe the origin and development of the major Indian cultures of the Americas.

3. explain the developments in Europe and Africa that led up to Columbus's voyage to America.

4. explain the changes and conflicts that occurred when the diverse worlds of Europe, Africa, and the Americas collided after 1492.

5. describe the Spanish conquest of Mexico and South America and identify the major features of Spanish colonization and expansion in North America.

B. GLOSSARY

To build your social science vocabulary, familiarize yourself with the following terms:

1. **nation-state** The form of political society that combines centralized government with a high degree of ethnic and cultural unity. ". . . the complex, large-scale, centralized Aztec and Incan nation-states that eventually emerged." (p. 8)

2. **matrilinear** The form of society in which family line, power, and wealth are passed primarily through the female side. ". . . many North American native peoples, including the Iroquois, developed matrilinear cultures. . . ." (p. 8)

3. **confederacy** An alliance or league of nations or peoples looser than a federation. "The Iroquois Confederacy developed the political and organizational skills. . . ." (p. 8)

4. **primeval** Concerning the earliest origin of things. ". . . the whispering, primeval forests. . . ." (p. 10)

5. **saga** A lengthy story or poem recounting the great deeds and adventures of a people and their heroes. ". . . their discovery was forgotten, except in Scandinavian saga and song." (p. 10)

6. **middlemen** In trading systems, those dealers who operate between the original buyers and the retail merchants who sell to consumers. "Muslim middlemen exacted a heavy toll en route." (p. 11)

7. **caravel** A small vessel with a high deck and three triangular sails. ". . . they developed the caravel, a ship that could sail more closely into the wind. . . ." (p. 11)

8. **plantation** A large-scale agricultural enterprise growing commercial crops and usually employing coerced or slave labor. "They built up their own systematic traffic in slaves to work the sugar plantations. . . ." (p. 12)

9.   **ecosystem** A naturally evolved network of relations among organisms in a stable environment. "Two ecosystems . . . commingled and clashed when Columbus waded ashore." (p. 14)

10.   **demographic** Concerning the general characteristics of a given population, including such factors as numbers, age, gender, birth and death rates, and so on. ". . . a demographic catastrophe without parallel in human history." (p. 15)

11.   **conquistador** A Spanish conqueror or adventurer in the Americas. "Spanish *conquistadores* (conquerors) fanned out across . . . American continents." (p. 16)

12.   **capitalism** An economic system characterized by private property, generally free trade, and open and accessible markets. ". . . the fuel that fed the growth of the economic system known as capitalism." (p. 17)

13.   **encomienda** The Spanish labor system in which persons were held to unpaid service under the permanent control of their masters, though not legally owned by them. ". . . the institution known as *encomienda*." (p. 17)

14.   **mestizo** A person of mixed Native American and European ancestry. "He intermarried with the surviving Indians, creating a distinctive culture of *mestizos*. . . ." (p. 21)

15.   **province** A medium-sized subunit of territory and governmental administration within a larger nation or empire. "They proclaimed the area to be the province of New Mexico. . . ." (p. 22)

PART II: CHECKING YOUR PROGRESS

A. True-False

Where the statement is true, circle **T**; where it is false, circle **F**.

1.   T   F   The geography of the North American continent was fundamentally shaped by the glaciers of the Great Ice Age.

2.   T   F   North America was first settled by people who came by boat across the waters of the Pacific Strait from Japan to Alaska.

3.   T   F   The early Indian civilizations of Mexico and Peru were built on the economic foundations of cattle and wheat growing.

4.   T   F   Most North American Indians lived in small, seminomadic agricultural and hunting communities.

5.   T   F   Many Indian cultures like the Iroquois traced descent through the female line.

6.   T   F   No Europeans had ever set foot on the American continents prior to Columbus's arrival in 1492.

7.   T   F   A primary motive for the European voyages of discovery was the desire to find a less expensive route to Asian goods and markets.

8.   T   F   The beginnings of African slavery developed in response to the Spanish conquest of the Americas.

9.   T   F   Columbus immediately recognized in 1492 that he had come across new continents previously unknown to Europeans.

10.   T   F   The greatest effect of the European intrusion on the Indians of the Americas was to increase the Indian population through intermarriage with the whites.

11. T F   Spanish gold and silver from the Americas fueled inflation and economic growth in Europe.

12. T F   The Spanish *conquistadores* had little to do with the native peoples of Mexico and refused to intermarry with them.

13. T F   The Spanish were able to defeat the Aztecs because they came from a more sophisticated, urban civilization.

14. T F   Spain expanded its empire into Florida and New Mexico partly to block French and English intrusions.

15. T F   The Spanish empire in the New World was larger, richer, and longer-lasting than that of the English.

B. Multiple Choice

Select the best answer and circle the corresponding letter.

1. The geologically oldest mountains in North America are
    a. the Appalachians.
    b. the Rockies.
    c. the Cascades.
    d. the Sierra Nevada.

2. The Indian peoples of the Americas
    a. developed no advanced forms of civilization.
    b. were divided into many diverse cultures speaking more than two thousand different languages.
    c. were all dominated by the two large empires of the Incas and the Aztecs.
    d. relied primarily on nomadic hunting for their sustenance.

3. The Iroquois Confederacy remained a strong political and military influence until
    a. the Spanish conquest of the Americas.
    b. the fur trade was wiped out in the early 1700s.
    c. King Philip's War.
    d. the American Revolution.

4. One of the important factors that first stimulated European interest in trade and discovery was
    a. the Christian crusaders who brought back a taste for the silks and spices of Asia.
    b. the Arab slave traders on the east coast of Africa.
    c. the Scandinavian sailors who had kept up continuous trade contacts with North America.
    d. the division of Spain into small kingdoms competing for wealth and power.

5. Among the most important American Indian products to spread to the Old World were
    a. animals such as buffalo and horses.
    b. technologies such as the compass and the wheel.
    c. economic systems such as plantation agriculture and livestock raising.
    d. foodstuffs such as maize, beans, and tomatoes.

6. The primary staples of Indian agriculture were
    a. potatoes, beets, and sugar cane.
    b. rice, manioc, and peanuts.
    c. maize, beans, and squash.
    d. wheat, oats, and barley.

7. The number of Indians in North America at the time Columbus arrived was approximately
    a. one million.

    b.   four million.

    c.   twenty million.

    d.   two hundred and fifty million.

8.   Before Columbus arrived, the only Europeans to have visited North America, temporarily, were

    a.   the Greeks.

    b.   the Irish.

    c.   the Norse.

    d.   the Italians.

9.   The Portuguese were the first to enter the slave trade and establish large-scale plantations using slave labor in

    a.   West Africa.

    b.   the Atlantic sugar islands.

    c.   the West Indies.

    d.   Brazil.

10. Much of the impetus for Spanish exploration and pursuit of glory in the early 1500s came from Spain's recent

    a.   successful wars with England.

    b.   national unification and expulsion of the Muslim Moors.

    c.   voyages of discovery along the coast of Africa.

    d.   conversion to Roman Catholicism.

11. A crucial political development that paved the way for the European colonization of America was

    a.   the rise of Italian city-states like Venice and Genoa.

    b.   the feudal nobles' political domination of the merchant class.

    c.   the rise of the centralized national monarchies such as that of Spain.

    d.   the political alliance between the Christian papacy and Muslim traders.

12. The primary reason for the drastic decline in the Indian population after the encounter with the Europeans was

    a.   the rise of intertribal warfare.

    b.   the Indians' lack of resistance to European diseases such as smallpox and malaria.

    c.   the sharp decline in the Indian birthrate due to the killing of many Indian males by the Europeans.

    d.   the sudden introduction of the deadly disease syphilis to the New World.

13. Cortés and his men were able to conquer the Aztec capital Tenochtitlán partly because

    a.   they had larger forces than the Aztecs.

    b.   the Aztec ruler Montezuma believed that Cortés was a god whose return had been predicted.

    c.   the Aztecs were peaceful people with no experience of war or conquest.

    d.   the city of Tenochtitlán already had been devastated by a disease epidemic.

14. The primary early colonial competitor with Spain in the Americas was

    a.   Portugal.

    b.   Italy.

    c.   France.

    d.   England.

15. The belief that the Spanish only killed, tortured, and stole in the Americas, while contributing nothing good, is called

    a.   the *encomienda.*

    b.   the mission of civilization.

    c.   the Evil Empire.

    d.   the Black Legend.

C. Identification

Supply the correct identification for each numbered description.

1. _____   Extended period when glaciers covered most of the North American continent

2. _____   Staple crop that formed the economic foundation of Indian civilizations

3. _____   Important Mississippian culture site, near present-day East St. Louis, Illinois

4. _____   First European nation to send explorers around the west coast of Africa

5. _____   Flourishing West African kingdom that had its capital and university at Timbuktu

6. _____   Mistaken term that the first European explorers gave to American lands because of the false belief that they were off the coast of Asia

7. _____   Animal introduced by Europeans that transformed the Indian way of life on the Great Plains

8. _____   Name one of the major European diseases that devastated Native American populations after 1492

9. _____   Disease originating in the Americas that was transmitted back to Europeans after 1492

10. _____   Treaty that proclaimed a Spanish title to lands in the Americas by dividing them with Portugal

11. _____   Wealthy capital of the Aztec empire

12. _____   Person of mixed European and Indian ancestry

13. _____   Indian uprising in New Mexico caused by Spanish efforts to suppress Indian religion

14. _____   Indian people of the Rio Grande Valley who were cruelly oppressed by the Spanish conquerors

15. _____   Roman Catholic religious order of friars that organized a chain of missions in California

D. Matching People, Places, and Events

Match the person, place, or event in the left column with the proper description in the right column by inserting the correct letter on the blank line.

1. ___   Ferdinand and Isabella

2. ___   Cortés and Pizarro

3. ___   Lake Bonneville

4. ___   Días and da Gama

5. ___   Columbus

6. ___   Malinche

7. ___   Montezuma

8. ___   Hiawatha

a.   Female Indian slave who served as interpreter for Cortés

b.   Legendary founder of the powerful Iroquois Confederacy

c.   Wealthy capital of the Aztec empire

d.   Financiers and beneficiaries of Columbus's voyages to the New World

e.   Portuguese navigators who sailed around the African coast

f.   Founded in 1565, the oldest continually inhabited

9. ___	Tenochtitlán		European settlement in United States territory
10. ___	St. Augustine	g.	Italian-born navigator sent by English to explore North American coast in 1498
11. ___	John Cabot		
12. ___	Junipero Serra	h.	Italian-born explorer who thought that he had arrived off the coast of Asia rather than on unknown continents

i. Powerful Aztec monarch who fell to Spanish conquerors

j. Spanish conquerors of great Indian civilizations

k. Franciscan missionary who settled California

l. Inland sea left by melting glaciers whose remnant is the Great Salt Lake

E. Putting Things in Order

Put the following events in correct order by numbering them from 1 to 5.

1. _____ The wealthy Aztec civilization falls to Cortés.

2. _____ Portuguese navigators sail down the west coast of Africa.

3. _____ The first human inhabitants cross into North America from Siberia across a temporary land bridge.

4. _____ The once-strong Iroquois Confederacy divides and collapses.

5. _____ Spanish conquerors move into the Rio Grande valley of New Mexico.

F. Matching Cause and Effect

Match the historical cause in the left column with the proper effect in the right column by writing the correct letter on the blank line.

	Cause		**Effect**
1. ___	The Great Ice Age	a.	Rapid expansion of global economic commerce and manufacturing
2. ___	Cultivation of corn (maize)		
3. ___	New sailing technology and desire for spices	b.	European voyages around Africa and across the Atlantic attempting to reach Asia
4. ___	Portugal's creation of sugar plantations on Atlantic coastal islands	c.	Establishment of Spanish settlements in Florida and New Mexico
5. ___	Columbus's first encounter with the New World	d.	Exposure of a "land bridge" between Asia and North America
6. ___	Native Americans' lack of immunity to smallpox, malaria, and yellow fever	e.	Formation of a chain of mission settlements in California
7. ___	The Spanish conquest of large quantities of New World gold and	f.	A global exchange of animals, plants, and diseases
		g.	The formation of large, sophisticated

silver

8. ___   Aztec legends of a returning god, Quetzalcoatl

9. ___   The Spanish need to protect Mexico against French and English encroachment

10. ___   Franciscan friars' desire to convert Pacific coast Indians to Catholicism

civilizations in Mexico and South America

h.   Cortés relatively easy conquest of Tenochtitlán

i.   A decline of 90 percent in the New World Indian population

j.   The rapid expansion of the African slave trade

G. Developing Historical Skills

Connecting History with Geology and Geography

Because human history takes place across the surface of the earth, both the physical science of geology and the social science of geography are important to historians. Answer the following questions about the geological and geographical setting of North American history.

1. What are the two major mountain chains that border the great mid-continental basin drained by the Mississippi River system?

2. What great geological event explains the formation of the Great Lakes, the St. Lawrence River system, the Columbia-Snake River system, and Great Salt Lake?

3. How did this same geological event isolate the human population of the Americas from that of Asia?

4. Given the original geographical origins of the Indian populations, in which direction did their earliest migrations across North America occur: from southeast to north and west, from southwest to north and east, or from northwest to south and east?

H. Map Mastery

Map Discrimination

Using the maps and charts in Chapter 1, answer the following questions:

1. *Chronological Chart*: The American Declaration of Independence occurred exactly 169 years between what other two major events in American history?

2. *The First Discoverers of America*: When the first migrants crossed the Bering Land Bridge from Siberia to North America, approximately how many miles did they have to walk before they were south of the large ice caps to either side of the only open route? a) 200 miles b) 500 miles c) 2000 miles d) 3000 miles

3. *North American Indian Peoples at the Time of First Contact with Europeans*: List five Indian tribes that lived in each of the following regions of North America: (a) Southwest (b) Great Plains (c) Northeast (d) Southeast.

4. *Trade Routes with the East*: In the early European trading routes with Asia and the East Indies, what one *common* destination could be reached by the Middle Route, the Southern route, and da Gama's ocean route? a) Constantinople b) Persia c) China

5. *Principal Early Spanish Explorations and Conquests*: Of the principal Spanish explorers— Columbus, Balboa, de León, Cortés, Pizarro, de Soto, and Coronado—which four *never* visited the territory or territorial waters of the land that eventually became part of the United States?

6. *Spain's North American Frontier, 1542–1823*: A) What were the two easternmost Spanish settlements on the northern frontier of Spanish Mexico? B) About how many years was Mission San Antonio founded before the first Spanish settlements in California? a) 10 b) 25 c) 50 d) 100

7. *Principal Voyages of Discovery:*

   A) Who was the first explorer of the Pacific Ocean?

   B) According to the 1494 Treaty of Tordesillas, about how much of North America was allotted to the Portuguese? a) one-half b) one-third c) one-tenth d) none

Map Challenge

Using the text and the map of *North American Indian Peoples at the Time of First Contact with Europeans*, write a brief essay describing the geographical distributions of the more *dense* North American Indian populations at the time of European arrival. Include some discussion of why certain regions were densely populated and others less so.

PART III: APPLYING WHAT YOU HAVE LEARNED[*]

1. How did the geographic setting of North America—including its relation to Asia, Europe, and Africa—affect its subsequent history?

2. What were the common characteristics of all Indian cultures in the New World, and what were the important differences among them?

3. What fundamental factors drew the Europeans to the exploration, conquest, and settlement of the New World?

4. What was the impact on the Indians, Europeans, and Africans when each of their previously separate worlds "collided" with one another?

5. Should the European encounter with the Indian peoples of the Americas be understood primarily as a story of conquest and exploitation, or as one of mutual cultural encounter that brought beneficial as well as tragic results for both?

---

[*]   Space is provided at the end of each chapter for answering the essay questions. Students needing more room should answer on separate sheets of paper.

CHAPTER 2

The Planting of English America, 1500–1733

PART I: REVIEWING THE CHAPTER

A. CHECKLIST OF LEARNING OBJECTIVES

After mastering this chapter, you should be able to

1. summarize the major factors that led England to begin colonization.

2. describe the development of the Jamestown colony from its disastrous beginnings to its later prosperity.

3. describe the cultural and social interaction and exchange between English settlers and Indians in Virginia, and the effects of the Virginians' policy of warfare and forced removal.

4. describe changes in the economy and labor system in Virginia and the other southern colonies.

5. indicate the similarities and differences among the southern colonies of Virginia, Maryland, North Carolina, South Carolina, and Georgia.

B. GLOSSARY

To build your social science vocabulary, familiarize yourself with the following terms:

1. **nationalism** Fervent belief and loyalty given to the political unit of the nation-state. "Indeed England now had . . . a vibrant sense of nationalism and national destiny." (p. 27)

2. **primogeniture** The legal principle that the oldest son inherits all family property or land. ". . . laws of primogeniture decreed that only eldest sons were eligible to inherit landed estates." (p. 28)

3. **joint-stock companies** An economic arrangement by which a number of investors pool their capital for investment. "Joint-stock companies provided the financial means." (p. 28)

4. **charter** A legal document granted by a government to some group or agency to implement a stated purpose, and spelling out the attending rights and obligations. ". . . the Virginia Company of London received a charter from King James I of England. . . ." (p. 28)

5. **census** An official count of population, often also including other information about the population. "By 1669 an official census revealed that only about two thousand Indians remained in Virginia. . . ." (p. 31)

6. **feudal** Concerning the decentralized medieval social system of personal obligations between rulers and ruled. "Absentee proprietor Lord Baltimore hoped that . . . Maryland . . . would be the vanguard of a vast new feudal domain." (p. 34)

7. **indentured servant** A poor person obligated to a fixed term of unpaid labor, often in exchange for a benefit such as transportation, protection, or training. "Also like Virginia, it depended for labor in its early years mainly on white indentured servants. . . ." (p. 34)

8.   **toleration** Originally, religious freedom granted by an established church to a religious minority. "Maryland's new religious statute guaranteed toleration to all Christians." (p. 34)

9.   **squatter** A frontier farmer who illegally occupied land owned by others or not yet officially opened for settlement. "The newcomers, who frequently were 'squatters' without legal right to the soil . . . ." (p. 40)

10. **buffer** In politics, a small territory or state between two larger, antagonistic powers and intended to minimize the possibility of conflict between them. "The English crown intended Georgia to serve chiefly as a buffer." (p. 41)

11. **melting pot** Popular American term for an ethnically diverse population that is presumed to be "melting" toward some eventual commonality. "The hamlet of Savannah, like Charleston, was a melting-pot community." (p. 41)

PART II: CHECKING YOUR PROGRESS

A. True-False

Where the statement is true, circle **T**; where it is false, circle **F**.

1.   T   F   Protestant England's early colonial ambitions were fueled by its religious rivalry with Catholic Spain.

2.   T   F   The earliest English colonization efforts experienced surprising success.

3.   T   F   The defeat of the Spanish Armada was important to North American colonization because it enabled England to conquer Spain's New World empire.

4.   T   F   Among the English citizens most interested in colonization were unemployed yeomen and the younger sons of the gentry.

5.   T   F   Originally, the primary purpose of the joint-stock Virginia Company was to provide for the well-being of the freeborn English settlers in the colony.

6.   T   F   The defeat of Powhatan's Indian forces in Virginia was achieved partly by Lord De La Warr's use of brutal "Irish tactics."

7.   T   F   The primary factor disrupting Indian cultures in the early years of English settlement was the introduction of Christianity.

8.   T   F   The Maryland colony was founded to establish a religious refuge for persecuted English Quakers.

9.   T   F   From the time of its founding, South Carolina had close economic ties with the British West Indies.

10. T   F   The principal export crop of the Carolinas in the early 1700s was wheat.

11. T   F   South Carolina prospered partly by selling African slaves in the West Indies.

12. T   F   In their early years, North Carolina and Georgia avoided reliance on slavery.

13. T   F   Compared with its neighbors Virginia and South Carolina, North Carolina was more democratic and individualistic in social outlook.

14. T   F   Britain valued the Georgia colony primarily as a rich source of gold and timber.

15. T   F   All the southern colonies eventually came to rely on staple-crop plantation agriculture for their economic prosperity.

B. Multiple Choice

Select the best answer and circle the corresponding letter.

1. After decades of religious turmoil, Protestantism finally gained permanent dominance in England after the succession to the throne of

    a. King Edward VI.
    b. Queen Mary I.
    c. Queen Elizabeth I.
    d. King James I.

2. Imperial England and English soldiers developed a contemptuous attitude toward "natives" partly through their colonizing experiences in

    a. Canada.
    b. Spain.
    c. India.
    d. Ireland.

3. England's victory over the Spanish Armada gave it

    a. control of the Spanish colonies in the New World.
    b. dominance of the Atlantic Ocean and a vibrant sense of nationalism.
    c. a stable social order and economy.
    d. effective control of the African slave trade.

4. At the time of the first colonization efforts, England

    a. was struggling under the political domination of Spain.
    b. was enjoying a period of social and economic stability.
    c. was undergoing rapid economic and social transformations.
    d. was undergoing sharp political conflicts between advocates of republicanism and the monarchy of Elizabeth I.

5. Many of the early Puritan settlers of America were

    a. displaced sailors from Liverpool and Bath.
    b. merchants and shopkeepers from the Midlands.
    c. urban laborers from Glasgow and Edinburgh.
    d. uprooted sheep farmers from eastern and western England.

6. England's first colony at Jamestown

    a. was an immediate economic success.
    b. was saved from failure by John Smith's leadership and by John Rolfe's introduction of tobacco.
    c. enjoyed the strong and continual support of King James I.
    d. depended on the introduction of African slave labor for its survival.

7. Representative government was first introduced to America in the colony of

    a. Virginia.
    b. Maryland.
    c. North Carolina.
    d. Georgia.

8. One important difference between the founding of the Virginia and Maryland colonies was that

    a. Virginia colonists were willing to come only if they could acquire their own land, while Maryland colonists labored for their landlords.
    b. Virginia depended primarily on its tobacco economy, while Maryland turned to rice cultivation.
    c. Virginia depended on African slave labor, while Maryland relied mainly on white indentured servitude.

    d.   Virginia was founded mainly as an economic venture, while Maryland was intended partly to secure religious freedom for persecuted Roman Catholics.

9.   After the Act of Toleration in 1649, Maryland provided religious freedom for all

    a.   Jews.
    b.   atheists.
    c.   Protestants and Catholics.
    d.   those who denied the divinity of Jesus.

10.   The primary reason that no new colonies were founded between 1634 and 1670 was

    a.   the severe economic conditions in Virginia and Maryland.
    b.   the civil war in England.
    c.   the continuous naval conflicts between Spain and England that disrupted sea-lanes.
    d.   the English kings' increasing hostility to colonial ventures.

11.   The early conflicts between English settlers and the Indians near Jamestown laid the basis for

    a.   the intermarriage of white settlers and Indians.
    b.   the incorporation of Indians into the "melting-pot" of American culture.
    c.   the forced separation of the Indians into the separate territories of the "reservation system."
    d.   the use of Indians as a slave-labor force on white plantations.

12.   The Indian peoples who most successfully adapted to the European incursion were

    a.   those whose organization and customs most resembled those of the invaders.
    b.   the coastal tribes like the Powhatans who first encountered the English colonizers.
    c.   the more nomadic and warlike tribes who put up the most effective military resistance to the English.
    d.   the interior Appalachian tribes who used their advantages of time, space, and numbers to create a "middle ground" of economic and cultural interaction.

13.   After the defeat of the coastal Tuscarora and Yamasee Indians by North Carolinians in 1711–1715,

    a.   there were almost no Indians left east of the Mississippi River.
    b.   the remaining southeastern Indian tribes formed an alliance to wage warfare against the whites.
    c.   the powerful Creeks, Cherokees, and Iroquois remained in the Appalachian Mountains as a barrier against white settlement.
    d.   the remaining coastal Indians migrated to the West Indies.

14.   Most of the early white settlers in North Carolina were

    a.   religious dissenters and poor whites fleeing aristocratic Virginia.
    b.   wealthy planters from the West Indies.
    c.   the younger, ambitious sons of English gentry.
    d.   ex-convicts and debtors released from English prisons.

15.   The high-minded philanthropists who founded the Georgia colony were especially interested in the causes of

    a.   women's rights and labor reform.
    b.   temperance and opposition to war.
    c.   prison reform and avoiding slavery.
    d.   religious and political freedom.

C. Identification

Supply the correct identification for each numbered description.

1. _____   Nation where English Protestant rulers employed brutal tactics against the local Catholic population

2. _____   Island colony founded by Sir Walter Raleigh that mysteriously disappeared in the 1580s

3. _____   Naval invaders defeated by English "sea dogs" in 1588

4. _____   Forerunner of the modern corporation that enabled investors to pool financial capital for colonial ventures

5. _____   Name of two wars, fought in 1614 and 1644, between the English in Jamestown and the nearby Indian leader

6. _____   The harsh system of laws governing African labor, first developed in Barbados and later officially adopted by South Carolina in 1696

7. _____   Royal document granting a specified group the right to form a colony and guaranteeing settlers their rights as English citizens

8. _____   Penniless people obligated to engage in unpaid labor for a fixed number of years, usually in exchange for passage to the New World or other benefits

9. _____   Powerful Indian confederation that dominated New York and the eastern Great Lakes area; comprised of several peoples (not the Algonquians)

10. _____   Poor farmers in North Carolina and elsewhere who occupied land and raised crops without gaining legal title to the soil

11. _____   Term for a colony under direct control of the English king or queen

12. _____   The primary staple crop of early Virginia, Maryland, and North Carolina

13. _____   The only southern colony with a slave majority

14. _____   The primary plantation crop of South Carolina

15. _____   A melting-pot town in early colonial Georgia

D. Matching People, Places, and Events

Match the person, place, or event in the left column with the proper description in the right column by inserting the correct letter on the blank line.

1. ____ Powhatan
2. ____ Raleigh and Gilbert
3. ____ Roanoke
4. ____ Smith and Rolfe
5. ____ Virginia
6. ____ Maryland
7. ____ Lord De La Warr
8. ____ Jamaica and Barbados
9. ____ Lord Baltimore
10. ____ South Carolina
11. ____ North Carolina
12. ____ Georgia
13. ____ James Oglethorpe
14. ____ Elizabeth I
15. ____ Jamestown

a. Founded as a haven for Roman Catholics

b. Indian leader who ruled tribes in the James River area of Virginia

c. Harsh military governor of Virginia who employed "Irish tactics" against the Indians

d. British West Indian sugar colonies where large-scale plantations and slavery took root

e. Founded as a refuge for debtors by philanthropists

f. Colony that was called "a vale of humility between two mountains of conceit"

g. The unmarried ruler who established English Protestantism and fought the Catholic Spanish

h. The Catholic aristocrat who sought to build a sanctuary for his fellow believers

i. The failed "lost colony" founded by Sir Walter Raleigh

j. Riverbank site where Virginia Company settlers planted the first permanent English colony

k. Colony that established a House of Burgesses in 1619

l. Virginia leader "saved" by Pocahantas and the prominent settler who married her

m. Elizabethan courtiers who failed in their attempts to found New World colonies

n. Philanthropic soldier-statesman who founded the Georgia colony

o. Colony that turned to disease-resistant African slaves for labor in its extensive rice plantations

Copyright © Houghton Mifflin Company. All rights reserved.

E. Putting Things in Order

Put the following events in correct order by numbering them from 1 to 5.

1. _____   A surprising naval victory by the English inspires a burst of national pride and paves the way for colonization.

2. _____   A Catholic aristocrat founds a colony as a haven for his fellow believers.

3. _____   Settlers from the West Indies found a colony on the North American mainland.

4. _____   An English colony is founded by philanthropists as a haven for imprisoned debtors.

5. _____   A company of investors launches a disaster-stricken but permanent English colony along a mosquito-infested river.

F. Matching Cause and Effect

Match the historical cause in the left column with the proper effect in the right column by writing the correct letter on the blank line.

Cause	**Effect**
1. ___ The English victory over the Spanish Armada	a. Led to the two Anglo-Powhatan wars that virtually exterminated Virginia's Indian population
2. ___ The English law of primogeniture	b. Enabled England to gain control of the North Atlantic sea-lanes
3. ___ The enclosing of English pastures and cropland	c. Forced gold-hungry colonists to work and saved them from total starvation
4. ___ Lord De La Warr's use of brutal "Irish tactics" in Virginia	d. Led Lord Baltimore to establish the Maryland colony
5. ___ The English government's persecution of Roman Catholics	e. Led to the founding of the independent-minded North Carolina colony
6. ___ The slave codes of England's Barbados colony	f. Led many younger sons of the gentry to seek their fortunes in exploration and colonization
7. ___ John Smith's stern leadership in Virginia	g. Contributed to the formation of powerful Indian coalitions like the Iroquois and the Algonquins
8. ___ The English settlers' near-destruction of small Indian tribes	h. Kept the buffer colony poor and largely unpopulated for a long time
9. ___ The flight of poor farmers and religious dissenters from planter-run Virginia	i. Became the legal basis for slavery in North America
10. ___ Georgia's unhealthy climate, restrictions on slavery, and vulnerability to Spanish attacks	j. Forced numerous laborers off the land and sent them looking for opportunities elsewhere

G. Developing Historical Skills

Understanding Historical Comparisons

To understand historical events, historians frequently compare one set of conditions with another so as to illuminate both similarities and differences. In this chapter, there are comparisons of English colonization in North America with (a) England's imperial activity in Ireland (p. 26), (b) Spanish colonization (pp. 26–27), and (c) England's colonies in the West Indies (pp.34–36). Examine these three comparisons, and then answer the following questions.

1. What similarity developed between the English attitude toward the Irish and the English attitude toward Native Americans?

2. What characteristics of England after the victory over the Spanish Armada were similar to Spain's condition one century earlier?

3. How was the sugar economy of the West Indies different from the tobacco economy of the Chesapeake?

H. Map Mastery

Map Discrimination

Using the maps and charts in Chapter 2, answer the following questions.

1. *Sources of the Great Puritan Migration to New England, 1620–1650*: List any five of the English woolen district counties from which the Puritans came.

2. *Early Maryland and Virginia*: The colony of Maryland was centered around what body of water?

3. *Early Carolina and Georgia Settlements*: Which southern colony bordered on foreign, non-English territory?

4. *Early Carolina and Georgia Settlements*: Which southern English colony had the smallest western frontier?

5. *Early Carolina and Georgia Settlements*: In which colony was each of the following cities located: Charleston, Savannah, Newbern, Jamestown?

Map Challenge

1.   Besides the James, what shorter river defines the peninsula where Jamestown was located?

2.   What river marked the border between the Virginia and Maryland colonies?

PART III: APPLYING WHAT YOU HAVE LEARNED

1.   What were the diverse purposes of England's American colonies and how were those purposes altered in the early years of settlement?

2.   What features were common to all of England's southern colonies, and what features were peculiar to each one?

3.   How did the interaction and conflict between English settlers and Indians affect both parties, and contribute to developments that neither group sought?

4.   How did the search for a viable labor force affect the development of the southern colonies? What was the role of African American slavery in the early colonial settlements? Why were two southern colonies initially resistant to slavery?

5.   Which was the most important factor shaping the development of England's southern colonies in the seventeenth century: Indian relations, the one-crop plantation economy, or slavery? Explain and support your answer.

6.   Compare and contrast the early colonial empires of Portugal, Spain, and England in terms of motives, economic foundations, and relations with Africans and Indians. (See Chapter 1.) What factors explain the similarities and differences in the two ventures?

CHAPTER 3

Settling the Northern Colonies, 1619–1700

PART I: REVIEWING THE CHAPTER

A. CHECKLIST OF LEARNING OBJECTIVES

After mastering this chapter, you should be able to

1. describe the Puritans and their beliefs and explain why they left England for the New World.

2. explain the basic religious and governmental ideas and practices of the Massachusetts Bay Colony.

3. explain how Massachusetts Bay's conflict with religious dissenters as well as economic opportunities led to the expansion of New England into Rhode Island, Connecticut, and elsewhere.

4. describe the conflict between the colonists and Indians in New England and the effects of King Philip's War.

5. summarize early New England attempts at intercolonial unity, and the consequences of England's Glorious Revolution in America.

6. describe the founding of New York and Pennsylvania, and explain why these two settlements as well as the other middle colonies became so ethnically, religiously, and politically diverse.

7. describe the central features of the middle colonies and explain how they differed from New England and the southern colonies.

B. GLOSSARY

To build your social science vocabulary, familiarize yourself with the following terms:

1. **predestination** The Calvinist doctrine that God has foreordained some people to be saved and some to be damned. "Good works could not save those whom 'predestination' had marked for the infernal fires." (p. 44)

2. **elect** In Calvinist doctrine, those who have been chosen by God for salvation. "But neither could the elect count on their predetermined salvation. . . ." (p. 44)

3. **conversion** A religious turn to God, thought by Calvinists to involve an intense, identifiable personal experience of grace. "They constantly sought, in themselves and others, signs of 'conversion.' . . ." (p. 44)

4. **visible saints** In Calvinism, those who publicly proclaimed their experience of conversion and were expected to lead godly lives. "The most devout Puritans . . . believed that only 'visible saints' . . . should be admitted to church membership." (p. 44)

5. **calling** In Protestantism, the belief that saved individuals have a religious obligation to engage in worldly work. "Like John Winthrop, [the Puritans] believed in the doctrine of a 'calling' to do God's work on this earth." (p. 47)

6.   **heresy** Departure from correct or officially defined belief. ". . . she eventually boasted that she had come by her beliefs through a direct revelation from God. This was even higher heresy." (p. 48)

7.   **seditious** Concerning resistance to or rebellion against the government. "[His was] a seditious blow at the Puritan idea of government's very purpose." (p. 48)

8.   **commonwealth** An organized civil government or social order united for a shared purpose. "They were allowed, in effect, to become semiautonomous commonwealths." (p . 53)

9.   **autocratic** Absolute or dictatorial rule. "An autocratic spirit survived, and the aristocratic element gained strength. . . ." (p. 59)

10.   **passive resistance** Nonviolent action or opposition to authority, often in accord with religious or moral beliefs. "As advocates of passive resistance, [the Quakers] would turn the other cheek and rebuild their meetinghouse on the site where their enemies had torn it down." (p. 60)

11.   **asylum** A place of refuge and security, especially for the persecuted or unfortunate. "Eager to establish an asylum for his people. . . ." (p. 60)

12.   **proprietary** Concerning exclusive legal ownership, as of colonies granted to individuals by the monarch. "Penn's new proprietary regime was unusually liberal. . . ." (p. 61)

13.   **naturalization** The granting of citizenship to foreigners or immigrants. "No restrictions were placed on immigration, and naturalization was made easy." (p. 61)

14.   **blue laws** Laws designed to restrict personal behavior in accord with a strict code of morality. "Even so, 'blue laws' prohibited 'ungodly revelers,' stage plays, playing cards, dice, games, and excessive hilarity." (p. 61)

15.   **ethnic** Concerning diverse peoples or cultures, specifically those of non-Anglo-Saxon background. ". . . Pennsylvania attracted a rich mix of ethnic groups." (p. 61)

PART II: CHECKING YOUR PROGRESS

A. True-False

Where the statement is true, circle **T**; where it is false, circle **F**.

1.   T   F   The most fervent Puritans believed that the Church of England was corrupt because it did not restrict its membership to "visible saints" who had experienced conversion.

2.   T   F   The Puritans all wanted to break away from the Church of England and establish a new "purified" church.

3.   T   F   The large, separatist Plymouth Colony strongly influenced Puritan Massachusetts Bay.

4.   T   F   Massachusetts Bay restricted the vote for elections to the General Court to adult male members of the Congregational Church.

5.   T   F   Roger Williams and Anne Hutchinson were both banished for organizing political rebellions against the Massachusetts Bay authorities.

6.   T   F   Rhode Island was the most religiously and politically tolerant of the New England colonies.

7.   T   F   The Wampanoag people of New England initially befriended the English colonists.

8.   T   F   Edmund Andros's autocratic Dominion of New England was overthrown in connection with the Glorious Revolution in England.

9.   T   F   King Philip's War enabled New England's Indians to recover their numbers and morale.

10.   T   F   New York became the most democratic and economically equal of the middle colonies.

11.   T   F   Dutch New Netherland was conquered in 1664 by Sweden.

12.   T   F   William Penn originally wanted his Pennsylvania colony to be settled exclusively by his fellow Quakers.

13.   T   F   Later non-Quaker immigrants to Pennsylvania welcomed the peaceful relations with the Indians established by William Penn's policies.

14.   T   F   The middle colonies' broad, fertile river valleys enabled them to develop a richer agricultural economy than that of New England.

15.   T   F   The middle colonies were characterized by tightly knit, ethically homogeneous communities that shared a common sense of religious purpose.

B. Multiple Choice

Select the best answer and circle the corresponding letter.

1. The principal motivation shaping the earliest settlements in New England was
   a. the desire for political freedom.
   b. religious commitment and devotion.
   c. economic opportunity and the chance for a better life.
   d. a spirit of adventure and interest in exploring the New World.

2. Compared with the Plymouth Colony, the Massachusetts Bay Colony was
   a. dedicated to complete separation from the Church of England.
   b. afflicted with corrupt and incompetent leaders.
   c. more focused on religious rather than political liberty.
   d. larger and more prosperous economically.

3. One reason that the Massachusetts Bay Colony was not a true democracy is that
   a. only church members could vote for the governor and the General Court.
   b. political offices were dominated by the clergy.
   c. people were not permitted to discuss issues freely in their own towns.
   d. the governor and his assistants were appointed rather than elected.

4. The most distinctive feature of the Rhode Island Colony was that
   a. it enjoyed the most complete religious freedom of all the English colonies.
   b. it secured an official charter from England.
   c. it contained a high proportion of well-educated and well-off colonists.
   d. it had a strong common sense of religious purpose.

5. Before the first English settlements in New England, Indians in the region had been devastated by
   a. constant warfare with the French.
   b. harsh weather that reduced the corn harvests and caused severe famine.
   c. disease epidemics caused by contact with English fishermen.
   d. intertribal conflicts caused by disputes over hunting grounds.

6. The Indian tribe that first encountered the Pilgrim colonists in New England were the
   a. Iroquois.
   b. Wampanoags.
   c. Narragansetts.

      d.   Hurons.

7. The Puritan missionary efforts to convert Indians to Christianity were

      a.   weak and mostly unsuccessful.
      b.   initially successful but undermined by constant warfare.
      c.   similar to the evangelistic efforts of the Catholic Spanish and French.
      d.   developed only after the Indians were defeated and confined to reservations.

8. King Philip's War represented

      a.   the first serious military conflict between New England colonists and the English King.
      b.   an example of the disastrous divisions among the Wampanoags, Pequots, and Narragansetts.
      c.   the last major Indian effort to halt New Englanders' encroachment on their lands.
      d.   a relatively minor conflict in terms of actual fighting and casualties.

9. The primary value of the New England Confederation lay in

      a.   restoring harmony between Rhode Island and the other New England colonies.
      b.   promoting better relations between New England colonists and their Indian neighbors.
      c.   providing the first small step on the road to intercolonial cooperation.
      d.   defending colonial rights against increasing pressure from the English monarchy.

10. The event that sparked the collapse of the Dominion of New England was

      a.   King Philip's War.
      b.   the revocation of the Massachusetts Bay Colony's charter.
      c.   Governor Andros's harsh attacks on colonial liberties.
      d.   the Glorious Revolution in England.

11. The Dutch Colony of New Netherland

      a.   was harshly and undemocratically governed.
      b.   contained little ethnic diversity.
      c.   was developed as a haven for Dutch Calvinists.
      d.   enjoyed prosperity and peace under the policies of the Dutch West India Company.

12. The short-lived colony conquered by Dutch New Netherland in 1655 was

      a.   New Jersey.
      b.   New France.
      c.   New England.
      d.   New Sweden.

13. William Penn's colony of Pennsylvania

      a.   sought settlers primarily from England and Scotland.
      b.   experienced continuing warfare with neighboring Indian tribes.
      c.   actively sought settlers from Germany and other non-British countries.
      d.   set up the Quaker religion as its tax-supported established church.

14. Besides Pennsylvania, Quakers were also heavily involved in the early settlement of both

      a.   New Jersey and New York.
      b.   New Jersey and Delaware.
      c.   New Netherland and New York.
      d.   Maryland and Delaware.

15. The middle colonies of New York, New Jersey, Pennsylvania, and Delaware

      a.   depended almost entirely on industry rather than agriculture for their prosperity.
      b.   all had powerful established churches that suppressed religious dissenters.
      c.   relied heavily on slave labor in agriculture.
      d.   had more ethnic diversity than either New England or the southern colonies.

C. Identification

Supply the correct identification for each numbered description.

1. _____   Sixteenth-century religious reform movement begun by Martin Luther

2. _____   English Calvinists who sought a thorough cleansing from within the Church of England

3. _____   Radical Calvinists who considered the Church of England so corrupt that they broke with it and formed their own independent churches

4. _____   The shipboard agreement by the Pilgrim Fathers to establish a body politic and submit to majority rule

5. _____   Puritans' term for their belief that Massachusetts Bay had a special arrangement with God to become a holy society

6. _____   Charles I's political action of 1629 that led to persecution of the Puritans and the formation of the Massachusetts Bay Company

7. _____   The *two* major nonfarming industries of Massachusetts Bay

8. _____   Anne Hutchinson's heretical belief that the truly saved need not obey human or divine law

9. _____   Common fate of Roger Williams and Anne Hutchinson after they were convicted of heresy in Massachusetts Bay

10. _____   Villages where New England Indians who converted to Christianity were gathered

11. _____   Successful military action by the colonies united in the New England Confederation

12. _____   English revolt that also led to the overthrow of the Dominion of New England in America

13. _____   River valley where vast estates created an aristocratic landholding elite in New Netherland and New York

14. _____   Required, sworn statements of loyalty or religious belief, resisted by Quakers

15. _____   Common activity in which the colonists engaged to avoid the restrictive, unpopular Navigation Laws

D. Matching People, Places, and Events

Match the person, place or event in the left column with the proper description in the right column by inserting the correct letter on the blank line.

1. ____ Martin Luther

2. ____ John Calvin

3. ____ Massasoit

4. ____ Plymouth

5. ____ Massachusetts Bay Colony

6. ____ John Winthrop

a. Dominant religious group in Massachusetts Bay

b. Founder of the most tolerant and democratic of the middle colonies

c. Mass flight by religious dissidents from the persecutions of Archbishop Laud and Charles I

d. Small colony that eventually merged

7. ___   Great Puritan Migration   into Massachusetts Bay

8. ___   General Court   e.   Religious dissenter convicted of the
                                       heresy of antinomianism
9. ___   Puritans

10. ___   Quakers   f.   Indian leader who waged an
                                       unsuccessful war against New
11. ___   Anne Hutchinson   England's white colonists

12. ___   Roger Williams   g.   German monk who began Protestant
                                       Reformation
13. ___   King Philip

14. ___   Peter Stuyvesant   h.   Religious group persecuted in
                                       Massachusetts and New York but not
15. ___   William Penn   in Pennsylvania

                                  i.   Representative assembly of
                                       Massachusetts Bay

                                  j.   Promoter of Massachusetts Bay as a
                                       holy "city upon a hill"

                                  k.   Conqueror of New Sweden who later
                                       lost New Netherland to the English

                                  l.   Reformer whose religious ideas
                                       inspired English Puritans, Scotch
                                       Presbyterians, French Huguenots, and
                                       Dutch Reformed

                                  m.   Wampanoag chieftain who befriended
                                       English colonists

                                  n.   Colony whose government sought to
                                       enforce God's law on believers and
                                       unbelievers alike

                                  o.   Radical founder of the most tolerant
                                       New England colony

E. Putting Things in Order

Put the following events in correct order by numbering them from 1 to 10.

1. _____   New England Confederation achieves a notable military success.

2. _____   English separatists migrate from Holland to America.

3. _____   Swedish colony on Delaware River is conquered by Dutch neighbor.

4. _____   Manhattan Island is acquired by non-English settlers.

5. _____   Protestant Reformation begins in Europe and England.

6. _____   Quaker son of an English admiral obtains a royal charter for a colony.

7. _____   Puritans bring a thousand immigrants and a charter to America.

8. _____   England conquers a colony on the Hudson River.

9. _____   Convicted Massachusetts Bay heretic founds a colony as a haven for dissenters.

10. _____   James II is overthrown in England and Edmund Andros is overthrown in America.

F. Matching Cause and Effect

Match the historical cause in the left column with the proper effect in the right column by writing the correct letter on the blank line.

Cause	Effect
1. ___ Charles I's persecution of the Puritans	a. Led to overthrow of Andros's Dominion of New England
2. ___ Puritans' belief that their government was based on a covenant with God	b. Encouraged development of Pennsylvania, New York, and New Jersey as rich, grain-growing "bread colonies"
3. ___ Puritan persecution of religious dissenters like Roger Williams	c. Secured political control of New York for a few aristocratic families
4. ___ The Glorious Revolution	d. Spurred formation of the Massachusetts Bay Company and mass migration to New England
5. ___ King Philip's War	
6. ___ The Dutch West India Company's search for quick profits	e. Encouraged large-scale foreign immigration to Pennsylvania
7. ___ Dutch and English creation of vast Hudson Valley estates	f. Led to restriction of political participation in colonial Massachusetts to "visible saints"
8. ___ The English government's persecution of Quakers	g. Spurred William Penn's founding of Pennsylvania
9. ___ William Penn's liberal religious and immigration policies	h. Meant that New Netherland was run as an authoritarian fur trading venture
10. ___ The middle colonies' cultivation of broad, fertile river valleys	i. Ended New England Indians' attempts to halt white expansion
	j. Led to the founding of Rhode Island as a haven for unorthodox faiths

G. Developing Historical Skills

Using Quantitative Maps

Some maps, like *The Great English Migration* on p. 46, present quantitative as well as geographical information. By making a few simple calculations, additional information and conclusions can be derived. Adding the figures on the map indicates that about 68,000 English people came to North America and the West Indies from about 1630–1642.

Study the map and answer the following questions:

1. About what percentage of the total English migration went to New England? (Divide the figure for New England by the total number of immigrants.)

2. How many *more* English settlers went to the West Indies than to New England?

H. Map Mastery

Map Discrimination

Using the maps and charts in Chapter 3, answer the following questions:

1. *Seventeenth-Century New England Settlements*: Which New England colony was largely centered on a single river valley?

2. *Seventeenth-Century New England Settlements*: Which New England colony was made part of Massachusetts Bay in 1641 but separated from the Bay Colony in 1679?

3. *Seventeenth-Century New England Settlements*: When Roger Williams fled Massachusetts to found a new colony, in which direction did he go?

4. *The Stuart Dynasty in England*: Which was the only New England colony founded during the Restoration regime of Charles II?

5. *The Stuart Dynasty in England*: Which New England colony was not founded during the reigns of Charles I or Charles II?

6. *Early Settlements in the Middle Colonies, with Founding Dates*: The territory that was once New Sweden became part of which three English colonies?

Map Challenge

Using the maps on p. 49 and p. 55, write a brief essay on the following question: In what ways did the colony of New Netherland have a historical-geographical relation to its neighboring middle colonies similar to the one Massachusetts Bay had to the other New England colonies, and in what ways were the relations different?

PART III: APPLYING WHAT YOU HAVE LEARNED

1. Compare and contrast the New England and middle colonies in terms of motives for founding, religious and social composition, and political development.

2. How did the Puritans' distinctive religious outlook affect the development of all the New England colonies?

3. "The dissent from Puritanism was as important in the formation of New England as Puritanism itself." How valid is this statement? Defend your answer.

4. Compare the pattern of relations between colonists and Indians in New England and Pennsylvania. Why did attempts at establishing friendly relations fail?

5. Describe and analyze the English government's relationship with the New England and middle colonies during the course of the seventeenth century. Is the term "benign neglect" an accurate description of English colonial policy?

6. Discuss the development of religious and political freedom in Massachusetts, Rhode Island, New York, and Pennsylvania. How did the greater degree of such freedoms enjoyed by Rhode Island and Pennsylvania affect life in those colonies?

7. What economic, social, and ethnic conditions typical of the early southern colonies (Chapter 2) were generally absent in the New England and middle colonies? What characteristics did the middle colonies have that were not generally present in the South?

CHAPTER 4

American Life in the Seventeenth Century, 1607–1692

PART I: REVIEWING THE CHAPTER

A. CHECKLIST OF LEARNING OBJECTIVES

After mastering this chapter, you should be able to

1. describe the basic economy, demographics, and social structure and life of the seventeenth-century colonies.

2. compare and contrast the different forms of society and ways of life of the southern colonies and New England.

3. explain how the practice of indentured servitude failed to solve the colonial labor problem, and why colonists then turned to African slavery.

4. describe the slave trade and the character of early African American slavery.

5. summarize the unique New England way of life centered on family, town, and church, and describe the changes that overcame this comfortable social order in the late seventeenth century.

6. describe the role of family life and the roles of women in the seventh century colonies, and indicate how these changed over time.

B. GLOSSARY

To build your social science vocabulary, familiarize yourself with the following terms:

1. **headright** The right to acquire a certain amount of land granted to the person who finances the passage of a laborer. "Masters—not servants themselves—thus reaped the benefits of landownership from the headright system." (p. 67)

2. **disfranchise** To take away the right to vote. "The Virginia Assembly in 1670 disfranchised most of the landless knockabouts. . . ." (p. 68)

3. **civil war** Any conflict between the citizens or inhabitants of the same country. "As this civil war in Virginia ground on . . . ." (p. 68)

4. **tidewater** The territory adjoining water affected by tides—that is, near the seacoast or coastal rivers. "Bacon . . . had pitted the hard scrabble backcountry frontiersmen against the haughty gentry of the tidewater plantations." (pp. 68, 70)

5. **middle passage** That portion of a slave ship's journey in which slaves were carried from Africa to the Americas. ". . . the captives were herded aboard sweltering ships for the gruesome 'middle passage.'. . . ." (p. 71)

6. **fertility** The ability to mate and produce abundant young. "The captive black population of the Chesapeake area soon began to grow not only through new imports but also through its own fertility. . . ." (p. 72)

7. **menial** Fit for servants; humble or low. "But chiefly they performed the sweaty toil of clearing swamps, grubbing out trees, and other menial tasks." (p. 73)

8. **militia** An armed force of citizens called out only in emergencies. "[They] tried to march to Spanish Florida, only to be stopped by the local militia." (p. 73)

9. **hierarchy** A social group arranged in ranks or classes. "The rough equality . . . was giving way to a hierarchy of wealth and status. . . ." (p. 73)

10. **corporation** A group or institution granted legal rights to carry on certain specified activities. ". . . the Massachusetts Puritans established Harvard College, today the oldest corporation in America. . . ." (p. 79)

11. **jeremiad** A sermon or prophecy recounting wrongdoing, warning of doom, and calling for repentance. "Jeremiads continued to thunder from the pulpits. . . ." (p. 80)

12. **lynching** The illegal execution of an accused person by mob action, without due process of law. "A hysterical 'witch-hunt' ensued, leading to the legal lynching in 1692 of twenty individuals. . . ." (p. 80)

13. **hinterland** An inland region set back from a port, river, or seacoast. ". . . their accusers came largely from subsistence farming families in Salem's hinterland." (p. 80)

14. **social structure** The basic pattern of the distribution of status and wealth in a society. ". . . many settlers . . . tried to re-create on a modified scale the social structure they had known in the Old World." (p. 83)

15. **blue blood** Of noble or upper-class descent. ". . . would-be American blue bloods resented the pretensions of the 'meaner sort.'. . ." (p. 83)

PART II: CHECKING YOUR PROGRESS

A. True-False

Where the statement is true, circle **T**; where it is false, circle **F**.

1. T F   Life expectancy among the seventeenth-century settlers of Maryland and Virginia was about sixty years.

2. T F   Because men greatly outnumbered women in the Chesapeake region, a fierce competition arose among men for scarce females.

3. T F   By the eighteenth century, the Chesapeake population was growing on the basis of natural increase.

4. T F   Chesapeake Bay tobacco planters responded to falling prices by cutting back production.

5. T F   The "headright" system of land grants to those who brought laborers to America primarily benefited wealthy planters rather than the poor indentured servants.

6. T F   Most of the European immigrants who came to Virginia and Maryland in the seventeenth century were indentured servants.

7. T F   Bacon's Rebellion involved an alliance of white indentured servants and Indians who attacked the elite planter class.

8. T F   African slaves began to replace white indentured servants as the primary labor supply in the plantation colonies in the 1680s.

9. T   F   Slaves brought to North America developed a culture that mixed African and American elements.

10. T   F   Directly beneath the wealthy slaveowning planters in the southern social structure were the white indentured servants.

11. T   F   New Englanders' long lives contributed to the general stability and order of their childrearing and family life.

12. T   F   New England expansion was carried out primarily by independent pioneers and land speculators who bought up large plots and then sold them to individual farmers.

13. T   F   New England women enjoyed fewer rights to inherit and own property than women in the South.

14. T   F   New England's commercial wealth was based on the export of agricultural crops to England and elsewhere.

15. T   F   Seventeenth-century American life was generally simple and lacking in displays of wealth or elaborate class distinctions.

B. Multiple Choice

Select the best answer and circle the corresponding letter.

1. For most of their early history, the colonies of Maryland and Virginia

    a. provided a healthy environment for child rearing.
    b. contained far more men than women.
    c. had harsh laws punishing premarital sexual relations.
    d. encouraged the formation of stable and long-lasting marriages.

2. The primary beneficiaries of the "headright" system were

    a. landowners who paid the transatlanic passage for indentured servants.
    b. widows who acquired new husbands from England.
    c. indentured servants who were able to acquire their own land.
    d. English ship owners who transported new laborers across the Atlantic.

3. The primary cause of Bacon's Rebellion was

    a. Governor Berkeley's harsh treatment of the Indians.
    b. the refusal of landlords to grant indentured servants their freedom.
    c. the poverty and discontent of many single young men unable to acquire land.
    d. the persecution of the colonists by King Charles II.

4. African slavery became the prevalent form of labor in the 1680s when

    a. planters were no longer able to rely on white indentured servants as a labor force.
    b. the first captives were brought from Africa to the New World.
    c. blacks could be brought to the New World in safer and healthier condition.
    d. the once-clear legal difference between a servant and a slave began to be blurred.

5. The culture that developed among the slaves in the English colonies of North America was

    a. derived primarily from that of the white masters.
    b. based mainly on the traditions of southern Africa.
    c. a combination of several African and American cultures.
    d. originally developed in the West Indies and spread northward.

6. Political and economic power in the southern colonies was dominated by

    a. urban professional classes such as lawyers and bankers.
    b. small landowners.
    c. wealthy planters.

    d.   the English royal governors.

7. Because there were few urban centers in the colonial South,

    a.   good roads between the isolated plantations were constructed early on.
    b.   a professional class of lawyers and financiers was slow to develop.
    c.   the rural church became the central focus of southern social and economic life.
    d.   there were almost no people of wealth and culture in the region.

8. Puritan lawmakers in New England prevented married women from having property rights because

    a.   they believed that property should be held by towns, not private citizens.
    b.   they feared that too much property would fall into the control of the numerous widows.
    c.   they feared that separate property rights for women would undercut the unity of married couples.
    d.   the Bible plainly prohibited women from owning property.

9. In New England, elementary education

    a.   was mandatory for any town with more than fifty families.
    b.   failed to provide even basic literacy to the large majority of citizens.
    c.   was less widespread than in the South.
    d.   was oriented to preparing students for entering college.

10. The Congregational Church of the Puritans contributed to

    a.   the development of basic democracy in the New England town meeting.
    b.   the extremely hierarchical character of New England life.
    c.   the social harmony and unity displayed throughout the seventeenth century in New England towns.
    d.   the growing movement toward women's rights in New England.

11. In contrast to the Chesapeake Bay colonists, those in New England

    a.   had fewer women and more men in their population.
    b.   had shorter life expectancies.
    c.   practiced birth control as a means of preventing overpopulation.
    d.   enjoyed longer lives and more stable families.

12. The focus of much of New England's politics, religion, and education was the institution of

    a.   the colonial legislature.
    b.   the town.
    c.   the militia company.
    d.   the college.

13. The "Half-Way Covenant" provided

    a.   baptism but not "full communion" to people who had not had a conversion experience.
    b.   partial participation in politics to people who were not church members.
    c.   admission to communion but not to voting membership in the church.
    d.   partial participation in church affairs for women.

14. Those people accused of being witches in Salem were generally

    a.   from the poorer and more uneducated segments of the town.
    b.   notorious for their deviation from the moral norms of the community.
    c.   outspoken opponents of the Puritan clergy.
    d.   from families associated with Salem's burgeoning market economy.

15. English settlers greatly altered the character of the New England environment by

    a.   raising wheat and oats rather than the corn grown by Indians.
    b.   their extensive introduction of livestock.
    c.   beating trails through the woods as they pursued seasonal hunting and fishing.
    d.   building an extensive system of roads and canals.

C. Identification

Supply the correct identification for each numbered description.

1. _____ Early Maryland and Virginia settlers had difficulty creating them and even more difficulty making them last

2. _____ Primary cause of death among tobacco-growing settlers

3. _____ Immigrants who received passage to America in exchange for a fixed term of labor

4. _____ Maryland and Virginia's system of granting land to anyone who would pay trans-Atlantic passage for laborers

5. _____ Fate of many of Nathaniel Bacon's followers, though not of Bacon himself

6. _____ American colony that was home to the Newport slave market and many slave traders

7. _____ English company that lost its monopoly on the slave trade in 1698

8. _____ African American dialect that blended English with Yoruba, Ibo, and Hausa

9. _____ Uprisings that occurred in New York City in 1712 and in South Carolina in 1739

10. _____ Wealthy extended clans like the Fitzhughs, Lees, and Washingtons that dominated politics in the most populous colony

11. _____ Approximate marriage age of most New England women

12. _____ The basic local political institution of New England, in which all freemen gathered to elect officials and debate local affairs

13. _____ Formula devised by Puritan ministers in 1662 to offer partial church membership to people who had not experienced conversion

14. _____ Late seventeenth-century judicial event that inflamed popular feelings, led to the deaths of twenty people, and weakened the Puritan clergy's prestige

15. _____ Primary occupation of most seventeenth-century Americans

D. Matching People, Places, and Events

Match the person, place, or event in the left column with the proper description in the right column by inserting the correct letter on the blank line.

1. ___ Chesapeake
2. ___ Indentured servants
3. ___ Nathaniel Bacon
4. ___ Governor Berkeley
5. ___ Royal African Company
6. ___ Middle passage
7. ___ Ringshout
8. ___ New York City slave revolt of 1712
9. ___ Nathanael Hawthorne
10. ___ "New England conscience"
11. ___ Harvard
12. ___ William and Mary
13. ___ Half-Way Covenant
14. ___ Salem witch trials
15. ___ Leisler's Rebellion

a. Major middle-colonies rebellion that caused thirty-three deaths

b. Helped erase the earlier Puritan distinction between the converted "elect" and other members of society

c. Small New York revolt of 1689–1691 that reflected class antagonism between landlords and merchants

d. Primary laborers in early southern colonies until the 1680s

e. Experience for which human beings were branded and chained, and which only 80 percent survived

f. Author of a novel about the early New England practice of requiring adulterers to wear the letter "A"

g. West African religious rite, retained by African Americans, in which participants responded to the shouts of a preacher

h. Phenomena started by adolescent girls' accusations that ended with the deaths of twenty people

i. Virginia-Maryland bay area, site of the earliest colonial settlements

j. The legacy of Puritan religion that inspired idealism and reform among later generations of Americans

k. Colonial Virginia official who crushed rebels and wreaked cruel revenge

l. The oldest college in the South, founded in 1793

m. Organization whose loss of the slave trade monopoly in 1698 led to free-enterprise expansion of the business

n. Agitator who led poor former indentured servants and frontiersmen on a rampage against Indians and colonial government

o. The oldest college in America, originally based on the Puritan commitment to an educated ministry

E. Putting Things in Order

Put the following events in correct order by numbering them from 1 to 10.

1. _____ "Legal lynching" of twenty accused witches occurs.

2. _____ Royal slave trade monopoly ends.

3. _____ First colonial college is founded.

4. _____ Landless whites in Virginia lose the right to vote.

5. _____ Major rebellion by African Americans occurs in one of the middle colonies.

6. _____ Southern slaves in revolt try but fail to march to Spanish Florida.

7. _____ Partial church membership is opened to the unconverted.

8. _____ African slaves begin to replace white indentured labor on southern plantations.

9. _____ Poor Virginia whites revolt against governor and rich planters.

10. _____ First Africans arrive in Virginia.

F. Matching Cause and Effect

Match the historical cause in the left column with the proper effect in the right column by writing the correct letter on the blank line.

Cause

1. ____ The severe shortage of females in southern colonies

2. ____ Poor white males' anger at their inability to acquire land or start families

3. ____ Planters' fears of indentured servants' rebellion, coupled with rising wages in England

4. ____ The dramatic increase in colonial slave population after 1680s

5. ____ The growing proportion of female slaves in the Chesapeake region after 1720

6. ____ New Englanders' introduction of livestock and intensive agriculture

7. ____ The healthier climate and more equal male-female ratio in New England

8. ____ The decline of religious devotion and in number of conversions in New England

Effect

a. Inspired passage of strict "slave codes"

b. Sparked Bacon's Rebellion

c. Produced large number of unattached males and weak family structure

d. Thwarted success in agriculture but helped create the tough New England character

e. Inspired the Half-Way Covenant and jeremiad preaching

f. Reduced forests and damaged the soil

g. Produced high birthrates and a very stable family structure

h. Fostered stronger slave families and growth of slave population through natural reproduction of children

i. Underlay the Salem witchcraft persecutions

j. Caused southern planters to switch from indentured-servant labor to African slavery

9. ___   Unsettled New England social
conditions and anxieties about the
decline of the Puritan religious
heritage

10. ___   The rocky soil and harsh climate
of New England

G. Developing Historical Skills

Learning from Historical Documents

The illustrations on pp. 69 and 79 reproduce parts of two colonial documents: excerpts from an indentured servant's contract and some pages from children's school materials.. By carefully examining even these small partial documents, you can learn more about early colonial culture and ideas.

Answering the following questions will illustrate the kind of information that historical documents can provide.

1.   What are the principal goals that both the master and the indentured servant are seeking in the contract?

2.   What potential problems does each side anticipate?

3.   What does the reference to the mother's consent suggest about this servant's condition?

PART III: APPLYING WHAT YOU HAVE LEARNED

1.   How did the factors of population, economics, disease, and climate shape the basic social conditions and ways of life of early Americans in both the South and New England?

2.   What was the underlying cause of the expansion of African slavery in English North America?

3.   Could the colonies' "labor problem" have been solved without slavery?

4.   How did African Americans develop a culture that combined African and American elements? What were some of the features of that culture?

5.   How did the numbers and condition of women affect family life and society in New England, among southern whites, and among African American slaves? Compare and contrast the typical family conditions and ways of life among various members of these three groups.

6.   How did the harsh climate and soil, stern religion, and tightly knit New England town shape the "Yankee character"?

7.   Compare the conditions of seventeenth-century social, economic, and religious life in New England and the Chesapeake region.

8.   How did the Salem witch episode reflect the tensions and changes in seventeenth-century New England life and thought?

9.   In what ways did the English and Africans who came to America in the seventeenth century have to shape their society and way of life to fit the conditions they faced in the New World?

CHAPTER 5

Colonial Society on the Eve of Revolution, 1700–1775

PART I: REVIEWING THE CHAPTER

A. CHECKLIST OF LEARNING OBJECTIVES

After mastering this chapter, you should be able to

1. describe the demographic, economic, and social structure of the eighteenth-century colonies and indicate how they had changed since the seventeenth century.

2. explain how the economic development of the colonies altered the patterns of social prestige and wealth.

3. identify the major religious denominations of the eighteenth-century colonies, and indicate their role in early American society.

4. explain the causes of the religious Great Awakening, and describe its effects on American education and politics.

5. describe the origins and development of education, culture, and journalism in the colonies.

6. describe the basic features of colonial politics, including the role of various official and informal political institutions.

7. indicate the key qualities of daily existence in eighteenth-century colonial America, including forms of socialization and recreation.

B. GLOSSARY

To build your social science vocabulary, familiarize yourself with the following terms:

1. **melting pot** The mingling of diverse ethnic groups in America, including the idea that these groups are or should be "melting" into a single culture or people. "Colonial America was a melting pot and had been from the outset." (p. 85)

2. **sect** A small religious group that has broken away from some larger mainstream church, often claiming superior or exclusive possession of religious truth. (A **denomination** is a branch of the church—usually Protestant—but makes no such exclusive claims.) "They belonged to several different Protestant sects. . . ." (p. 85)

3. **agitators** Those who seek to excite or persuade the public on some issue. "Already experienced colonizers and agitators in Ireland, the Scots-Irish proved to be superb frontiersmen. . . ." (p. 86)

4. **stratification** The visible arrangement of society into a hierarchical pattern, with distinct social groups layered one on top of the other. ". . . colonial society . . . was beginning to show signs of stratification. . . ." (p. 87)

5. **mobility** The capacity to pass readily from one social or economic condition to another. ". . . barriers to mobility . . . raised worries about the 'Europeanization' of America." (p. 87)

6. **elite** The smaller group at the top of a society or institution, usually possessing wealth, power, or special privileges. ". . . these elites now feathered their nests more finely." (p. 87)

7. **almshouse** A home for the poor, supported by charity or public funds. "Both Philadelphia and New York built almshouses in the 1730s. . . ." (p. 87)

8. **gentry** Landowners of substantial property, social standing, and leisure, but not titled nobility. "Wealth was concentrated in the hands of the largest slaveowners, widening the gap between the prosperous gentry and the 'poor whites'. . . ." (p. 90)

9. **tenant farmer** One who rents rather than owns land. ". . . the 'poor whites' . . . were increasingly forced to become tenant farmers." (p. 90)

10. **penal code** The body of criminal laws specifying offenses and prescribing punishments. "But many convicts were the unfortunate victims . . . of a viciously unfair English penal code. . . ." (p. 90)

11. **veto** The executive power to prevent acts passed by the legislature from becoming law. "Thomas Jefferson, himself a slaveholder, assailed the British vetoes. . . ." (p. 90)

12. **apprentice** A person who works under a master to acquire instruction in a trade or profession. "Aspiring young doctors served for a while as apprentices to older practitioners. . . ." (p. 90)

13. **speculation** Buying land or anything else in the hope of profiting by an expected rise in price. "Commercial ventures and land speculation . . . were the surest avenues to speedy wealth." (p. 91)

14. **revival** In religion, a movement of renewed enthusiasm and commitment, often accompanied by special meetings or evangelical activity. "The stage was thus set for a rousing religious revival." (p. 96)

15. **secular** Belonging to the worldly sphere rather than to the specifically sacred or churchly. "A more secular approach was evident late in the eighteenth century. . . ." (p. 98)

PART II: CHECKING YOUR PROGRESS

A. True-False

Where the statement is true, circle **T**; where it is false, circle **F**.

1. T F   Most of the spectacular growth of the colonial population came from immigration rather than natural increase.

2. T F   The most numerous white ethnic groups in the colonies were the Germans and the Scots-Irish.

3. T F   Compared with the seventeenth-century colonies, the eighteenth-century colonies were becoming more socially equal and democratic.

4. T F   The lowest class of whites in the colonies consisted of the convicted criminals and prisoners shipped to America by British authorities.

5. T F   Thomas Jefferson's condemnation of British support of the slave trade was removed from the Declaration of Independence by other members of Congress.

6. T F   The most highly regarded professionals in the colonies were doctors and lawyers.

7. T F   Besides agriculture, the most important colonial economic activities were fishing, shipping, and ocean-going trade.

8.   T   F   Colonial merchants were generally satisfied to trade in protected British markets and accepted imperial restrictions on trade with other countries.

9.   T   F   The established Anglican Church was a more powerful force in colonial life than the Congregational Church of New England.

10. T   F   The Great Awakening was a revival of fervent religion after a period of religious decline caused by clerical over-intellectualism and lay liberalism in doctrine.

11. T   F   Great Awakening revivalists like Jonathan Edwards and George Whitefield tried to replace the older Puritan ideas of conversion and salvation with more rational and less emotional beliefs.

12. T   F   The Great Awakening broke down denominational and sectional barriers, creating a greater sense of a common American identity and a united destiny.

13. T   F   Most early colonial education, including that at the college level, was closely linked with religion.

14. T   F   The greatest colonial cultural achievements came in art and imaginative literature rather than in theology and political theory.

15. T   F   The central point of conflict in colonial politics was the relation between the democratically elected lower house of the assembly and the governors appointed by the king or colonial proprietor.

B. Multiple Choice

Select the best answer and circle the corresponding letter.

1.   The primary reason for the spectacular growth of America's population in the eighteenth century was

   a.   the conquering of new territories.
   b.   the natural fertility of the population.
   c.   the increased importation of white indentured servants and black slaves.
   d.   new immigration from Europe.

2.   German settlement in the colonies was especially heavy in

   a.   Massachusetts.
   b.   Maryland.
   c.   New York.
   d.   Pennsylvania.

3.   The Scots-Irish eventually became concentrated especially in

   a.   coastal areas of the Middle Colonies and the South.
   b.   the New England colonies.
   c.   the frontier areas.
   d.   the cities.

4.   Compared with the seventeenth century, American colonial society in the eighteenth century showed

   a.   greater domination by small farmers and artisans.
   b.   greater equality of wealth and status.
   c.   greater gaps in wealth and status between rich and poor.
   d.   greater opportunity for convicts and indentured servants to climb to the top.

5.   The most honored professional in colonial America was the

   a.   lawyer.

    b.   clergyman.

    c.   doctor.

    d.   journalist.

6.   The primary source of livelihood for most colonial Americans was

    a.   manufacturing.

    b.   agriculture.

    c.   lumbering.

    d.   commerce and trade.

7.   Indians and African Americans shared in the common American experience of

    a.   migrating westward in search of free land.

    b.   creating new cultures and societies out of the mingling of diverse ethnic groups.

    c.   forming closed, settled communities that resisted outsiders.

    d.   clinging to traditional cultural values brought from the Old World.

8.   An unfortunate group of involuntary immigrants who ranked even below indentured servants on the American social scale were

    a.   the younger sons of English gentry.

    b.   French-Canadian fur traders.

    c.   convicts and paupers.

    d.   single women.

9.   The "triangular trade" involved the sale of rum, molasses, and slaves among the ports of

    a.   Virginia, Canada, and Britain.

    b.   the West Indies, France, and South America.

    c.   New England, Britain, and Spain.

    d.   New England, Africa, and the West Indies.

10.   The passage of British restrictions on trade encouraged colonial merchants to

    a.   organize political resistance in the British Parliament.

    b.   find ways to smuggle and otherwise evade the law by trading with other countries.

    c.   turn to domestic trade within the colonies.

    d.   turn from trading to such other enterprises as fishing and manufacturing.

11.   Besides offering rest and refreshment, colonial taverns served an important function as centers of

    a.   news and political opinion.

    b.   trade and business.

    c.   medicine and law.

    d.   religious revival.

12.   The Anglican Church suffered in colonial America because of

    a.   its strict doctrines and hierarchical church order.

    b.   its poorly qualified clergy and close ties with British authorities.

    c.   its inability to adjust to conditions of life in New England.

    d.   its reputation for fostering fanatical revivalism.

13.   The two denominations that enjoyed the status of "established" churches in various colonies were the

    a.   Quakers and Dutch Reformed.

    b.   Baptists and Lutherans.

    c.   Anglicans and Congregationalists.

    d.   Roman Catholics and Presbyterians.

14.   Among the many important results of the Great Awakening was that it

    a.   broke down sectional boundaries and created a greater sense of common American identity.

    b.   contributed to greater religious liberalism and toleration in the churches.

    c.   caused a decline in colonial concern for education.

    d.   moved Americans closer to a single religious outlook.

15. A primary weapon used by colonial legislatures in their conflicts with royal governors was

    a.   extending the franchise to include almost all adult white citizens.
    b.   passing laws prohibiting the governors from owning land or industries.
    c.   voting them out of office.
    d.   using their power of the purse to withhold the governor's salary.

C. Identification

Supply the correct identification for each numbered description.

1.   _____   Corruption of a German word used as a term for German immigrants in Pennsylvania

2.   _____   Ethnic group that had already relocated once before immigrating to America and settling largely on the Western frontier of the middle and southern colonies

3.   _____   Rebellious movement of frontiersmen in the southern colonies that included future President Andrew Jackson

4.   _____   Popular term for convicted criminals dumped on colonies by British authorities

5.   _____   Term for New England settlements where Indians from various tribes were gathered to be Christianized

6.   _____   A once-despised profession that rose in prestige after 1750 because its practitioners defended colonial rights

7.   _____   Small but profitable trade route that linked New England, Africa, and the West Indies

8.   _____   Popular colonial centers of recreation, gossip, and political debate

9.   _____   Term for tax-supported condition of Congregational and Anglican churches, but not of Baptists, Quakers, and Roman Catholics

10.   _____   Spectacular, emotional religious revival of the 1730s and 1740s

11.   _____   Ministers who supported the Great Awakening against the "old light" clergy who rejected it

12.   _____   Institutions that were founded in greater numbers as a result of the Great Awakening, although a few had been founded earlier

13.   _____   The case that established the precedent that true statements about public officials could not be prosecuted as libel

14.   _____   The upper house of a colonial legislature, appointed by the crown or the proprietor

15.   _____   Benjamin Franklin's highly popular collection of information, parables, and advice

D. Matching People, Places, and Events

Match the person, place, or event in the left column with the proper description in the right column by inserting the correct letter on the blank line.

1. ___ Philadelphia

2. ___ African Americans

3. ___ Scots-Irish

4. ___ Paxton Boys and Regulators

5. ___ Patrick Henry

6. ___ Molasses Act

7. ___ Anglican church

8. ___ Jonathan Edwards

9. ___ George Whitefield

10. ___ Phillis Wheatley

11. ___ Benjamin Franklin

12. ___ John Peter Zenger

13. ___ Quakers

14. ___ Baptists

15. ___ John Singleton Copley

a. Itinerant British evangelist who spread the Great Awakening throughout the colonies

b. Colonial printer whose case helped begin freedom of the press

c. Colonial painter who studied and worked in Britain

d. Leading city of the colonies; home of Benjamin Franklin

e. Largest non-English group in the colonies

f. Dominant religious group in colonial Pennsylvania, criticized by others for their attitudes toward Indians

g. Former slave who became a poet at an early age

h. Scots-Irish frontiersmen who protested against colonial elites of Pennsylvania and North Carolina

i. Attempt by British authorities to squelch colonial trade with French West Indies

j. Brilliant New England theologian who instigated the Great Awakening

k. Group that settled the frontier, made whiskey, and hated the British and other governmental authorities

l. Nonestablished religious group that benefited from the Great Awakening

m. Author, scientist, printer; "the first civilized American"

n. Eloquent lawyer-orator who argued in defense of colonial rights

o. Established religion in southern colonies and New York; weakened by lackadaisical clergy and too-close ties with British crown

E. Putting Things in Order

Put the following events in correct order by numbering them 1 to 10.

1. _____ Epochal freedom of the press case is settled.

2. _____ First southern college to train Anglican clergy is founded.

3. _____   Britain vetoes colonial effort to halt slave importation.

4. _____   Scots-Irish protestors stage armed marches.

5. _____   First medical attempts are made to prevent dreaded disease epidemics.

6. _____   Parliament attempts to restrict colonial trade with French West Indies.

7. _____   Princeton College is founded to train "new light" ministers.

8. _____   An eloquent British preacher spreads evangelical religion through the colonies.

9. _____   Benjamin Franklin starts printing his most famous publication.

10. _____   A fiery, intellectual preacher sets off a powerful religious revival in New England.

F. Matching Cause and Effect

Match the historical cause in the left column with the proper effect in the right column by writing the correct letter on the blank line.

Cause	Effect
1. ___ The high natural fertility of the colonial population	a. Prompted colonial assemblies to withhold royal governors' salaries
2. ___ The heavy immigration of Germans, Scots-Irish, Africans, and others into the colonies	b. Created the conditions for the Great Awakening to erupt in the early eighteenth century
3. ___ The large profits made by merchants as military suppliers for imperial wars	c. Resulted in the development of a colonial "melting pot," only one-half English by 1775
4. ___ American merchants' search for non-British markets	d. Was met by British attempts to restrict colonial trade, e.g., the Molasses Act
5. ___ Dry over-intellectualism and loss of religious commitment	e. Increased the wealth of the eighteenth-century colonial elite
6. ___ The Great Awakening	f. Led to the increase of American population to one-third of England's in 1775
7. ___ The Zenger case	g. Forced the migration of colonial artists to Britain to study and pursue artistic careers
8. ___ The appointment of unpopular or incompetent royal governors to colonies	h. Marked the beginnings of freedom of printed political expression in the colonies
9. ___ Upper-class fear of "democratic excesses" by poor whites	i. Reinforced colonial property qualifications for voting
10. ___ The lack of artistic concerns, cultural tradition, and leisure in the colonies	j. Stimulated a fervent, emotional style of religion, denominational divisions, and a greater sense of inter-colonial American identity

G. Developing Historical Skills

Learning from Map Comparison

By comparing two similar maps dealing with the same historical period, you can derive additional information about the relations between the two topics the maps emphasize. The map on p. 85 shows immigrant groups in 1775, and the map on p. 91 shows the colonial economy. By examining both maps, you can learn about the likely economic activities of various immigrant groups.

Answer the following questions:

1. To what extent were Scots-Irish immigrants involved in tobacco cultivation?

2. What agricultural activities were most of the Dutch immigrants involved in?

3. With what part of the agricultural economy were African American slaves most involved?

4. Which major immigrant group may have had some involvement in the colonial iron industry?

H. Map Mastery

Map Discrimination

Using the maps and charts in Chapter 5, answer the following questions:

1. Which section contained the fewest non-English minorities?

2. The Scots-Irish were concentrated most heavily on the frontiers of which four colonies?

3. In which colony were German and Swiss immigrants most heavily concentrated?

4. Which colony contained the largest concentration of French immigrants?

5.   Which *four* colonies had the greatest concentration of tobacco growing?

6.   Which was the larger minority in the colonies: all the non-English white ethnic groups together, or the African Americans?

7.   Which *two* social groups stood between the landowning farmers and the slaves in the colonial social pyramid?

8.   Which of the following religious groups were most heavily concentrated in the middle colonies: Lutherans, Dutch Reformed, Quakers, Baptists, Roman Catholics?

9.   How many years after the Declaration of Independence in 1776 was the last church officially disestablished?

10.   How many of the colonial colleges were originally founded by "established" denominations?

Map Challenge

Using the map on p. 85, write a brief essay in which you compare the "ethnic mix" in each of the following colonies: North Carolina, Virginia, Pennsylvania, New York, Massachusetts.

PART III: APPLYING WHAT YOU HAVE LEARNED

1.   What factors contributed to the growing numbers and wealth of the American colonists in the eighteenth century?

2.   Describe the structure of colonial society in the eighteenth century. What developments tended to make society less equal and more hierarchical?

3.   What attitudes toward education and the "higher" forms of culture were prevalent in eighteenth century colonial America? To what extent were these products of a basically rural society, and to what extent did they derive from popular ideas and attitudes?

4.   What were the causes and consequences of the Great Awakening?

5.   What features of colonial politics contributed to the development of popular democracy, and what kept political life from being more truly democratic?

6.   How did the various churches, established and nonestablished, fundamentally shape eighteenth-century colonial life, including education and politics?

7.   What made American society far more equal than Britain's, but seemingly less equal than it had been in the seventeenth century?

8.   Compare and contrast the social structure and culture of the eighteenth century with that of the seventeenth century (see Chapter 4). In what ways was eighteenth-century society more complex, and in what ways did it clearly continue earlier ideas and practices?

CHAPTER 6

The Duel for North America, 1608–1763

PART I: REVIEWING THE CHAPTER

A. CHECKLIST OF LEARNING OBJECTIVES

After mastering this chapter, you should be able to

1. explain what caused the great contest for North America between Britain and France, and why Britain won.

2. describe France's colonial settlements and their expansion, and compare New France with Britain's colonies in North America.

3. explain how the series of wars with France helped foster greater unity among the British colonies.

4. explain how North American political and military events were affected by developments on the larger European stage.

5. indicate how and why the Seven Years' War (French and Indian War) became one of the background causes of the American Revolution.

B. GLOSSARY

To build your social science vocabulary, familiarize yourself with the following terms:

1. **domestic** Concerning the internal affairs of a country. "It was convulsed . . . by foreign wars and domestic strife. . . ." (p. 106)

2. **minister** In politics, a person appointed by the head of state to take charge of some department or agency of government. "France blossomed . . . led by a series of brilliant ministers. . . ." (p. 107)

3. **autocratic** Marked by strict authoritarian rule, without consent or participation by the populace. "This royal regime was almost completely autocratic." (p. 107)

4. **peasant** A farmer or agricultural laborer, sometimes legally tied to the land. "Landowning French peasants . . . had little economic motive to move." (pp. 107–108)

5. **coureurs des bois** French-Canadian fur trappers; literally, "runners of the woods." "These colorful coureurs des bois . . . were also runners of risks. . . ." (p. 108)

6. **voyageurs** French-Canadian explorers, adventurers, and traders. "Singing, paddle-swinging French *voyageurs* also recruited Indians. . . ." (p. 108)

7. **flotilla** A fleet of boats, usually smaller vessels. "The Indian fur flotilla . . . numbered four hundred canoes." (p. 108)

8. **ecological** Concerning the relations between the biological organisms and their environment. ". . . they extinguished the beaver population in many areas, inflicting incalculable ecological damage." (p. 109)

9. **mutinous** Concerning revolt by subordinate soldiers or seamen against their commanding officers. "But he failed to find the Mississippi delta, . . . and was murdered by his mutinous men." (p. 109)

10. **strategic** Concerning the placement and planned movement of large-scale military forces so as to gain advantage, usually prior to actual engagement with the enemy. "Commanding the mouth of the Mississippi River, this strategic semitropical outpost also tapped the fur trade of the huge interior valley." (p. 109)

11. **guerilla warfare** Unconventional combat waged by small military units using hit-and-run tactics. ". . . so the combatants waged a kind of primitive guerilla warfare." (p. 110)

12. **sallies (sally)** In warfare, very rapid military movements, usually by small units, against an enemy force or position. "For their part the British colonists failed miserably in sallies against Quebec and Montreal. . . ." (p. 110)

13. **siege** A military operation of surrounding and attacking a fortified place, often over a sustained period. "After a ten-hour siege he was forced to surrender. . . ." (p. 113)

14. **regulars** Trained professional soldiers, as distinct from militia or conscripts. ". . . they had fought bravely alongside the crack British regulars. . . ." (p. 116)

15. **commissions** An official certification granting a commanding rank in the armed forces. ". . . the British refused to recognize any American militia commission. . . ." (p. 117)

PART II: CHECKING YOUR PROGRESS

A. True-False

Where the statement is true, circle **T**; where it is false, circle **F**.

1. T F French colonization was late developing because of internal religious and political conflict.

2. T F The French empire in North America rested on an economic foundation of forestry and sugar production.

3. T F Early imperial conflicts in North America often saw the French and their Indian allies engaging in guerrilla warfare against British frontier outposts.

4. T F Colonists in British North America managed to avoid direct involvement in most of Britain's "world wars" until the French and Indian War.

5. T F In the early seventeenth century, both France and England committed large regular forces to what they considered the crucial struggle for control of North America.

6. T F George Washington's battle at Fort Necessity substantially resolved the issue of control of the Ohio Valley.

7. T F The Albany Congress demonstrated a strong desire among some English colonists to overcome their differences and control their own affairs.

8. T F William Pitt's successful strategy in the French and Indian War was to concentrate British forces and try to capture the strongholds of Louisbourg, Quebec, and Montreal.

9. T F British regular troops under General Braddock succeeded in capturing the key French forts in the Ohio Valley.

10. T F   The French and Indian War left France with only Louisiana as a remnant of its once-mighty North American empire.

11. T F   American soldiers gained new respect for British military men after the British success against the French.

12. T F   The American colonists enthusiastically united in patriotic support of the British cause against the French.

13. T F   The removal of the French threat made American colonists more secure and therefore less reliant on the mother country for protection.

14. T F   A British commander used the harsh tactics of distributing blankets infected with smallpox to suppress Pontiac's Indian uprising.

15. T F   The British government's attempt to prohibit colonial expansion across the Appalachian Mountains aroused colonial anger and defiance of the law.

B. Multiple Choice

Select the best answer and circle the corresponding letter.

1.   Compared with the English colonies, New France was
     a.   more wealthy and successful.
     b.   better able to maintain consistently friendly relations with the Indians.
     c.   more heavily populated.
     d.   more autocratically governed.

2.   The expansion of New France occurred especially
     a.   in the interior mountain areas.
     b.   along the paths of lakes and rivers.
     c.   in areas already occupied by English settlers.
     d.   to the north of the original St. Lawrence River settlement.

3.   Colonial Americans were unhappy after the peace treaty following the "War of Jenkins's Ear" because
     a.   it failed to settle the issue that had caused the war.
     b.   it gave the Louisbourg fortress they had captured back to France.
     c.   it created further conflicts with Spain.
     d.   it failed to deal with the issue of Indian attacks on the frontier.

4.   The original cause of the French and Indian War was
     a.   conflict in Europe between Britain and France.
     b.   British removal of the "Acadian" French settlers from Nova Scotia.
     c.   competition between French and English colonists for land in the Ohio River valley.
     d.   a French attack on George Washington's Virginia headquarters.

5.   The French and Indian War eventually became part of the larger world conflict known as
     a.   the Seven Years' War.
     b.   the War of Jenkins's Ear.
     c.   the War of the Austrian Succession.
     d.   King George's War.

6.   Benjamin Franklin's attempt to create intercolonial unity at the Albany Congress resulted in
     a.   a permanent cooperative organization of the colonies.
     b.   rejection of the congress's proposal for colonial home rule both by London and by the individual colonies.
     c.   a sharp increase in Indian attacks on colonial settlements.

d. a growing colonial sympathy with France in the war against Britain.

7. The British forces suffered early defeats in the French and Indian War under the overall command of

   a. General Braddock.
   b. General Washington.
   c. General Wolfe.
   d. General Montcalm.

8. William Pitt's strategy in the assault on New France finally succeeded because

   a. he was able to arouse more support for the war effort from the colonists.
   b. he gave full support to General Braddock as commander of the British forces.
   c. he concentrated British forces on attacking the vital strong points of Quebec and Montreal.
   d. he was able to gain the support of the British aristocracy for the war effort.

9. The decisive event in the French-British contest for North America was

   a. the British capture of Fort Duquesne.
   b. the British victory in the Battle of Quebec.
   c. the American capture of the Louisbourg fortress.
   d. the British attack on the West Indies.

10. Among the factors that tended to promote intercolonial unity during the French and Indian War was

   a. religious unity.
   b. common language and wartime experience.
   c. ethnic and social harmony.
   d. improved transportation and settlement of boundary disputes.

11. The French and Indian War weakened interior Indian peoples like the Iroquois and Creeks by

   a. establishing new American settlements on their territory.
   b. eliminating their most effective leaders.
   c. ending their hopes for diplomatic recognition in Europe.
   d. removing their French and Spanish allies from Canada and Florida.

12. Pontiac's fierce attack on frontier outposts in 1763 had the effect of

   a. ending good American-Indian relations on the frontier.
   b. reviving French hopes for a new war.
   c. convincing the British to keep troops stationed in the colonies.
   d. stopping the flow of westward settlement.

13. The British Proclamation of 1763

   a. was welcomed by most American colonists.
   b. angered colonists who thought that it deprived them of the fruits of victory.
   c. was aimed at further suppressing the French population of Canada.
   d. halted American westward settlement for several years.

14. The French and Indian War created conflict between the British and the American military because

   a. the American soldiers had failed to support the British military effort.
   b. the British regulars had carried the brunt of the fighting.
   c. British officers treated the American colonial militia with contempt.
   d. American soldiers refused to accept orders from British officers.

15. The effect on the colonists of the French removal from North America was

   a. to increase their gratitude to Britain for defending them in the war.
   b. to create new threats to colonial expansion from Spain and the Indians.
   c. to reduce the colonies' reliance on Britain and increase their sense of independence.
   d. to focus colonial energies on trade.

C. Identification

Supply the correct identification for each numbered description.

1. _____ French Protestants who were granted toleration by the Edict of Nantes in 1598 but not permitted to settle in New France

2. _____ Absolute French monarch who reigned for seventy-two years

3. _____ Animal whose pelt provided great profits for the French empire and enhanced European fashion at enormous ecological cost

4. _____ French Catholic religious order that explored the North American interior and sought to protect and convert the Indians

5. _____ Far-running, high-living French fur trappers

6. _____ Part of a certain British naval officer's anatomy that set off an imperial war with Spain

7. _____ Strategic French fortress conquered by New England settlers, handed back to the French, and finally conquered again by the British in 1759

8. _____ Inland river territory, scene of fierce competition between the French and land-speculating English colonists

9. _____ Bloodiest European theater of the Seven Years' War, where Frederick the Great's troops drained French strength away from North America

10. _____ Unification effort that Benjamin Franklin nearly led to success by his eloquent leadership and cartoon artistry

11. _____ Military aide of British General Braddock and defender of the frontier after Braddock's defeat

12. _____ Fortress boldly assaulted by General Wolfe, spelling doom for New France

13. _____ The "buckskin" colonial soldiers whose military success did nothing to alter British officers' contempt

14. _____ Allies of the French against the British, who continued to fight under Pontiac even after the peace settlement in 1763

15. _____ The larger European struggle of which the French and Indian War was part

D. Matching People, Places, and Events

Match the person, place, or event in the left column with the proper description in the right column by inserting the correct letter on the blank line.

1. ___ Samuel de Champlain

2. ___ Robert de la Salle

3. ___ Albany

4. ___ War of Austrian Succession

5. ___ Fort Duquesne

6. ___ George Washington

7. ___ Benjamin Franklin

a. Advocate of colonial unity at a 1754 meeting in upstate New York

b. British document that aroused colonial anger but failed to stop frontier expansion

c. French colonists in Nova Scotia brutally uprooted by the victorious British and shipped to Louisiana

d. Conflict that started with the War of

8. ___   General Braddock
9. ___   William Pitt
10. ___   Plains of Abraham
11. ___   Seven Years' War
12. ___   Pontiac
13. ___   Proclamation of 1763
14. ___   New Orleans
15. ___   Acadians (Cajuns)

Jenkins's Ear and ended with the return of Louisbourg to France

e.   Strategic French outpost at the mouth of the Mississippi

f.   Indian leader whose frontier uprising caused the British to attempt to limit colonial expansion

g.   Blundering British officer whose defeat gave the advantage to the French and Indians in the early stages of their war

h.   The Father of New France, who established a crucial alliance with the Huron Indians

i.   Site of the death of Generals Wolfe and Montcalm, where France's New World empire also perished

j.   Strategic French stronghold; later renamed after a great British statesman

k.   Militia commander whose frontier skirmish in Pennsylvania touched off a world war

l.   Site of a meeting that proposed greater unity and home rule among Britain's North American colonies

m.   Conflict that began with George Washington's skirmish in Ohio and ended with the loss of France's North American empire

n.   French empire builder who explored the Mississippi Basin and named it after his monarch

o.   Splendid British orator and organizer of the winning strategy against the French in North America

E. Putting Things in Order

Put the following events in correct order by numbering them from 1 to 10.

1. _____   A Virginia militia commander attempts an unsuccessful invasion of the Ohio Valley.

2. _____   The "Great Commoner" takes command of the British government and its war effort.

3. _____   Toleration of French Huguenots brings religious peace to France.

4. _____   New France is founded, one year after Jamestown.

5. _____ Britain issues a proclamation to prohibit colonial expansion and thereby prevent another Indian war.

6. _____ The second "world war" between France and Britain ends in British victory and the acquisition of Acadia.

7. _____ British victory on the Plains of Abraham seals the fate of New France.

8. _____ Return of Louisbourg fortress at the end of King George's War angers colonial New Englanders.

9. _____ War begins badly for the British when Braddock fails to take Fort Duquesne.

10. _____ A great empire builder explores Louisiana and claims it for the French king.

F. Matching Cause and Effect

Match the historical cause in the left column with the proper effect in the right column by writing the correct letter on the blank line.

Cause	**Effect**
1. ___ The French fur trade	a. Resulted in decisive French defeat and British domination of North America
2. ___ The four "world wars" between 1688 and 1763	b. Prompted widespread Indian assaults on the weakly defended colonial frontier
3. ___ Competition for land and furs in the Ohio Valley	c. Led to Washington's expedition and battle with the French at Fort Necessity
4. ___ The summoning of the Albany Congress by the British	d. Heightened colonial anger and encouraged illegal westward expansion
5. ___ William Pitt's assumption of control of British government and strategy	e. Increased American military confidence and resentment of British redcoats
6. ___ Wolfe's victory over Montcalm at Quebec	f. Decimated beaver populations while spreading the French empire
7. ___ The colonial militia's military success in the French and Indian War	g. Were echoed by four small wars between French and British subjects in North America
8. ___ Colonial American smuggling and trading with French enemy	h. Represented the first major attempt at intercolonial unity
9. ___ British issuance of the Proclamation of 1763	i. Increased British government's disdain for colonial Americans and raised doubts about their loyalty to the empire
10. ___ Braddock's defeat at Fort Duquesne	j. Ended a string of defeats and turned the French and Indian War in Britain's favor

G. Developing Historical Skills

Using a Map to Understand the Text

Reading maps frequently aids in understanding a point being made in the text—especially when it involves geography or strategy. On p.115, the text emphasizes that the British did not turn the tide in the French and Indian War until Pitt altered strategy to concentrate on the strategic points of Louisbourg, Montreal, and Quebec. Examining the map on p. 115 helps you to understand why this was so.

Answer the following questions:

1. Why is Quebec more important than, say, Fort Duquesne in relation to the St. Lawrence River and the Atlantic Ocean?

2. Why was it essential to capture Louisbourg before attacking Quebec?

3. What was the strategic situation of remaining French forces in the Great Lakes area once Montreal and Quebec were captured?

H. Map Mastery

Map Discrimination

Using the maps and charts in Chapter 6, answer the following questions:

1. *France's American Empire at the Greatest Extent, 1700*: Around which great river valley was New France first colonized?

2. *France's American Empire at the Greatest Extent, 1700*: Which French colonial settlement on the Great Lakes linked the St. Lawrence and Mississippi river basins?

3. *Fur-Trading Posts*: Along which river, besides the Mississippi, were the greatest number of French fur-trading posts located?

4. *The Nine World Wars*: How many years of peace did Britain and France enjoy between France's loss of Acadia in the War of Spanish Succession and the beginning of the War of Austrian Succession?

5. *Scenes of the French Wars*: The attacks on Schenectady and Deerfield occurred during attacks from which French Canadian city?

6. *The Ohio Country, 1753–1754*: Fort Duquesne was located at the intersection of which two rivers (which unite at that point to form a third river)?

7. *Events of 1755–1760*: Which French Canadian stronghold did not finally fall until a year after Wolfe's defeat of Montcalm on the Plains of Abraham at Quebec?

8. *North America Before 1754/After 1763*: In the peace treaty of 1763, which nation besides Britain acquired North American territory from France?

9. *North America Before 1754/After 1763*: Which North American territory owned by Spain before 1754 was acquired by Britain in the peace of 1763?

Map Challenge

Using the maps in this chapter, write a brief essay explaining why the St. Lawrence River valley was the strategic key to control of the whole center of North America.

PART III: APPLYING WHAT YOU HAVE LEARNED

1. Why did the British and their American colonial subjects win the contest with the French for control of North America?

2. In what ways were the American colonists involved in the mother country's struggle with France?

3. How did French relations with the Indians compare with those of Britain and Spain?

4. Why did most Indian peoples fight with the French against Britain and its American colonists in the French and Indian War?

5. Explain why Britain's *success* in defeating the French empire led to *failures* in dealing with its colonial subjects.

6. How did events in France, Britain, and elsewhere in Europe affect the history of North America in this period?

7. Compare France's colonizing efforts in the New World with Spain's and England's colonies. (See especially Chapters 1 and 2.) What factors explain France's relatively weak impact on the New World compared with that of England's and Spain's?

8. When the Seven Years' War (French and Indian War) began, most American colonists were extremely proud and happy to be part of the world's greatest empire. When it ended many of them no longer felt that way, even though the British empire was greater than ever. Why?

CHAPTER 7

The Road to Revolution, 1763–1775

PART I: REVIEWING THE CHAPTER

A. CHECKLIST OF LEARNING OBJECTIVES

After mastering this chapter, you should be able to

1. explain the deeply rooted historical factors that moved America toward independence from Britain.

2. describe the theory and practice of mercantilism and explain why Americans resented it.

3. explain why Britain attempted tighter control and taxation of Americans after 1763 and why Americans resisted these efforts.

4. describe the major British efforts to impose taxes and tighten control of the colonies.

5. describe the methods of colonial resistance that forced repeal of all taxes except the tax on tea.

6. explain how sustained agitation and resistance to the tea tax led to the Intolerable Acts and the outbreak of war.

7. assess the balance of forces between the British and the American rebels as the two sides prepared for war.

B. GLOSSARY

To build your social science vocabulary, familiarize yourself with the following terms:

1. **patronage** A system in which benefits, including jobs, money, or protection are granted in exchange for political support. "The Whigs mounted withering attacks on the use of patronage and bribes by the king's ministers. . . ." (p. 123)

2. **mercantilism** The economic theory that all parts of an economy should be coordinated for the good of the whole state; hence, that colonial economics should be subordinated for the benefit of an empire. "The British authorities nevertheless embraced a theory called mercantilism. . . ." (p. 123)

3. **depreciate** To decrease in value, as in the decline of the purchasing power of money. ". . . dire financial need forced many of the colonies to issue paper money, which swiftly depreciated." (p. 124)

4. **veto** The constitutional right of a ruler or executive to block legislation passed by another unit of government. "This royal veto was used rather sparingly. . . ." (p. 124)

5. **monopoly** The complete control of a product or sphere of economic activity by a single producer or business. "Virginia tobacco planters enjoyed a monopoly in the British market. . . ." (p. 125)

6. **admiralty courts** In British law, special administrative courts designed to handle maritime cases without a jury. "Both the Sugar Act and the Stamp Act provided for trying offenders in the hated admiralty courts. . . ." (p. 126)

7. **virtual representation** The political theory that a class of persons is represented in a lawmaking body without direct vote. "Elaborating the theory of 'virtual representation,' Grenville claimed that every member of Parliament represented all British subjects, even . . . Americans. . . ." (p. 127)

8. **nonimportation agreement** Pledges to boycott, or decline to purchase, certain goods from abroad. "More effective than the congress was the widespread adoption of nonimportation agreements. . . ." (p. 127)

9. **mulatto** A person of mixed African and European ancestry. ". . . Crispus Attucks [was] described . . . as a powerfully built runaway 'mulatto.'. . . " (p. 130)

10. **duty (duties)** A customs tax on the export or import of goods. ". . . finally persuaded Parliament to repeal the Townshend revenue duties." (p. 131)

11. **propaganda (propagandist)** A systematic program or particular materials designed to promote certain ideas; sometimes but not always the term is used negatively, implying the use of manipulative or deceptive means. (A propagandist is one who engages in such practices.) "Resistance was further kindled by a master propagandist and engineer of rebellion, Samuel Adams of Boston. . . ." (p. 131)

12. **boycott** An organized refusal to deal with some person, organization, or product. "The Association called for a *complete* boycott of British goods. . . ." (p. 134)

13. **inflation** An increase in the supply of currency relative to the goods available, leading to a decline in the purchasing power of money. "Inflation of the currency inevitably skyrocketed prices." (p. 137)

14. **desert** To leave official government or military service without permission. ". . . hundreds of anxious husbands and fathers deserted." (p. 137)

PART II: CHECKING YOUR PROGRESS

A. True-False

Where the statement is true, circle **T**; where it is false, circle **F**.

1. T F   The republican idea of a just society in which selfish interests were subordinated to the common good took deep root in Britain's North American colonies.

2. T F   The theory of mercantilism held that colonies existed primarily to provide the mother country with raw materials as well as a market for exports.

3. T F   British mercantilism forbade the importation of any non-British goods into the colonies.

4. T F   In practice, British mercantilism provided the colonies with substantial economic benefits such as military protection and guaranteed markets for certain goods.

5. T F   The fundamental motive behind the steep new taxes in the 1760s was to repay the large debt that Britain had incurred in defending its North American colonies.

6. T F   Americans generally accepted the right of Parliament to tax the colonies to provide money for defense but denied its right to legislate about colonial affairs.

7. T F   When Americans first cried "no taxation without representation," what they wanted was to be represented in the British Parliament.

8. T   F   The colonies finally forced repeal of the Stamp Act by organizing political protests and enforcing nonimportation agreements against British goods.

9. T   F   Colonial rebellion against the new Townshend Acts was more highly organized and successful than the earlier Stamp Act protests.

10. T   F   The Boston Massacre provoked outrage because the British troops had been unprovoked when they opened fire on peaceful Boston citizens.

11. T   F   Massachusetts Governor Thomas Hutchinson provoked a crisis in Boston by enforcing the importation of British tea even though he believed that the tea tax was unjust.

12. T   F   The colonists considered the Quebec Act especially oppressive because they thought it would extend the domain of Roman Catholicism.

13. T   F   The First Continental Congress proclaimed that the colonies would declare independence from Britain unless their grievances were redressed.

14. T   F   One fundamental American asset in the impending war with Britain was an extensive stockpile of military weapons and supplies.

15. T   F   A key British advantage was that they did not have to defeat all the American forces but only fight to a draw in order to crush the Revolution.

B. Multiple Choice

Select the best answer and circle the corresponding letter.

1. The British theory of mercantilism, by which the colonies were governed, held that
    a.   the economy should be shaped by market forces, without government interference.
    b.   the colonies should develop by becoming as economically self-sufficient as possible.
    c.   the colonial economy should be carefully controlled to serve the mother country's needs.
    d.   colonists should promote economic growth by free trade with other countries.

2. One of the ways in which mercantilism harmed the colonial economy was
    a.   by prohibiting colonial merchants from owning and operating their own ships.
    b.   by inhibiting the development of banking and paper currency in the colonies.
    c.   by forcing the colonists to fall into debt through the purchase of goods on credit.
    d.   by forcing Virginia tobacco planters to sell their product only in Britain.

3. The mobilization of "nonimportation" policies against the Stamp Act was politically important because
    a.   it aroused the first French support for the American cause.
    b.   it aroused revolutionary fervor among many ordinary American men and women.
    c.   it reinforced the completely nonviolent character of the anti-British movement.
    d.   it helped stimulate the development of colonial manufacturing.

4. When British officials decided to enforce the East India Company's tea monopoly and the three-pence tax on tea,
    a.   they were successful in landing the tea everywhere except Boston.
    b.   colonists were outraged because their favorite beverage would cost more than ever before.
    c.   the colonists persuaded friendly Indian tribes to dump the tea into Boston harbor.
    d.   colonists were outraged because they saw it as a trick to undermine their principled resistance to the tax.

5. The British reacted to the Boston Tea Party by
    a.   shipping the colonial protestors to Britain for trial.
    b.   closing the Port of Boston until damages were paid and order restored.

c. passing the Quebec Act prohibiting trial by jury and permitting the practice of Catholicism.
d. granting a monopoly on the sale of tea to the British East India Company.

6. American colonists especially resented the Townshend Acts because
   a. they strongly disliked the British minister, "Champagne Charley" Townshend, who proposed them.
   b. the revenues from the taxation would go to support British officials and judges in America.
   c. they called for the establishment of the Anglican church throughout the colonies.
   d. the taxes were to be imposed directly by the king without an act of Parliament.

7. The passage of the Quebec Act aroused intense American fears because
   a. it put the French language on an equal standing with English throughout the colonies.
   b. it involved stationing British troops throughout the colonies.
   c. it extended Catholic jurisdiction and a non-jury judicial system into the western Ohio country.
   d. it threatened to make Canada the dominant British colony in North America.

8. The most important action the Continental Congress took to protest the Intolerable Acts was
   a. forming The Association to impose a complete boycott of all British goods.
   b. organizing a colonial militia to prepare for military resistance.
   c. forming Committees of Correspondence to communicate among all the colonies and develop political opposition to British rule.
   d. sending petitions to the British Parliament demanding repeal of the laws.

9. The event that precipitated the first real shooting between the British and American colonists was
   a. the British attempt to seize Bunker Hill and the Old North Church.
   b. the British attempt to seize colonial supplies and leaders at Lexington and Concord.
   c. the Boston Tea Party.
   d. the Boston Massacre.

10. The British parliamentary government at the time of the American Revolution was headed by
    a. William Pitt.
    b. "Champagne Charley" Townshend.
    c. Edmund Burke.
    d. Lord North.

11. The American rebellion was especially dangerous to the British because they were also worried about
    a. possible revolts in Ireland and war with France.
    b. labor unrest in British industrial cities.
    c. maintaining sufficient troops in India.
    d. their ability to maintain naval control of the oceans.

12. The British political party that was generally more sympathetic to the American cause was
    a. the Tory Party.
    b. the Labor Party.
    c. the Country Party.
    d. the Whig Party.

13. One of the advantages the British enjoyed in the impending conflict with the colonies was
    a. a determined and politically effective government.
    b. the ability to enlist foreign soldiers, Loyalists, and Native Americans in their military forces.
    c. a highly motivated and efficiently run military force in America.
    d. the concentration of colonial resistance in a few urban centers.

14. One of the advantages the colonists enjoyed in the impending conflict with Britain was
    a. fighting defensively on a large, agriculturally self-sufficient continent.
    b. a well-organized and effective political leadership.

    c.   a strong sense of unity among the various colonies.

    d.   the fact that nearly all Americans owned their own firearms.

15. In the Revolutionary War, African Americans

    a.   unanimously supported the American patriot cause.

    b.   were generally neutral between the British and American forces.

    c.   fought in both the American patriot and British loyalist military forces.

    d.   took the opportunity to stage substantial slave revolts.

C. Identification

Supply the correct identification for each numbered description.

1. _____ The basic economic and political theory by which seventeenth- and eighteenth-century European powers governed their overseas colonies

2. _____ The set of Parliamentary laws, first passed in 1650, that restricted colonial trade and directed it to the benefit of Britain

3. _____ The term for products, such as tobacco, that could be shipped only to England and not to foreign markets

4. _____ Hated British courts in which juries were not allowed and defendants were assumed guilty until proven innocent

5. _____ British governmental theory that Parliament spoke for all British subjects, including Americans, even if they did not vote for its members

6. _____ The effective form of organized colonial resistance against the Stamp Act, which made homespun clothing fashionable

7. _____ The product taxed under the Townshend Acts that generated the greatest colonial resistance

8. _____ Underground networks of communication and propaganda, established by Samuel Adams, that sustained colonial resistance

9. _____ Religion that was granted toleration in the trans-Allegheny West by the Quebec Act, arousing deep colonial hostility

10. _____ British political party opposed to Lord North's Tories and generally more sympathetic to the colonial cause

11. _____ German mercenaries hired by George III to fight the American revolutionaries

12. _____ Paper currency authorized by Congress to finance the Revolution depreciated to near worthlessness

13. _____ Effective organization created by the First Continental Congress to provide a total, unified boycott of all British goods

14. _____ Rapidly mobilized colonial militiamen whose refusal to disperse sparked the first battle of the Revolution

15. _____ Popular term for British regular troops, scorned as "lobster backs" and "bloody backs" by Bostonians and other colonials

D. Matching People, Places, and Events

Match the person, place, or event in the left column with the proper description in the right column by inserting the correct letter on the blank line.

1. ___ John Hancock

2. ___ George Grenville

3. ___ Stamp Act

4. ___ Sons and Daughters of Liberty

5. ___ "Champagne Charley" Townshend

6. ___ Crispus Attucks

7. ___ George III

8. ___ Samuel Adams

9. ___ Boston Tea Party

10. ___ Intolerable Acts

11. ___ Thomas Hutchinson

12. ___ First Continental Congress

13. ___ Marquis de Lafayette

14. ___ Baron von Steuben

15. ___ Quartering Act

a. British minister who raised a storm of protest by passing the Stamp Act

b. Legislation passed in 1765 but repealed the next year, after colonial resistance made it impossible to enforce

c. Body led by John Adams that issued a Declaration of Rights and organized The Association to boycott all British goods

d. Legislation that required colonists to feed and shelter British troops; disobeyed in New York and elsewhere

e. Nineteen-year-old major general in the Revolutionary army

f. Wealthy president of the Continental Congress and "King of the Smugglers"

g. Minister whose clever attempt to impose import taxes nearly succeeded, but eventually brewed trouble for Britain

h. Zealous defender of the common people's rights and organizer of underground propaganda committees

i. Harsh measures of retaliation for a tea party, including the Boston Port Act closing that city's harbor

j. Stubborn ruler, lustful for power, who promoted harsh ministers like Lord North

k. Alleged leader of radical protesters killed in Boston Massacre

l. Organizational genius who turned raw colonial recruits into tough professional soldiers

m. Male and female organizations that enforced the nonimportation agreements, sometimes by coercive means

n. British governor of Massachusetts whose stubborn policies helped provoke the Boston Tea Party

o.   Event organized by disguised "Indians"
to sabotage British support of a British
East India Company monopoly

E. Putting Things in Order

Put the following events in correct order by numbering them from 1 to 10.

1. _____   Britain attempts to gain revenue by a tax on papers and documents, creating a colonial uproar.

2. _____   Britain closes the port of Boston and opens the western frontier to Catholicism.

3. _____   Crispus Attucks leads a crowd in an attack on British troops, and eleven people are killed.

4. _____   Colonial Minute Men fire "the shot heard around the world" in the first battle of the Revolution.

5. _____   A British minister cleverly attempts to gain revenue and dampen colonial protest by imposing an import tax only on certain specialized products.

6. _____   A British agency is established with broad but generally ineffective power over colonial commerce.

7. _____   Samuel Adams and others organize revolutionary cells of communication and agitation across the colonies.

8. _____   Parliament repeals a direct tax in response to colonial protest but declares that it has the right to tax colonies.

9. _____   A band of "Indians" dumps the rich cargo of the British East India Company into Boston Harbor, provoking a harsh British response.

10. _____   First acts are passed by Parliament to regulate colonial trade based on mercantilist principles.

F. Matching Cause and Effect

Match the historical cause in the left column with the proper effect in the right column by writing the correct letter on the blank line.

Cause		Effect
1. ___ America's distance from Britain and the growth of colonial self-government	a.	Prompted the summoning of the First Continental Congress
2. ___ British mercantilism	b.	Led Grenville to propose the Sugar Act, Quartering Act, and Stamp Act
3. ___ The large British debt incurred defending the colonies in the French and Indian War	c.	Precipitated the Battle of Lexington and Concord
4. ___ Passage of the Stamp Act	d.	Fired on colonial citizens in the Boston Massacre
5. ___ British troops sent to enforce order in Boston	e.	Prompted passage of the Intolerable Acts, including the Boston Port Act

6. ___ The British government's attempt to maintain the East India Company's tea monopoly

f. Resulted in the printing of large amounts of paper currency and skyrocketing inflation

7. ___ The Boston Tea Party

g. Enforced restrictions on colonial manufacturing, trade, and paper currency

8. ___ The Intolerable Acts

9. ___ A British attempt to seize the colonial militia's gunpowder supplies

h. Led to gradual development of a colonial sense of independence years before the Revolution

10. ___ The Continental Congress's reluctance to tax Americans for war

i. Spurred patriots to stage Boston Tea Party

j. Was greeted in the colonies by the nonimportation agreements, the Stamp Act Congress, and the forced resignation of stamp agents

G. Developing Historical Skills

Interpreting Historical Illustrations

Contemporary illustrations of historical events may not only give us information about those events but tell us something about the attitude and intention of those who made the illustrations. The caption to the engraving of the Boston Massacre by Paul Revere (p.130) observes that it is "both art and propaganda." Drawing on the account of the massacre in the text (pp. 129–130) enables you to see the ways in which Revere's engraving combines factual information with a political point of view.

Answer the following questions:

1. What parts of the encounter between the British redcoats and the colonists does the engraving entirely leave out?

2. The text says that the British troops fired "without orders." How does the engraving suggest the opposite?

3. How does Revere's presentation of the colonial victims seem especially designed to inflame the feelings of the viewer?

PART III: APPLYING WHAT YOU HAVE LEARNED

1. Why did the American colonies move from loyalty to protest to rebellion in the twelve years following the end of the French and Indian War?

2. How and why did the Americans and the British differ in their views of taxation and of the relationship of colonies to the empire?

3. What was the theory and practice of mercantilism? What were its actual effects on the colonies, and why did the colonists resent it so much?

4. What methods did the colonists use in their struggle with British authorities, and how did the British try to counteract them?

5. What advantages and disadvantages did the American rebels and the British each possess as the war began? What did each side do to mobilize its resources most effectively?

6. Is it correct to argue that the British possessed an overwhelming military advantage at the outbreak of the Revolutionary War, but that the Americans possessed the political advantage in ideology and leadership?

7. Could the American people have won their independence without George Washington and the small, professional Continental Army? Why have the myths of the militiamen and the part-time citizen-soldiers loomed so large in American memories of the Revolutionary War?

8. Was the American Revolution inevitable? Or could the thirteen colonies have remained attached to Britain for many years and then peacefully achieved their independence as the British colonies of Canada and Australia later did? How would the "meaning of America" have been different without this violent revolt from the mother country?

CHAPTER 8

America Secedes from the Empire, 1775–1783

PART I: REVIEWING THE CHAPTER

A. CHECKLIST OF LEARNING OBJECTIVES

After mastering this chapter, you should be able to

1. describe how Americans engaged in major military hostilities with Britain after April 1775, even while proclaiming their loyalty to the British crown.

2. explain why Paine's *Common Sense* finally propelled Americans to declare their independence in the summer of 1776, and outline the principal ideas of "republicanism" that Paine and other American revolutionary leaders promoted.

3. explain the specific reasons and general principles used in the Declaration of Independence to justify America's separation.

4. understand the American Revolution as a civil war as well as a war with Britain, and describe the motivations and eventual fate of the Loyalists.

5. describe how the British attempt to crush the Revolution quickly was foiled, especially by the Battle of Saratoga.

6. describe the military and political obstacles Washington and his generals faced, and how they were able to overcome them.

7. outline the course and conduct of the Revolutionary War after 1778, and describe the key role played by France in the final victory at Yorktown.

8. describe the terms of the Treaty of Paris and explain why America was able to achieve such a stunning diplomatic victory.

B. GLOSSARY

To build your social science vocabulary, familiarize yourself with the following terms:

1. **mercenary** A professional soldier who serves in a foreign army for pay. ". . . the Americans called all the European mercenaries Hessians." (p. 143)

2. **indictment** A formal written accusation charging someone with a crime. "The overdrawn bill of indictment included imposing taxes without consent. . . ." (p. 148)

3. **dictatorship** A form of government characterized by absolute state power and the unlimited authority of the ruler. "The [charges] included . . . establishing a military dictatorship. . . ." (p. 148)

4. **neutral** A nation or person not taking sides in a war. "Many colonists were apathetic or neutral. . . ." (p. 148)

5. **civilian** A citizen not in military service. "The opposing forces contended . . . for the allegiance . . . of the civilian population." (p. 148)

6. **traitor** One who betrays a country by aiding an enemy. ". . . they regarded their opponents, not themselves, as traitors." (p. 152)

7. **confiscate** To seize private property for public use, often as a penalty. "The estates of many of the fugitives were confiscated. . . ." (p. 152)

8. **envoy** A messenger or agent sent by a government on official business. "Benjamin Franklin, recently sent to Paris as an envoy, truthfully jested that Howe had not captured Philadelphia. . . ." (p. 155)

9. **rabble** A mass of disorderly and crude common people. "This rabble was nevertheless whipped into a professional army. . . ." (p. 155)

10. **arsenal** A place for making or storing weapons and ammunition. "About 90 percent of all the gunpowder . . . came from French arsenals." (p. 155)

11. **isolationist** Concerning the belief that a country should take little or no part in foreign affairs, especially through alliances or wars. "The American people, with ingrained isolationist tendencies, accepted the French entanglement with distaste." (p. 156)

12. **hereditary** Passed down from generation to generation. "They were painfully aware that it bound them to a hereditary foe that was also a Roman Catholic power." (p. 156)

13. **blockade** The isolation of a place by hostile ships or troops. "Now the French had powerful fleets. . . in a position to jeopardize Britain's blockade and lines of supply." (p. 157)

14. **privateer** A private vessel temporarily authorized to capture or plunder enemy ships in wartime. "More numerous and damaging than ships of the regular American navy were swift privateers." (p. 159)

15. **graft** Taking advantage of one's official position to gain money or property by illegal means. "It had the unfortunate effect of . . . involving Americans, including Benedict Arnold, in speculation and graft." (p. 159)

PART II: CHECKING YOUR PROGRESS

A. True-False

Where the statement is true, circle **T**; where it is false, circle **F**.

1. T   F   George Washington was chosen commander of the American army primarily because of his military abilities and experience.

2. T   F   Following the Battle of Bunker Hill, King George and the Continental Congress made one last attempt at reconciliation.

3. T   F   The American army that invaded Canada falsely believed that oppressed French Canadians would join them in revolt and make Canada the fourteenth state.

4. T   F   Tom Paine's *Common Sense* was most important because it pushed the colonies into violent rebellion against the king as well as against Parliament.

5. T   F   The Declaration of Independence was especially important because it enabled the Americans to appeal for direct aid from France.

6. T   F   American militiamen proved politically very effective in pushing their apathetic or neutral fellow citizens into supporting the Patriot cause.

7.   T   F   The Loyalists considered the "Patriots" to be the traitors to their country and themselves to be the true patriots.

8.   T   F   Most Loyalists were executed or driven from the country after the Patriot victory.

9.   T   F   The Loyalists were strongest in New England and Virginia.

10.   T   F   General Burgoyne's defeat at Saratoga in 1777 was critical for the American cause because it led to the alliance with France.

11.   T   F   Americans' enlightened revolutionary idealism made them reluctant to enter into a military and political alliance with monarchical France.

12.   T   F   During much of the Revolutionary War, the British controlled cities like New York, Boston, Philadelphia, and Charleston, while the Americans conducted their campaigns primarily in the countryside.

13.   T   F   At Yorktown, the Americans finally showed that they could win an important battle without French assistance.

14.   T   F   American diplomats were successful in guaranteeing American political independence but failed to gain the territorial concessions they wanted.

15.   T   F   American success in the Revolutionary War and the peace treaty was due in significant measure to political developments in Europe.

B. Multiple Choice

Select the best answer and circle the corresponding letter.

1.   During the period of fighting between April 1775 and July 1776, the colonists claimed that their goal was
   a.   the removal of all British troops from America.
   b.   to restore their rights within the British Empire.
   c.   complete independence from Britain.
   d.   to end the power of King George III to rule them.

2.   George Washington proved to be an especially effective commander of American forces in the Revolution because
   a.   he was able to rally previously skeptical New Englanders to the Patriot cause.
   b.   of his exceptionally brilliant military mind.
   c.   of his integrity, courage, and moral forcefulness.
   d.   his humble background inspired the ordinary soldiers in the Revolutionary army.

3.   The bold American military strategy that narrowly failed in December 1775 involved
   a.   a two-pronged attack on British forces in New Jersey.
   b.   an invasion of Canada by generals Arnold and Montgomery.
   c.   an attack on British forts in the Ohio country.
   d.   a naval assault on British warships in Boston harbor.

4.   Many of the German Hessian soldiers hired by King George III to fight for the British
   a.   hated the American revolutionaries and their cause.
   b.   helped draw in the Prussian King Frederick II as a British ally.
   c.   were ineffective in battle against American militiamen.
   d.   had little loyalty to the British cause and ended up deserting.

5. Thomas Paine's appeal for a new republican form of government attracted many Americans because
    a. they believed that social class differences promoted by monarchy were wrong.
    b. their own experience with local and colonial democratic governance had prepared them for the idea.
    c. they were impressed that Paine was drawing on the best classical ideas from Plato's *Republic*.
    d. they were fearful that wealthy southern planters like Washington wanted to establish nobility in America.

6. Paine's *Common Sense* was crucial in convincing many Americans that what they should fight for was
    a. American representation in the British Parliament.
    b. an alliance with the French against Britain.
    c. a federal constitution and bill of rights.
    d. an independent and republican America separate from Britain.

7. The Loyalists were particularly strong among
    a. conservative and well-off Americans.
    b. the younger generation.
    c. Presbyterians and Congregationalists.
    d. citizens of New England.

8. Besides George Washington, the most militarily effective American officer in the early campaigns of 1776 and 1777 was
    a. General Nathanael Greene.
    b. General von Steuben.
    c. General Benedict Arnold.
    d. General William Howe.

9. The Battle of Saratoga was a key turning point of the War for Independence because
    a. it prevented the British from keeping control of the key port of New York City.
    b. it brought about crucial French assistance to the Revolutionary cause.
    c. it ended the possibility of a peaceful settlement with Britain.
    d. if effectively destroyed British military power in the middle colonies.

10. The primary reason that Americans were willing to enter a military and diplomatic alliance with France in 1778 was
    a. the practical self-interest of needing assistance to defeat the British.
    b. to spread republican government and the principles of the Declaration of Independence among the oppressed French people.
    c. that Benjamin Franklin was able to construct an alliance treaty based completely on revolutionary idealism.
    d. that the French king agreed that the United States could seek a separate peace with Britain if it wanted to.

11. The British especially relied on the numerous Loyalists to aid them in fighting the Patriots
    a. in Rhode Island and the rest of New England.
    b. in the western Illinois country.
    c. in the warfare at sea.
    d. in the Carolinas.

12. Most of the Six Nations of the Iroquois under Joseph Brant fought against the American revolutionaries because

   a.   they disagreed with the principles of the Declaration of Independence.
   b.   they believed that a victorious Britain would contain westward American expansion.
   c.   they were paid as mercenary soldiers by the British government.
   d.   they hoped to drive the American colonists off the North American continent.

13. The British defeat at Yorktown was brought about by George Washington's army and

   a.   the French navy under Admiral de Grasse.
   b.   the American navy under John Paul Jones.
   c.   the American militia under George Rogers Clark.
   d.   the Armed Neutrality under Catherine the Great.

14. In the peace negotiations at Paris, the French wanted the Americans

   a.   to stop short of demanding full independence.
   b.   to negotiate a separate peace with Britain.
   c.   to acquire only the territory east of the Appalachian Mountains.
   d.   to help them regain Quebec from the British.

15. The British yielded the Americans a generous peace treaty that included the western territories primarily because of

   a.   the desire of the weak Whig ministry in London for friendly future relations with the United States.
   b.   the threat of further war with France.
   c.   the military power of the United States.
   d.   the willingness of the Americans to yield on other issues like trade and fishing rights.

C. Identification

Supply the correct identification for each numbered description.

1. _____   The body that chose George Washington commander of the Continental Army

2. _____   The British colony that Americans invaded in hopes of adding it to the rebellious thirteen

3. _____   The inflammatory pamphlet that demanded independence and heaped scorn on "the Royal Brute of Great Britain"

4. _____   The document that provided a lengthy explanation and justification of Richard Henry Lee's resolution that was passed by Congress on July 2, 1776

5. _____   The term by which the American Patriots were commonly known, to distinguish them from the American "Tories"

6. _____   Another name for the American Tories

7. _____   The church body most closely linked with Tory sentiment, except in Virginia

8. _____   The river valley that was the focus of Britain's early military strategy and the scene of Burgoyne's surrender at Saratoga in 1777

9. _____   Term for the alliance of Catherine the Great of Russia and other European powers who did not declare war but assumed a hostile neutrality toward Britain

10. _____   The region that saw some of the Revolution's most bitter fighting, from 1780 to 1782, between American General Greene and British General Cornwallis

11. _____   "Legalized pirates," more than a thousand strong, who inflicted heavy damage on British shipping

12. _____   British political party that replaced Lord North's Tories in 1782 and made a generous treaty with the United States

13. _____   The western boundary of the United States established in the Treaty of Paris

14. _____   The irregular American troops who played a crucial role in swaying the neutral civilian population toward the Patriot cause

15. _____   The other European nation besides France and Spain that supported the American Revolution by declaring war on Britain

D. Matching People, Places, and Events

Match the person, place, or event in the left column with the proper description in the right column by inserting the correct letter on the blank line.

1. ___ George Washington

2. ___ Bunker Hill

3. ___ Benedict Arnold

4. ___ Thomas Paine

5. ___ Richard Henry Lee

6. ___ Thomas Jefferson

7. ___ Loyalists

8. ___ General Burgoyne

9. ___ General Howe

10. ___ Benjamin Franklin

11. ___ George Rogers Clark

12. ___ John Paul Jones

13. ___ Saratoga

14. ___ Yorktown

15. ___ Joseph Brant

a. British general who chose to enjoy himself in New York and Philadelphia rather than vigorously pursue the American enemy

b. Brilliant American general who invaded Canada, foiled Burgoyne's invasion, and then betrayed his country in 1780

c. American naval commander who successfully harassed British shipping

d. Author of an explanatory indictment, signed on July 4, 1776, that accused George III of establishing a military dictatorship

e. Shrewd and calculatingly "homespun" American diplomat who forged the alliance with France and later secured a generous peace treaty

f. Mohawk chief who led many Iroquois to fight with Britain against American revolutionaries

g. The decisive early battle of the American Revolution that led to the alliance with France

h. Military engagement that led King George III officially to declare the colonists in revolt

i. Americans who fought for King George and earned the contempt of Patriots

j. A wealthy Virginian of great character

and leadership abilities who served his country without pay

k.   The British defeat that led to the fall of North's government and the end of the war

l.   Leader whose small force conquered key British forts in the West

m.   A radical British immigrant who put an end to American toasts to King George

n.   Fiery Virginian and author of the official resolution of July 2, 1776, formally authorizing the colonies' independence

o.   Blundering British general whose slow progress south from Canada ended in disaster at Saratoga

E. Putting Things in Order

Put the following events in correct order by numbering them from 1 to 6.

1.   _____   Lord North's military collapses, and Britain's Whigs take power ready to make peace.

2.   _____   Thomas Jefferson writes an eloquent justification of Richard Henry Lee's resolution.

3.   _____   Burgoyne and Howe are defeated both by the generalship of Washington and Arnold and by their own blundering.

4.   _____   The Treaty of Paris is signed, guaranteeing American independence.

5.   _____   The British launch a frontal attack on entrenched American forces near Boston and suffer drastic losses in their "victory."

6.   _____   Washington's army and the French navy trap General Cornwallis, spelling the end for the British.

F. Matching Cause and Effect

Match the historical cause in the left column with the proper effect in the right column by writing the correct letter on the blank line.

Cause		Effect	
1. ___	The Battle of Bunker Hill	a.	Led to American acquisition of the West up to the Mississippi River
2. ___	Thomas Paine's *Common Sense*		
3. ___	Jefferson's *Declaration of Independence*	b.	Caused King George to proclaim the colonies in revolt and import Hessian troops to crush them
4. ___	The Patriot militia's political education and recruitment	c.	Led to a favorable peace treaty for the United States and the end of French

5. ___   The blundering of Burgoyne and Howe and the superb military strategy of Arnold and Washington

6. ___   The Battle of Saratoga

7. ___   Clark's military conquests and Jay's diplomacy

8. ___   The trapping of Cornwallis between Washington's army and de Grasse's navy

9. ___   The collapse of the North ministry and the Whig takeover of the British government

10. ___   Jay's secret and separate negotiations with Britain

schemes for a smaller, weaker America

d.   Caused the British to begin peace negotiations in Paris

e.   Inspired universal awareness of the American Revolution as a fight for the belief that "all men are created equal"

f.   Caused the British defeat at Yorktown and the collapse of North's Tory government

g.   Led to the failure of Britain's grand strategy and the crucial American victory at Saratoga

h.   Made France willing to become an ally of the United States

i.   Stirred growing colonial support for declaring independence from Britain

j.   Won neutral or apathetic Americans over to the Patriot cause

G. Developing Historical Skills

Distinguishing Historical Fact and Historical Meaning

Some historical events can be understood as simple facts requiring little explanation. But other historical events have meaning only when their significance is analyzed. The text on pp. 142–148 contains examples of both kinds of historical events. Comparing them will help sort out the difference between the two.

Indicate which of these pairs of historical events is (a) a simple factual event requiring little explanation and which is (b) an event whose meaning needs to be interpreted in order to be understood. In each case, list the meaning the text gives to the second kind of event.

1.   The British burning of Falmouth (Portland), Maine, and King George's proclamation that the colonies were in rebellion.

2.   Tom Paine's *Common Sense* and the death of General Richard Montgomery.

3.   Richard Henry Lee's resolution of July 2, 1776, and Thomas Jefferson's Declaration of Independence.

H. Map Mastery

Map Discrimination

Using the maps and charts in Chapter 8, answer the following questions.

1. *Revolution in the North, 1775–1776*: Which two British strong points in Canada did the American generals Arnold and Montgomery attack in 1775?

2. *New York-Pennsylvania Theater, 1777–1778*: When Washington recrossed the Delaware River before the Battle of Trenton on December 26, 1776, which state did he come from, and which state did he go to?

3. *New York-Pennsylvania Theater, 1777–1778*: Which of the three British generals who were supposed to meet near Albany, New York moved in the opposite direction and failed to get to the appointed gathering?

4. *Britain Against the World*: Besides France, which two European nations directly declared war on Britain during the American Revolution?

5. *War in the South, 1780–1781*: Name three cities in the South occupied at one time or another by General Cornwallis.

6. *George Rogers Clark's Campaign, 1778–1779*: Which river did George Rogers Clark move down as he went to conquer western forts from the British?

7. *George Rogers Clark's Campaign, 1778–1779*: Which three British posts did Clark capture?

Map Challenge

Using the maps on p. 144 and p. 154 as a basis, write a brief essay explaining why control of the Hudson River–Lake Champlain Valley was strategically crucial to both the British and the Americans in the Revolutionary War.

PART III: APPLYING WHAT YOU HAVE LEARNED

1.   Why was the Battle of Saratoga such a key to American success in the Revolutionary War?

2.   What were the causes and consequences of the American Declaration of Independence in 1776?

 Why were Americans so long reluctant to break with Britain? How does the Declaration of Independence explain their reasons for separation (see Appendix)?

3.   Describe the different courses of the Revolutionary War in New England, the middle Atlantic states, and the South. What role did the battles in each region play in the eventual American victory?

4.   Why did Americans choose not only to break from Britain, but to adopt a republican form of government in 1776? What republican ideas did they share, and what did they disagree about?

5.   In what ways was the Revolution a civil war among Americans as well as a fight between Britain and those Americans seeking independence? Why have the Loyalists generally been "forgotten" in the story of America's beginnings?

6.   How did the idealism and "self-evident truths" of the Declaration of Independence shape Americans' outlook and conduct during the Revolutionary War? Why did so many Americans believe that they were establishing "a new order for the ages"?

7.   Argue for and against: the idealistic American Revolution was really because of the self-interest of the reactionary French monarchy.

8.   Argue for and against: Washington was a great general not so much because of his victories but because of his brilliant strategic retreats.

9.   How did economic and social self-interest compete with revolutionary idealism during the course of the Revolution? In what ways was the conflict about economic self-interest and social class as well as the principles of liberty and equality?

CHAPTER 9

The Confederation and the Constitution, 1776–1790

PART I: REVIEWING THE CHAPTER

A. CHECKLIST OF LEARNING OBJECTIVES

After mastering this chapter, you should be able to

1. explain the movement toward social and political equality that flourished after the Revolution, and indicate why certain social and racial inequalities remained in place.

2. describe the government of the Articles of Confederation and summarize its achievements and failures.

3. explain the crucial role of Shays's Rebellion in sparking the movement for a new Constitution.

4. describe the basic intentions and ideas of the Founding Fathers, and how they incorporated their fundamental principles into the Constitution.

5. grasp the central concerns that motivated the antifederalists, and indicate their social, economic, and political differences with the federalists.

6. describe the difficult political fight over ratification of the Constitution between federalists and antifederalists, and explain why the federalists won.

7. explain why the new Constitutional government represented a conservative reaction to the American Revolution and at the same time institutionalized its central radical principles.

B. GLOSSARY

To build your social science vocabulary, familiarize yourself with the following terms:

1. **disestablish** To separate an official state church from its connection with the government. ". . . the Protestant Episcopal church . . . was everywhere disestablished." (p. 167)

2. **emancipation** Setting free from servitude or slavery. "Several northern states . . . provided for the gradual emancipation of blacks." (p. 167)

3. **chattel** An article of personal or movable property; hence a term applied to slaves, since they were considered the personal property of their owners. ". . . a few idealistic masters freed their human chattels." (p. 167)

4. **abolitionist** An advocate of the end of slavery. "In this . . . were to be found the first frail sprouts of the later abolitionist movement." (p. 167)

5. **ratification** The confirmation or validation of an act (such as a constitution) by authoritative approval. "Massachusetts . . . submitted the final draft directly to the people for ratification." (p. 168)

6. **bill of rights** A list of fundamental freedoms assumed to be central to society. "Most of these documents included bills of rights. . . ." (p. 168)

7. **speculators (speculation)** Those who buy property, goods, or financial instruments not primarily for use but in anticipation of profitable resale after a general rise in value. "States seized control of former crown lands . . . although rich speculators had their day." (p. 169)

8. **township** In America, a surveyed territory six miles square; the term also refers to a unit of local government, smaller than a county, that is often based on these survey units. "The sixteenth section of each township was set aside to be sold for the benefit of the public schools. . . ." (p. 174)

9. **territory** In American government, an organized political entity not yet enjoying the full and equal status of a state. ". . . when a territory could boast sixty thousand inhabitants, it might be admitted by Congress as a state. . . ." (p. 174)

10. **annex** To make a smaller territory or political unit part of a larger one. "They . . . sought to annex that rebellious area to Britain." (p. 175)

11. **requisition** A demand for something issued on the basis of public authority. "The requisition system of raising money was breaking down. . . ." (p. 176)

12. **foreclosure** Depriving someone of the right to redeem mortgaged property because the legal payments on the loan have not been kept up. ". . . Revolutionary war veterans were losing their farms through mortgage foreclosures." (p. 176)

13. **quorum** The minimum number of persons who must be present in a group before it can conduct valid business. "A quorum of the fifty-five emissaries from twelve states finally convened at Philadelphia. . . ." (p. 177)

14. **anarchy** The theory that formal government is unnecessary and wrong in principle; the term is also used generally for lawlessness or antigovernmental disorder. "Delegates were determined to preserve the union [and] forestall anarchy. . . ." (p. 179)

15. **bicameral, unicameral** Referring to a legislative body with two houses (bicameral) or one (unicameral). ". . . representation in both houses of a bicameral Congress should be based on population. . . ." "This provided for equal representation in a unicameral Congress. . . ." (p. 179)

PART II: CHECKING YOUR PROGRESS

A. True-False

Where the statement is true, circle **T**; where it is false, circle **F**.

1. T F   The American Revolution created a substantial though not radical push in the direction of social and political equality.

2. T F   The movement toward the separation of church and state was greatly accelerated by the disestablishment of the Anglican church in Virginia.

3. T F   After the Revolution, slavery was abolished in New York and Pennsylvania, but continued to exist in New England and the South.

4. T F   Drawing up a written fundamental law in a special constitutional convention and then submitting the document directly to the people for ratification was an important new idea of the Revolutionary period.

5. T F   The state governments after the Revolution stayed mostly under the tight political control of the eastern seaboard elite.

6. T F   The United States experienced hard economic times and some social discontent during the years of the Confederation (1781–1787).

7. T F   The greatest failure of the national government under the Articles of Confederation was its inability to deal with the issue of western lands.

8. T F   The Articles of Confederation were weak because they contained neither an executive nor power to tax and regulate commerce.

9. T F   The Northwest Ordinance originally attempted to make the western territories permanent colonial possessions of the United States.

10. T F   Shays's Rebellion significantly strengthened the movement for a stronger central government by raising the fear of anarchy among conservatives.

11. T F   The states sent their delegates to Philadelphia in 1787 for the purpose of writing a new Constitution with a strong central government.

12. T F   The delegates to the Constitutional Convention were all extremely wealthy slaveholders.

13. T F   The "Great Compromise" between large and small states at the convention resulted in a bicameral legislature with different principles of representation in each.

14. T F   The antifederalists opposed the Constitution partly because they thought it gave too much power to the states and not enough to Congress.

15. T F   The federalists used tough political maneuvering and the promise of a bill of rights to win a narrow ratification of the Constitution in key states.

B. Multiple Choice

Select the best answer and circle the corresponding letter.

1. Among the important changes brought about by the American Revolution was
    a. the abolition of slavery everywhere except South Carolina and Georgia.
    b. a strong movement toward equality of property rights.
    c. the increasing separation of church and state.
    d. full equality and voting rights for women.

2. A major new political innovation that emerged in the Revolutionary era was
    a. the election of legislative representatives capable of voting on taxation.
    b. the shifting of power from the legislative to the executive branch of government.
    c. the idea of a written constitution drafted by a convention and ratified by direct vote of the people.
    d. the extension of voting rights to indentured servants.

3. Despite the Revolution's emphasis on human rights and equality, the Founding Fathers failed to abolish slavery because
    a. they saw it as necessary to maintain American power.
    b. they feared black rebellion if slavery were removed.
    c. of their fear that a fight over slavery would destroy fragile national unity.
    d. almost none of them believed that slavery was wrong.

4. The ideal of "republican motherhood" that emerged from the American Revolution held that
    a. women should be rewarded politically for having helped establish the American republic.

b.   women had a special responsibility to cultivate the "civic virtues" of republicanism in their children.

c.   the government should establish social services to help mothers raise their children.

d.   mothers should be granted full political and economic rights in the American republic.

5.   In the new state constitutions written after the Revolution, the most powerful branch of government was

a.   the legislative branch.

b.   the executive branch.

c.   the judicial branch.

d.   the military branch.

6.   One way that American independence actually harmed the nation's economic fortunes was by

a.   ending British trade and investment in America.

b.   abolishing the stable currency system that had existed under the empire.

c.   cutting off American trade with the British empire.

d.   weakening the manufacturing efforts begun under the British.

7.   Attempts to establish strong governments in post-Revolutionary America were seriously hindered by

a.   the lack of strong leadership available in the new nation.

b.   the revolutionary ideology that preached natural rights and suspicion of all governmental authority.

c.   the hostility of the clergy toward the idea of separation of church and state.

d.   the fear that a strong government would suppress economic development.

8.   The primary political obstacle to the formation of the first American government under the Articles of Confederation was

a.   disputes among the jealous states over control of western lands.

b.   disagreement over the relative power of Congress and the executive branch.

c.   conflict over the right of Congress to regulate trade and manufacturing.

d.   conflict over slavery between northern and southern states.

9.   The greatest weakness of the government under the Articles of Confederation was that

a.   it was unable to deal with the issue of western lands.

b.   it had no power to regulate commerce or collect taxes from the sovereign states.

c.   it had no power to establish relations with foreign governments.

d.   there was no judicial branch to balance the legislative and executive branches.

10. The Northwest Ordinance of 1787 provided that

a.   the states should retain permanent control of their western lands.

b.   money from the sale of western lands should be used to promote manufacturing.

c.   after sufficient population growth, western territories could be organized and then join the union as states.

d.   the settlers in the northwest could vote on whether or not they should have slavery.

11. Shays's Rebellion contributed to the movement for a new constitution by

a.   revealing that Revolutionary War veterans like Shays wanted a more powerful federal government.

b.   raising the fear of anarchy and disorder among wealthy conservatives.

c.   raising the prospect of British or French interference in American domestic affairs.

d.   showing that state legislatures could effectively resist the demands of radical farmers.

12. Besides George Washington, the most influential figures in the Constitutional Convention were

a.   John Jay, Thomas Jefferson, and John Hancock.

b.   Samuel Adams, Patrick Henry, and Thomas Paine.

c.   John Adams, Abigail Adams, and Gouverneur Morris.

d.   Benjamin Franklin, James Madison, and Alexander Hamilton.
13.   The "Great Compromise" finally agreed to by the Constitutional Convention provided that
   a.   the House of Representatives would be elected by the people and the Senate by the state legislatures.
   b.   the large states would be taxed on the basis of population and the small states on the basis of territory.
   c.   there would be separation of powers between the executive and legislative branches of government.
   d.   there would be representation by population in the House of Representatives but equal representation of all states in the Senate.
14.   Antifederalists generally found their greatest support among
   a.   small states like Delaware and New Jersey.
   b.   the commercial areas of the eastern seaboard.
   c.   the poorer debtors and farmers.
   d.   the wealthy and well educated.
15.   The crucial federalist successes in the fight for ratification occurred in the states of
   a.   Georgia, Maryland, and Delaware.
   b.   Massachusetts, Virginia, and New York.
   c.   Pennsylvania, North Carolina, and Rhode Island.
   d.   Connecticut, South Carolina, and New Hampshire.

C. Identification

Supply the correct identification for each numbered description.

1.   _____   New name for the Anglican Church after it was disestablished and de-Anglicized in Virginia and elsewhere

2.   _____   The idea that American women had a special responsibility to cultivate "civic virtue" in their children

3.   _____   A type of special assembly, originally developed in Massachusetts, for drawing up a fundamental law that would be superior to ordinary law

4.   _____   The first constitutional government of the United States

5.   _____   The territory north of the Ohio and east of the Mississippi governed by the acts of 1785 and 1787

6.   _____   In the new territories, six-mile by six-mile square areas consisting of thirty-six sections, one of which was set aside for public schools

7.   _____   The status of a western area under the Northwest Ordinance after it established an organized government but before it became a state

8.   _____   A failed revolt in 1786 by poor debtor farmers that raised fears of "mobocracy"

9.   _____   The plan proposed by Virginia at the Constitutional Convention for a bicameral legislature with representation based on population

10. _____   The plan proposed by New Jersey for a unicameral legislature with equal representation of states regardless of size and population

11. _____   The compromise between North and South that resulted in each slave being counted as 60 percent of a free person for purposes of representation

12. _____   The opponents of the Constitution who argued against creating such a strong central government

13. _____   A masterly series of pro-Constitution articles printed in New York by Jay, Madison, and Hamilton

14. _____   The official under the new Constitution who would be commander-in-chief of the armed forces, appoint judges and other officials, and have the power to veto legislation

15. _____   A list of guarantees that federalists promised to add to the Constitution in order to win ratification

D. Matching People, Places, and Events

Match the person, place, or event in the left column with the proper description in the right column by inserting the correct letter on the blank line.

1. ___ Society of the Cincinnati

2. ___ Virginia Statute for Religious Freedom

3. ___ Articles of Confederation

4. ___ Northwest Ordinance of 1787

5. ___ Benjamin Franklin

6. ___ Daniel Shays

7. ___ George Washington

8. ___ James Madison

9. ___ federalists

10. ___ antifederalists

11. ___ Patrick Henry

12. ___ Alexander Hamilton

13. ___ John Jay

14. ___ Massachusetts

15. ___ New York

a.   Group that failed to block the central government they feared but did force the promise of a bill of rights

b.   Father of the Constitution and author of *Federalist* No. 10

c.   An exclusive order of military officers that aroused strong democratic opposition

d.   Wealthy conservatives devoted to republicanism who engineered a nonviolent political transformation

e.   Legislation passed by an alliance of Jefferson and the Baptists that disestablished the Anglican church

f.   Revolutionary War veteran who led poor farmers in a revolt that failed but had far-reaching consequences

g.   Elder statesman who lent his prestige to the Constitutional Convention and promoted the "Great Compromise"

h.   The only state to allow a direct vote on the Constitution

i.   Frustrated foreign affairs secretary under the Articles; one of the three authors of *The Federalist*

j.   Legislation that provided for the orderly transformation of western territories into states

k.   First of key states where federalists won by a narrow margin over the opposition of antifederalist Sam Adams

l.   Virginia antifederalist leader who thought the Constitution spelled the end of liberty and equality

m.   Unanimously elected chairman of the secret convention of "demi-gods"

n.   Young New Yorker who argued eloquently for the Constitution even though he favored an even stronger central government

o.   Document of 1781 that was put out of business by the Constitution

E. Putting Things in Order

Put the following events in correct order by numbering them from 1 to 5.

1. _____   Fifty-five "demi-gods" meet secretly in Philadelphia to draft a new charter of government.

2. _____   The first American national government, more a league of states than a real government, goes into effect.

3. _____   At the request of Congress, the states draft new constitutions based on the authority of the people.

4. _____   The Constitution is ratified by the nine states necessary to put it into effect.

5. _____   Debtor farmers fail in a rebellion, setting off conservative fears and demands for a stronger government to control anarchy.

F. Matching Cause and Effect

Match the historical cause in the left column with the proper effect in the right column by writing the correct letter on the blank line.

Cause

1. ___   The American Revolution

2. ___   Agreement among states to give up western land claims

3. ___   The weakness of the Articles of Confederation

4. ___   Shays's Rebellion

5. ___   The conflict in the Constitutional Convention between large and small states

6. ___   The North-South conflict in the Constitutional Convention over counting slaves for representation

Effect

a.   Forced acceptance of the "Three-Fifths Compromise," counting each slave as three-fifths of a person for purposes of representation

b.   Made the federalists promise to add a bill of rights to the Constitution

c.   Nearly bankrupted the national government and invited assaults on American interests by foreign powers

d.   Laid the basis for the Virginia Statute for Religious Freedom and the separation of church and state

e.   Brought about somewhat greater social

7. ___   A meeting in Annapolis to discuss revising the Articles of Confederation

8. ___   Antifederalist fears that the Constitution would destroy liberties

9. ___   *The Federalist* and fears that New York would be left out of the Union

10. ___   The disestablishment of the Anglican Church

and economic equality and the virtual end of slavery in the North

f.   Finally brought New York to ratify the Constitution by a narrow margin

g.   Issued a call to Congress for a special convention to revise the Articles of Confederation

h.   Forced the adoption of the "Great Compromise," which required a bicameral legislature with two different bases of representation

i.   Scared conservatives and made them determined to strengthen the central government against debtors

j.   Made possible the approval of the Articles of Confederation and the passage of two important laws governing western lands

G. Developing Historical Skills

Interpreting a Chart

Analyzing a chart in more detail can enhance understanding of the historical information in the text and add further information. The chart on p. 182 provides information on the voting for ratification of the Constitution in the states.

Answer the following questions:

1. Look carefully at the vote in the five most populous states. What conclusions can you draw about the relation between population and support for ratification?

2. Look at the vote in the five least populous states. In what ways would the figures support your conclusion about the relation between population and support for ratification in #1? How would the results in New Hampshire and Rhode Island partially qualify that conclusion?

3. Look at the relation between region and date of ratification. Which region—New England, the middle Atlantic states, or the South—had only *one* state ratify after January of 1788? Which region had only *one* state ratify before April of 1788? In which region was opinion more evenly divided?

4.   The text indicates that four states—Pennsylvania, Massachusetts, Virginia, and New York—were the keys to ratification. How many *total* delegates would have had to switch sides in order for all of those states to have opposed ratification? (Remember that each change subtracts from one side and adds to the other.)

H. Map Mastery

Map Discrimination

Using the maps and charts in Chapter 9, answer the following questions:

1.   *Western Land Cessions to the United States*: Which two of the thirteen states had the largest western land claims?

2.   *Western Land Cessions to the United States*: Which states had claims in the area that became the Old Northwest Territory?

3.   *Surveying the Old Northwest*: How many square miles were there in each township established by the Land Ordinance of 1785?

4.   *Main Centers of British and Spanish Influence After 1783*: Which nation exercised the greatest foreign influence in the American Southwest from 1783 to 1787?

5.   *Strengthening the Central Government*: Of the measures that strengthened the central government under the Constitution as compared with the Articles of Confederation, how many dealt with economic matters?

6.   *Ratification of the Constitution*: In which three states was there no opposition to the Constitution?

7.   *Ratification of the Constitution*: In which state was there only slender opposition?

8.   *Ratification of the Constitution*: In which four states was support for the Constitution strong—by a ratio of two to one or three to one—but not overwhelming?

9.   *Ratification of the Constitution*: In which five states was the Constitution ratified by very slender margins?

10. *Ratification of the Constitution*: Of the top five states in population, how many had extremely narrow votes in favor of the Constitution (less than twenty votes difference)?

11. *The Struggle Over Ratification*: The map shows that western frontier residents were generally antifederalist. In which two large states, though, was western opinion divided over, or even inclined to favor, adoption of the Constitution?

Map Challenge

Using the map of *The Struggle over Ratification* on p.183, write a brief essay describing how the factors of (a) nearness to the commercial seacoast and (b) size of state influenced profederalist or antifederalist views. Indicate which states were exceptions to the general pattern.

PART III: APPLYING WHAT YOU HAVE LEARNED

1.   How did the revolutionary American ideas of natural human rights, equality, and freedom from governmental tyranny affect developments in the immediate post-Revolutionary period (1783–1789)?

2.   How were women and African Americans affected by the ideas of the American Revolution? Why was slavery abolished in the North but not in the entire nation?

3.   Which problems of the post-Revolutionary period and weaknesses of the Articles of Confederation lead to the adoption of a new Constitution?

4.   What were the basic features of the new Constitution, and how did they differ from the government under the Articles of Confederation?

5.   Who were the federalists and the antifederalists, what were the issues that divided them, and why did the federalists win?

6.   Should the Constitution be seen as a conservative reaction to the Revolution, an enshrinement of revolutionary principles, or both? What was most truly *original* about the Constitution?

7.   In Chapters 4 and 5, the basic structure of early American society and economy was described. How was that structure changed by the political developments during the period after the Revolution? How did the Constitution itself reflect issues concerning social structure, economic equality, and the distribution of power?

8. What social, economic, and political forces contributed to the movement for a new Constitution? Would such a Constitution have come about even if Daniel Shays or foreign assaults on American sovereignty and shipping had never existed?

9. Americans have traditionally revered the Constitution, and viewed its writers as "demigods." Does the historical account of the actual initiation, writing, and ratification of the Constitution confirm or detract from that view? Why or why not?

CHAPTER 10

Launching the New Ship of State, 1789–1800

PART I: REVIEWING THE CHAPTER

A. CHECKLIST OF LEARNING OBJECTIVES

After mastering this chapter, you should be able to

1. state why George Washington was pivotal to inaugurating the new federal government.

2. describe the methods and policies Alexander Hamilton used to put the federal government on a sound financial footing.

3. explain how the conflict between Hamilton and Jefferson led to the emergence of the first political parties.

4. describe the polarizing effects of the French Revolution on American foreign policy and politics from 1790 to 1800.

5. explain the rationale for Washington's neutrality policies, the conciliatory Jay's Treaty, and why the treaty provoked Jeffersonian outrage.

6. describe the causes of the undeclared war with France and explain Adams's decision to seek peace rather than declare war.

7. describe the poisonous political atmosphere that produced the Alien and Sedition Acts and the Kentucky and Virginia resolutions.

8. describe the contrasting membership and principles of the Hamiltonian Federalists and the Jeffersonian Republicans, and how they laid the foundations of the American political party system.

B. GLOSSARY

To build your social science vocabulary, familiarize yourself with the following terms:

1. **census** An official count of population; in the United States, the federal census occurs every ten years. ". . . the first official census of 1790 recorded almost 4 million people." (p. 190)

2. **public debt** The debt of a government or nation to individual creditors, also called the national debt. ". . . the public debt, with interest heavily in arrears, was mountainous." (p. 190)

3. **cabinet** The body of official advisers to the head of a government; in the United States, it consists of the heads of the major executive departments. "The Constitution does not mention a cabinet. . . ." (p. 191)

4. **circuit court** A court that hears cases in several designated locations rather than a single place. "The act organized . . . federal district and circuit courts. . . ." (p. 193)

5. **fiscal** Concerning public finances—expenditures and revenues. "His plan was to shape the fiscal policies of the administration. . . ." (p. 193)

6. **assumption** The appropriation or taking on of obligations not originally one's own. "The secretary made a convincing case for 'assumption.' " (p. 194)

7. **excise** A tax on the manufacture, sale, or consumption of certain products. "Hamilton . . . secured from Congress an excise tax on a few domestic items, notably whiskey." (p. 195)

8. **stock** The shares of capital ownership gained from investing in a corporate enterprise; the term also refers to the certificates representing such shares. "Stock was thrown open to public sale." (p. 196)

9. **medium of exchange** Any item, paper or otherwise, used as money. "They regarded [whiskey] as a . . . medium of exchange." (p. 196)

10. **despotism** Arbitrary or tyrannical rule. "The American people, loving liberty and deploring despotism, cheered." (p. 198)

11. **impress** To force people or property into public service without choice; conscript. "They . . . impressed scores of seamen into service on British vessels. . . ." (p. 200)

12. **assimilation** The merging of diverse cultures or peoples into one. "The drastic new law violated the traditional American policy of open-door hospitality and speedy assimilation." (p. 205)

13. **witch-hunt** An investigation carried on with much publicity, supposedly to uncover dangerous activity but actually intended to weaken the political opposition. "Anti-French hysteria played directly into the hands of witch-hunting conservatives." (p. 206)

14. **compact** An agreement or covenant between states to perform some legal act. "Both Jefferson and Madison stressed the compact theory. . . ." (p. 207)

15. **nullification** In American politics, the assertion that a state may legally invalidate a federal act deemed inconsistent with its rights or sovereignty. "[The] resolutions concluded that . . . 'nullification' was the 'rightful remedy.' " (p. 207)

PART II: CHECKING YOUR PROGRESS

A. True-False

Where the statement is true, circle **T**; where it is false, circle **F**.

1. T F   One immediate concern for the new federal government was the questionable loyalty of people living in the western territories of Kentucky, Tennessee, and Ohio.

2. T F   The passage of the first ten amendments to the Constitution demonstrated the Federalist determination to develop a powerful central government.

3. T F   Hamilton's basic purpose in all his financial measures was to strengthen the federal government by building up a larger national debt.

4. T F   Both "funding at par" of the federal debt and assumption of state debts were designed to give wealthier interests a strong stake in the success of the federal government.

5. T F   Hamilton financed his large national debt by revenues from tariffs and excise taxes on products such as whiskey.

6. T F   In the battle over the Bank of the United States, Jefferson favored a "loose construction" of the Constitution and Hamilton favored a "strict construction."

7. T F   The first American political parties grew mainly out of the debate over Hamilton's fiscal policies and U. S. foreign policy toward Europe.

8. T   F   The French Revolution's radical political goals were greeted with great approval by both Jeffersonian Republicans and Federalists.

9. T   F   Washington's Neutrality Proclamation was based on a mistaken belief that the United States could not really compete militarily with the major world powers.

10. T   F   The Indians of the Miami Confederacy northwest of the Ohio River were easily defeated by U.S. forces and removed across the Mississippi.

11. T   F   Washington supported John Jay's unpopular treaty with Britain because he feared a disastrous war if it were rejected.

12. T   F   Adams decided to seek a negotiated peace with France in order to unite his party and enhance his own popularity with the public.

13. T   F   The Alien Laws were a conservative Federalist attempt to prevent radical French immigrants and spies from supporting the Jeffersonians and stirring up anti-British sentiment.

14. T   F   Jeffersonian Republicans believed that the common people were not to be trusted and had to be led by those who were wealthier and better educated.

15. T   F   The Jeffersonian Republicans generally sympathized with Britain in foreign policy, while the Hamiltonian Federalists sympathized with France and the French Revolution.

B. Multiple Choice

Select the best answer and circle the corresponding letter.

1. A key addition to the new federal government that had been demanded by many of the ratifying states was

    a. a cabinet to aid the president.
    b. a written bill of rights to guarantee liberty.
    c. a supreme court.
    d. federal assumption of state debts.

2. One immediate innovation not mentioned in the Constitution that was developed by George Washington's administration was

    a. the cabinet.
    b. the military joint chiefs of staff.
    c. the Supreme Court.
    d. the vice presidency.

3. The Bill of Rights is the name given to provisions whose actual form is

    a. an executive proclamation of President George Washington.
    b. Article II, Section 3 of the U.S. Constitution.
    c. a set of rulings issued by the Supreme Court.
    d. the first ten amendments to the federal Constitution.

4. Which of the following sets of rights are *not* included in the Bill of Rights?

    a. freedom of religion, speech, and the press.
    b. rights to freedom of education and freedom of travel.
    c. rights to bear arms and to be tried by a jury.
    d. rights to assemble and petition the government for redress of grievances.

5. The Ninth and Tenth Amendments partly reversed the federalist momentum of the Constitution by declaring that

    a. the federal government had no power to restrict the action of local governments.

    b.   the powers of the presidency did not extend to foreign policy.

    c.   all rights not mentioned in the federal Constitution were retained by the states or by the people themselves.

    d.   the Supreme Court had no power to rule in cases affecting property rights.

6.   Hamilton's first financial policies were intended

    a.   to finance the new government through the sale of western lands.

    b.   to fund the national debt and to have the federal government assume the debts owed by the states.

    c.   to repudiate the debts accumulated by the government of the Articles of Confederation.

    d.   to create a sound federal currency backed by gold.

7.   The essential disagreement between Hamilton and Jefferson over the proposed Bank of the United States was

    a.   whether the Constitution granted the federal government the power to establish such a bank.

    b.   whether it would be economically wise to create a single national currency.

    c.   whether the bank should be under the control of the federal government or the states.

    d.   whether such a Bank violated the Bill of Rights.

8.   The first American political parties developed primarily out of

    a.   the disagreement of Jefferson and his states' rights followers with Hamilton's economic policies.

    b.   the belief of the Founding Fathers that organized political opposition was a necessary part of good government.

    c.   the continuing hostility of the antifederalists to the legitimacy of the new federal Constitution.

    d.   patriotic opposition to foreign intervention in American domestic affairs.

9.   The Whiskey Rebellion was most significant because

    a.   it showed that American citizens would rise up against unfair taxation.

    b.   it showed that the new federal government would use force if necessary to uphold its authority.

    c.   it demonstrated the efficiency of the American military.

    d.   it showed the strength of continuing antifederalist hostility to the new constitutional government.

10.   Regarding the French Revolution, most Jeffersonian Democratic-Republicans believed that

    a.   the violence was regrettable but necessary.

    b.   the overthrow of the king was necessary, but the Reign of Terror went much too far.

    c.   the Revolution should be supported by American military aid.

    d.   the Revolution represented a complete distortion of American ideals of liberty.

11.   Washington's foreign policy rested on the basic belief that

    a.   there should be an end to European colonialism in the Americas.

    b.   it was in America's interest to stay neutral in all European wars.

    c.   America needed to adhere to its Revolutionary alliance with France.

    d.   America ought to enter the French-British war only if republican ideals were at stake.

12.   The United States became involved in undeclared hostilities with France in 1797 because of

    a.   fierce American opposition to the concessions of Jay's Treaty.

    b.   American anger at attempted French bribery in the XYZ Affair.

    c.   French interference with American shipping and freedom of the seas.

    d.   President Adams's sympathy with Britain and hostility to Revolutionary France.

13.   The Alien and Sedition Acts were aimed primarily at

    a.   the Jeffersonians and their allegedly pro-French activities and ideas.

    b.   the opponents of President Adams's peace settlement with France.

c.   Napoleon's French agents who were infiltrating the country.

d.   the Hamiltonian Federalists and their pro-British activities and ideas.

14.   In foreign policy, the Jeffersonians essentially believed that

a.   the United States should seek an international organization that could mediate great-power conflicts.

b.   that the "Anglo-Saxon" nations of Britain and the United States shared a common language and political heritage.

c.   the United States should turn westward, away from old Europe, and strengthen democracy at home.

d.   that the United States should pursue an aggressively anti-colonial policy in Spanish-owned Latin America.

15.   The Federalists essentially believed that

a.   most governmental power should be retained by the states.

b.   government should provide no special aid to private enterprise.

c.   the common people could, if educated, participate in government affairs.

d.   there should be a strong central government controlled by the wealthy and well educated.

C. Identification

Supply the correct identification for each numbered description.

1.   _____   The official body designated to choose the President under the new Constitution, which in 1789 unanimously elected George Washington

2.   _____   The constitutional office into which John Adams was sworn on April 30, 1789

3.   _____   The cabinet office in Washington's administration headed by a brilliant young West Indian immigrant who distrusted the people

4.   _____   Alexander Hamilton's policy of paying off all federal bonds at face value in order to strengthen the national credit

5.   _____   Hamilton's policy of having the federal government pay the financial obligations of the states

6.   _____   The first ten amendments to the Constitution

7.   _____   Political organizations not envisioned in the Constitution and considered dangerous to national unity by most of the Founding Fathers

8.   _____   Political and social upheaval supported by most Americans during its moderate beginnings in 1789, but the cause of bitter divisions after it took a radical turn in 1792

9.   _____   Agreement signed between two anti-British countries in 1778 that increasingly plagued American foreign policy in the 1790s

10.   _____   Alliance of eight Indian nations led by Little Turtle that inflicted major defeats on American forces in the early 1790s.

11.   _____   Document signed in 1794 whose terms favoring Britain outraged Jeffersonian Republicans

12.   _____   The nation with which the United States fought an undeclared war from 1798 to 1800

13. _____ The political theory on which Jefferson and Madison based their antifederalist resolutions declaring that the thirteen sovereign states had created the Constitution

14. _____ The doctrine, proclaimed in the Virginia and Kentucky resolutions, that a state can block a federal law it considers unconstitutional

15. _____ The nation to which most Hamiltonian Federalists were sentimentally attached and which they favored in foreign policy

D. Matching People, Places, and Events

Match the person, place, or event in the left column with the proper description in the right column by inserting the correct letter on the blank line.

1. ___ Neutrality Proclamation of 1793

2. ___ Alexander Hamilton

3. ___ Thomas Jefferson

4. ___ James Madison

5. ___ Supreme Court

6. ___ Funding and assumption

7. ___ Bank of the United States

8. ___ Whiskey Rebellion

9. ___ Federalists

10. ___ Republicans

11. ___ XYZ

12. ___ Treaty of Greenville

13. ___ Alien and Sedition Acts

14. ___ Bill of Rights

15. ___ Farewell Address

a. A protest by poor western farmers that was firmly suppressed by Washington and Hamilton's army

b. Body organized by the Judiciary Act of 1789 and first headed by John Jay

c. Brilliant administrator and financial wizard whose career was plagued by doubts about his character and belief in popular government

d. Political party that believed in the common people, no government aid for business, and a pro-French foreign policy

e. President Washington's statement of the basic principles of American foreign policy in his administration

f. Skillful politician-scholar who drafted the Bill of Rights and moved it through the First Congress

g. Institution established by Hamilton to create a stable currency and bitterly opposed by states' rights advocates

h. Hamilton's aggressive financial policies of paying off all federal bonds and taking on all state debts

i. Harsh and probably unconstitutional laws aimed at radical immigrants and Jeffersonian writers

j. Agreement between the United States and Miami Indians that ceded much of Ohio and Indiana while recognizing a limited sovereignty for the Miamis

k. Message telling America that it should

avoid unnecessary foreign entanglements—a reflection of the foreign policy of its author

l.   Secret code names for three French agents who attempted to extract bribes from American diplomats in 1797

m.   Washington's secretary of state and the organizer of a political party opposed to Hamilton's policies

n.   Ten constitutional amendments designed to protect American liberties

o.   Political party that believed in a strong government run by the wealthy, government aid to business, and a pro-British foreign policy

E. Putting Things in Order

Put the following events in correct order by numbering them from 1 to 5.

1. _____   Revolutionary turmoil in France causes the U.S. president to urge Americans to stay out of foreign quarrels.

2. _____   Envoys sent to make peace in France are insulted by bribe demands from three mysterious French agents.

3. _____   First ten amendments to the Constitution are adopted.

4. _____   Western farmers revolt against a Hamiltonian tax and are harshly suppressed.

5. _____   Jefferson organizes a political party in opposition to Hamilton's financial policies.

F. Matching Cause and Effect

Match the historical cause in the left column with the proper effect in the right column by writing the correct letter on the blank line.

Cause		Effect
1. ___ The need to gain support of wealthy groups for the federal government	a.	Led to the formation of the first two American political parties
2. ___ Passage of the Bill of Rights	b.	Caused the Whiskey Rebellion
3. ___ The need for federal revenues to finance Hamilton's ambitious policies	c.	Led Hamilton to promote the fiscal policies of funding and assumption
4. ___ Hamilton's excise tax on western farmers' products	d.	Guaranteed basic liberties and indicated some swing away from Federalist centralizing
5. ___ Clashes between Hamilton and Jefferson over fiscal policy and foreign affairs	e.	Led to imposition of the first tariff in 1789 and the excise tax on whiskey in 1791
	f.	Aroused Jeffersonian Republican

6. ___   The French Revolution

7. ___   The danger of war with Britain

8. ___   Jay's Treaty

9. ___   The XYZ Affair

10. ___   The Federalist fear of radical French immigrants

outrage at the Washington administration's pro-British policies

g. Created bitter divisions in America between anti-Revolution Federalists and pro-Revolution Republicans

h. Caused an undeclared war with France

i. Led Washington to support Jay's Treaty

j. Caused passage of the Alien Acts

G. Developing Historical Skills

Reading for Main Idea and Supporting Details

Any historical generalization must be backed up by supporting details and historical facts. For example, the text states that "the key figure in the new government was smooth-faced Alexander Hamilton. . ." (p. 193). This generalization is then supported by details and facts showing Hamilton's importance, such as his policy of funding and assumption, his customs and excise taxes, and his establishment of the Bank of the United States. (pp. 193–196)

List at least two supporting details or facts that support each of the following general assertions in the text.

1. "President Washington's far-visioned policy of neutrality was sorely tried by the British." (p. 200)

2. "True to Washington's policy of steering clear of war at all costs, [President Adams] tried again to reach an agreement with the French. . . ." (p. 203)

3. "Exulting Federalists had meanwhile capitalized on the anti-French frenzy to drive through Congress in 1798 a sheaf of laws designed to reduce or gag their Jeffersonian foes." (p. 205)

4. "Resentful Jeffersonians naturally refused to take the Alien and Sedition Laws lying down." (p. 207)

5. "As the presidential contest of 1800 approached, the differences between Federalists and Democratic-Republicans were sharply etched." (p. 207) (Indicate two clear differences between the parties.)

PART III: APPLYING WHAT YOU HAVE LEARNED

PART III: APPLYING WHAT YOU HAVE LEARNED

1. What were the most important issues facing the new federal government, and how did the Washington administration address them?

2. Explain the purpose and significance of the Bill of Rights. Did these Ten Amendments significantly weaken federal authority, or actually enhance it?

3. What were Hamilton's basic economic and political goals, and how did he attempt to achieve them?

4. What were the philosophical and political disagreements between Hamilton and Jefferson that led to the creation of the first American political parties?

5. What were the basic goals of Washington's and Adams's foreign policies, and how successful were they in achieving them?

6. How did divisions over foreign policy create the poisonous political atmosphere that produced both the Alien and Sedition Acts and the Kentucky and Virginia resolutions?

7. In foreign policy, the Federalists believed that the United States needed to build a strong national state to pursue American interests in Europe and elsewhere, while the Republicans believed the country should turn inward, away from Europe and toward the West. Which was the wiser policy in 1800? Which view generally prevailed in the nineteenth century, and why? Which view generally prevailed in the twentieth century, and why?

8. Although Federalists and Republicans engaged in extremely bitter political struggles during this period, they both retained their basic commitment to republican government, and at the end of the decade, the Federalists peacefully handed over power to the Republicans. What characteristics of American politics and society enabled them to keep their conflict within bounds?

CHAPTER 11

The Triumphs and Travails of the Jeffersonian Republic, 1800–1812

PART I: REVIEWING THE CHAPTER

A. CHECKLIST OF LEARNING OBJECTIVES

After mastering this chapter, you should be able to

1. explain how Jefferson's moderation and compromises turned the "Revolution of 1800" into a relatively smooth transition of party control from Federalists to Republicans.

2. describe the conflicts between Federalists and Republicans over the judiciary and the important legal precedents that developed from these conflicts.

3. describe Jefferson's basic foreign-policy goals and how he attempted to achieve them.

4. analyze the causes and effects of the Louisiana Purchase.

5. describe how America came to be caught up in the turbulent international crisis of the Napoleonic Wars.

6. describe the original intentions and actual results of Jefferson's embargo and explain why it failed.

7. explain why President Madison saw a new war with Britain as essential to maintain America's experiment in republican government.

B. GLOSSARY

To build your social science vocabulary, familiarize yourself with the following terms:

1. **lame duck** A political official during the time he or she remains in office after a defeat or inability to seek another term, and whose power is therefore diminished. "This body was controlled for several more months by the lame-duck Federalists. . . ." (p. 214)

2. **commission** The official legal authorization appointing a person to an office or military position, indicating the nature of the duty, term of office, chain of command, and so on. "When Marbury learned that his commission was being shelved by the new secretary of state, James Madison, he sued for its delivery." (p. 218)

3. **writ** A formal legal document ordering or prohibiting some act. ". . . his Jeffersonian rivals . . . would hardly enforce a writ to deliver the commission. . . ." (p. 218)

4. **impeachment** The charge of a public official with improper conduct in office. "Jefferson urged the impeachment of an arrogant and tart-tongued Supreme Court justice. . . ." (p. 219)

5. **pacifist** Characterized by principled opposition to all war and belief in nonviolent solutions to conflict. "A challenge was thus thrown squarely into the face of Jefferson—the non-interventionist, the pacifist. . . ." (p. 220)

6. **consulate (consul)** A place where a government representative is stationed in a foreign country, but not the main headquarters of diplomatic representation headed by an ambassador (the embassy). "The pasha of Tripoli . . . informally declared war on the United States by cutting down the flagstaff of the American consulate." (p. 220)

7. **cede** To yield or grant something, often upon request or under pressure. (Anything ceded is a *cession*.) "Napoleon Bonaparte induced the king of Spain to cede to France . . . the immense trans-Mississippi region. . . ." (p. 220)

8. **precedent** In law and government, a decision or action that establishes a sanctioned rule for determining similar cases in the future. ". . . the transfer established a precedent that was to be followed repeatedly. . . ." (p. 222)

9. **secession** The withdrawal, by legal or illegal means, of one portion of a political entity from the government to which it has been bound. "Burr joined with a group of Federalist extremists to plot the secession of New England and New York." (p. 223)

10. **conscription** Compulsory enrollment of men and women into the armed forces. "Impressment . . . was a crude form of conscription. . . ." (p. 226)

11. **broadside** The simultaneous firing of all guns on one side of a ship. "The British warship thereupon fired three devastating broadsides. . . ." (p. 226)

12. **embargo** A government order prohibiting commerce in or out of a port. "The hated embargo was not continued long enough or tightly enough to achieve the desired result. . . ." (p. 227)

PART II: CHECKING YOUR PROGRESS

A. True-False

Where the statement is true, circle **T**, where it is false, circle **F**.

1. T F   The "Revolution of 1800" involved a radical transfer of power from the Federalist merchant class to farmers and urban artisans and craftsmen.

2. T F   An unexpected deadlock with Aaron Burr meant that Jefferson had to be elected by the House of Representatives.

3. T F   Jefferson and his Treasury Secretary, Albert Gallatin, kept in place most of the Federalist financial policies.

4. T F   The Jeffersonian Republicans showed their hostility to the Federalist Supreme Court by trying to impeach Chief Justice John Marshall.

5. T F   The case of *Marbury* v. *Madison* established the principle that the president could appoint but not remove Supreme Court justices.

6. T F   Jefferson cut the size of the United States Army to twenty-five hundred men because he believed that a large standing army was a threat to liberty and economy.

7. T F   Jefferson's envoys to Paris initially intended to buy only New Orleans and the immediate vicinity.

8. T F   Jefferson's deepest doubt about the Louisiana Purchase was that the price of $15 million was too high.

9. T F   The Lewis and Clark expedition demonstrated the viability of an overland American route to the Pacific.

10. T F   Aaron Burr's various conspiracies to break apart the United States demonstrated the fragility of the American government's control of the trans-Appalachian West.

11. T F   The most explosive issue between Britain and the United States was the British blockade of American shipments to Europe.

12. T F   After the *Chesapeake* affair, Jefferson could easily have declared war on Britain with the enthusiastic support of both Federalists and Republicans.

13. T F   Jefferson's embargo badly hurt southern and western farmers as well as Federalist New England.

14. T F   The Shawnee leaders Tecumseh and Tenskwatawa successfully organized a great Indian confederacy aimed at stemming white expansion and reviving Indian culture.

15. T F   The War of 1812 was promoted largely by New Englanders angry over British violation of American freedom of the seas.

B. Multiple Choice

Select the best answer and circle the corresponding letter.

1. The most "revolutionary" development in the critical election of 1800 was

    a.   the nasty campaign smears against Jefferson.
    b.   Jefferson's radical proposals for overturning the existing political system.
    c.   the peaceful transition of power from one political party to its opponent.
    d.   the electoral stalemate between Jefferson and his running mate, Burr.

2. One Federalist policy that Jefferson quickly overturned was

    a.   funding and assumption.
    b.   the excise tax.
    c.   the Bank of the United States.
    d.   the protective tariff.

3. The case of *Marbury* v. *Madison* established the principle that

    a.   the Supreme Court has the right to determine the constitutionality of legislation.
    b.   federal laws take precedence over state legislation.
    c.   the president has the right to appoint the federal judiciary.
    d.   the Supreme Court is the final court of appeal in the federal judiciary.

4. Jefferson was forced to reverse his strong opposition to substantial military forces because of

    a.   growing French intervention in Santo Domingo and Louisiana.
    b.   the plunder and blackmailing of American shipping by North African states.
    c.   the threat to America posed by the British-French wars.
    d.   the political attacks by his Federalist opponents.

5. Jefferson's greatest concern in purchasing Louisiana was

    a.   whether it was in America's interest to acquire the territory.
    b.   whether the cost was excessive for his small-government philosophy.
    c.   whether the purchase was permissible under the Constitution.
    d.   how to defend and govern the territory once it was part of the United States.

6. The greatest political beneficiary of the Louisiana Purchase was

    a.   Thomas Jefferson.
    b.   Aaron Burr.
    c.   the Federalist party.
    d.   Napoleon.

7.   Although greatly weakened after Jefferson's election, the Federalist party's philosophy continued to have great influence through

   a.   the propaganda efforts of Federalist agitators.
   b.   the Federalist control of the U.S. Senate.
   c.   the Federalist judicial rulings of John Marshall.
   d.   Federalist sympathies within the U.S. army and navy.

8.   The term "midnight judges" refers to

   a.   Federalist judges appointed by President John Adams at the last moments of his administration.
   b.   federal judges who held late-night court sessions to hear controversial cases.
   c.   judges like William Marbury who sued to have their late-night appointment commissions confirmed.
   d.   states' rights judges appointed by President Jefferson moments after his inauguration.

9.   The Republicans' failure to impeach Supreme Court Justice Samuel Chase established the principle that

   a.   the Supreme Court had the power to declare laws unconstitutional.
   b.   presidents could appoint but not remove federal justices.
   c.   impeachment should be used only for "high crimes and misdemeanors" and not as a political weapon.
   d.   the constitutional power of impeachment was in effect impossible to carry out.

10.   Jefferson focused his military construction policy primarily on

   a.   building large naval frigates like the *Constitution*.
   b.   building several hundred small gunboats.
   c.   building up coastal forts and defense works.
   d.   constructing light and medium artillery capable of use on land or sea.

11.   Which of the following was *not* among the consequences of the Louisiana Purchase—

   a.   the geographical and scientific discoveries of the Lewis and Clark expedition?
   b.   the weakening of the power of the presidency in foreign affairs?
   c.   the expansion of the United States as a great "democratic empire" with new states admitted to equal membership with the old?
   d.   allowing the United States to pursue an isolationist policy by removing the last major foreign threat from North America?

12.   Jefferson's Embargo Act provided that

   a.   America would not trade with Britain until it ended impressment.
   b.   American goods could be carried only in American ships.
   c.   America would sell no military supplies to either warring nation, Britain or France.
   d.   America would prohibit all foreign trade.

13.   A crucial foreign policy goal for many "war hawks" in the War of 1812 was

   a.   the end of all Spanish colonization in the Americas.
   b.   the capture and annexation of Canada.
   c.   the conquest and settlement of Texas.
   d.   the destruction of the British navy.

14.   Besides creating a pan-Indian military alliance against white expansion, Tecumseh and Tenskwatawa (the Prophet) urged American Indians to

   a.   resist white ways and revive their traditional culture.
   b.   demonstrate their legal ownership of the lands that whites were entering.
   c.   adopt the whites' culture and technology as a way of resisting their further expansion.
   d.   declare independence and form an alliance with Spain.

15. Most Indian military resistance east of the Mississippi River was effectively crushed in the two battles of
    a. the Thames and Lake Erie.
    b. Fort McHenry and New Orleans.
    c. Tippecanoe and Horseshoe Bend.
    d. Plattsburgh and Bladensburg.

C. Identification

Supply the correct identification for each numbered description.

1. _____ Hamiltonian economic measure repealed by Jefferson and Gallatin

2. _____ Action Jefferson took toward Republican "martyrs" convicted under the Federalist Sedition Law

3. _____ Derogatory Republican term for Federalist judges appointed at the last minute by President Adams

4. _____ Precedent-setting Supreme Court case in which Marshall declared part of the Judiciary Act of 1789 unconstitutional

5. _____ The principle, established by Chief Justice Marshall in a famous case, that the Supreme Court can declare laws unconstitutional

6. _____ Action voted by the House of Representatives against Supreme Court Justice Samuel Chase

7. _____ Branch of military service that Jefferson considered least threatening to liberty and most necessary to suppressing the Barbary states

8. _____ Sugar-rich island where Toussaint L'Ouverture's slave rebellion disrupted Napoleon's dreams of a vast New World empire

9. _____ Territory beyond Louisiana, along the Columbia River, explored by Lewis and Clark

10. _____ Price paid by the United States for the Louisiana Purchase

11. _____ American ship fired on by British in 1807, nearly leading to war between the two countries

12. _____ Jefferson's policy of forbidding the shipment of any goods in or out of the United States

13. _____ Militantly nationalistic western congressmen eager for hostilities with the Indians, Canadians, and British

14. _____ Battle in 1811 where General Harrison defeated the Indian forces under Tecumseh and Tenskwatawa (the Prophet)

15. _____ Derisive Federalist name for the War of 1812 that blamed it on the Republican president

D. Matching People, Places, and Events

Match the person, place, or event in the left column with the proper description in the right column by inserting the correct letter on the blank line.

1. ___ Thomas Jefferson

2. ___ Albert Gallatin

3. ___ John Marshall

4. ___ *Marbury* v. *Madison*

5. ___ Samuel Chase

6. ___ Pasha of Tripoli

7. ___ Napoleon Bonaparte

8. ___ Robert Livingston

9. ___ Toussaint L'Ouverture

10. ___ William Clark

11. ___ Aaron Burr

12. ___ *Chesapeake* affair

13. ___ Embargo Act of 1807

14. ___ Tecumseh

15. ___ William Henry Harrison

a. Former vice-president, killer of Alexander Hamilton, and plotter of mysterious secessionist schemes

b. Military leader who defeated Tecumseh's brother, "the Prophet," at the Battle of Tippecanoe

c. Swiss-born treasury secretary who disliked national debt but kept most Hamiltonian economic measures in effect

d. American minister to Paris who joined James Monroe in making a magnificent real estate deal

e. Strong believer in strict construction, weak government, and antimilitarism who was forced to modify some of his principles in office

f. Shawnee leader who organized a major Indian confederation against U.S. expansion

g. Federalist Supreme Court justice impeached by the House in 1804 but acquitted by the Senate

h. British attack on American sailors that aroused angry demands for war

i. Young army officer who joined Jefferson's personal secretary in exploring the Louisiana Purchase and Oregon country

j. Restrictive trade policy that hurt Britain but hurt American shippers and farmers even more

k. Ruling based on a "midnight judge" case that established the right of the Supreme Court to declare laws unconstitutional

l. North African leader who fought an undeclared war with the United States from 1801 to 1805

m. Gifted black revolutionary whose successful slave revolution indirectly led to Napoleon's sale of Louisiana

n. French ruler who acquired Louisiana from Spain only to sell it to the United States

o. Federalist Supreme Court justice whose brilliant legal efforts established the principle of judicial review

E. Putting Things in Order

Put the following events in correct order by numbering them from 1 to 5.

1. ___ Rather than declare war after a British attack on an American ship, Jefferson imposes a ban on all American trade.

2. ___ President Adams appoints a host of "midnight judges" just before leaving office, outraging Republicans.

3. ___ The foreign difficulties of a French dictator lead him to offer a fabulous real estate bargain to the United States.

4. ___ After four years of naval war, the Barbary state of Tripoli signs a peace treaty with the United States.

5. ___ A deceitful French dictator and aggressive western Congressmen maneuver a reluctant president into a war with Britain.

F. Matching Cause and Effect

Match the historical cause in the left column with the proper effect in the right column by writing the correct letter on the blank line.

Cause

1. ___ Jefferson's moderation and continuation of many Federalist policies

2. ___ Adams's appointment of "midnight judges"

3. ___ Marshall's ruling in *Marbury* v. *Madison*

4. ___ The Barbary pirates' attacks on American shipping

5. ___ France's acquisition of Louisiana from Spain

6. ___ Napoleon's foreign troubles with Britain and Santo Domingo

7. ___ The Louisiana Purchase

8. ___ British impressment of American sailors and anger at American harboring of British deserters

9. ___ French compliance with Macon's Bill No. 2

10. ___ Western war hawks' fervor for acquiring Canada and removing resisting Indians

Effect

a. Provoked Federalists to charge Jefferson with unconstitutional expansionism

b. Aroused Jeffersonian hostility to the Federalist judiciary and led to repeal of the Judiciary Act of 1801

c. Forced Madison to declare a policy of nonimportation that accelerated the drift toward war

d. Led to an aggressive and deadly assault on the American ship *Chesapeake*

e. Created stability and continuity in the transition of power from one party to another

f. Caused Harrison's and Jackson's military ventures and contributed to the declaration of war in 1812

g. Established the principle of "judicial review" of laws by the Supreme Court

h. Made Americans eager to purchase New Orleans in order to protect their Mississippi River shipping

i. Led to a surprise offer to sell Louisiana to the United States for $15 million

j. Forced a reluctant Jefferson to send the

U.S. Navy into military action

G. Developing Historical Skills

Reading and Election Map: Reading an election map carefully yields additional information about voting patterns and political alignments. Using the map of the *Presidential Election of 1800* on p. 214, answer the following questions:

1. How many electoral votes did Adams get from the five New England states?

2. Which was the only state north of Virginia that went completely for Jefferson?

3. How many electoral votes were there in the three states that divided between Adams and Jefferson?

4. The text records the final electoral vote as 73 for Jefferson to 65 for Adams, and notes that Jefferson carried New York only by a very slender margin. *If* Adams had carried New York, what would the electoral result have been?

PART III: APPLYING WHAT YOU HAVE LEARNED

1. What was the significance of the Jeffersonian "Revolution of 1800" in relation to the new republican experiment and the fierce political battles of the 1790s? (See Chapter 10.)

2. How did the conflict between Federalists and Republicans over the judiciary lead to a balance of power among political interests and different branches of government?

3. What were the political and economic consequences of the Louisiana Purchase?

4. Argue for and against: the Louisiana Purchase made possible the success of nineteenth-century American democracy as well as America's effective isolation from the world.

5. What was the essential idea behind Jefferson's imposition of the embargo, and why did it finally fail?

6. What were the real causes of the War of 1812? Was the declaration of war a "mistake," or the result of President Madison's genuine fear that the American republican experiment could fail?

7. How would the key events of this period—the spread of Jeffersonian democracy, the Louisiana Purchase, and the new war with Britain—look in the eyes of an American Indian leader like Tecumseh?

8. Thomas Jefferson prided himself on the principles of democracy, local self-rule, and limited government. How effectively did he and his friend and successor Madison transform those principles into policy? Could it be argued that Jefferson ironically laid the foundations for an imperial United States and a powerful federal government?

CHAPTER 12

The Second War for Independence and the Upsurge of Nationalism, 1812–1824

PART I: REVIEWING THE CHAPTER

A. CHECKLIST OF LEARNING OBJECTIVES

After mastering this chapter, you should be able to

1. explain why the War of 1812 was so politically divisive and poorly fought by the United States.

2. describe the crucial military developments of the War of 1812, and explain why Americans experienced more success on water than on land.

3. describe the terms of the Treaty of Ghent and the long-term results of the War of 1812 for the United States at home and abroad.

4. describe and explain the burst of American nationalism that followed the War of 1812.

5. describe the major political and economic developments of the period, including the death of the Federalist Party and the depression following the Panic of 1819.

6. describe the conflict over slavery that arose in 1819 and the terms of the Missouri Compromise that temporarily resolved it.

7. indicate how John Marshall's Supreme Court promoted the spirit of nationalism through its rulings in favor of federal power.

8. describe the Monroe Doctrine and explain its real and symbolic significance for American foreign policy and for relations with the new Latin American republics.

B. GLOSSARY

To build your social science vocabulary, familiarize yourself with the following terms:

1. **regiment** A medium-sized military unit, larger than a company or battalion and smaller than a division. "Among the defenders were two Louisiana regiments of free black volunteers. . . ." (p. 236)

2. **mediation** An intervention, usually by consent of the parties, to aid in voluntarily settling differences between groups or nations. (**Arbitration** involves a *mandatory* settlement determined by a third party.) "Tsar Alexander I of Russia . . . proposed mediation between the clashing Anglo-Saxon cousins in 1812." (p. 237)

3. **armistice** A temporary stopping of warfare by mutual agreement, usually in preparation for an actual peace negotiation between the parties. "The Treaty of Ghent, signed on Christmas Eve in 1814, was essentially an armistice." (p. 237)

4. **dynasty** A succession of rulers in the same family line; by extension, any system of predetermined succession in power. "This last clause was aimed at the much-resented 'Virginia Dynasty.' . . ." (p. 239)

5. **reaction (reactionary)** In politics, extreme conservatism, looking to restore the political or social conditions of some earlier time. ". . . the Old World took the rutted road back to conservatism, illiberalism, and reaction." (p. 240)

6. **protection (protective)** In economics, the policy of stimulating or preserving domestic producers by placing barriers against imported goods, often through high tariffs. "The infant industries bawled lustily for protection." (p. 241)

7. **raw materials** Products in their natural, unmanufactured state. "Through these new arteries of transportation would flow foodstuffs and raw materials. . . ." (p. 241)

8. **internal improvements** The basic public works, such as roads and canals, that create the structure for economic development. "Congress voted . . . for internal improvements." (p. 242)

9. **intrastate** Something existing wholly within a state of the United States. (**Interstate** refers to movement between two or more states.) "Jeffersonian Republicans . . . choked on the idea of direct federal support of intrastate internal improvements." (p. 242)

10. **depression** In economics, a severe and very prolonged period of declining economic activity, high unemployment, and low wages and prices. "It brought deflation, depression, [and] bankruptcies. . . ." (p. 243)

11. **boom** In economics, period of sudden, spectacular expansion of business activity or prices. "The western boom was stimulated by additional developments." (p. 244)

12. **wildcat bank** An unregulated, speculative bank that issues notes without sufficient capital to back them. "Finally, the West demanded cheap money, issued by its own 'wildcat' banks. . . ." (p. 244)

13. **peculiar institution** Widely used term for the institution of American black slavery. "If Congress could abolish the 'peculiar institution' in Missouri, might it not attempt to do likewise in the older states of the South?" (p. 245)

14. **demagogic (demagogue)** Concerning a leader who stirs up the common people by appeals to emotion and prejudice, often for selfish or irrational ends. ". . . Marshall's decisions bolstered judicial barriers against democratic or demagogic attacks on property rights." (p. 250)

15. **contract** In law, an agreement in which each of two or more parties binds themselves to perform some act in exchange for what the other party similarly pledges to do. ". . . the legislative grant was a contract . . . and the Constitution forbids state laws 'impairing' contracts." (p. 250)

PART II: CHECKING YOUR PROGRESS

A. True-False

Where the statement is true, circle **T**; where it is false, circle **F**.

1. T F President Madison cleverly manipulated Napoleon into repealing his blockade decrees.

2. T F The large western delegation in Congress was not concerned about foreign-policy issues such as Canada and maritime rights.

3. T F Western hostility to Britain arose partly because the war hawks believed the British were supplying Indians with weapons for war.

4. T F New Englanders opposed the War of 1812 because they believed that Canada should be acquired by peaceful negotiation rather than war.

5.   T   F   The most effective branch of the American military in the War of 1812 proved to be the U.S. Army.

6.   T   F   The American strategy for conquering Canada was well conceived but failed because of a lack of equipment and troops.

7.   T   F   American naval forces under Perry and Macdonough thwarted British-Canadian invasion threats to Detroit and upstate New York.

8.   T   F   Andrew Jackson's victory at the Battle of New Orleans was crucial to the American military and political gains in the Treaty of Ghent.

9.   T   F   Clay's and Calhoun's plans for an extensive system of federally funded roads and canals were blocked by the western states' objections to federal involvement in their affairs.

10.   T   F   The Federalist Party remained a sturdy center of opposition to the expansion of slavery and Monroe's anti-British foreign policies.

11.   T   F   Because of its wildcat banking practices and land speculation, the West was hit especially hard in the panic of 1819.

12.   T   F   The Missouri Compromise admitted Missouri to the Union as a free state, in exchange for the admission of Louisiana as a slave state.

13.   T   F   John Marshall's Supreme Court rulings generally defended the power of the federal government against the power of the states.

14.   T   F   Secretary of State John Quincy Adams successfully acquired both Oregon and Florida for the United States.

15.   T   F   The Monroe Doctrine declaring that the United States would permit no new European colonialism in the Americas was most enthusiastically welcomed in Latin America.

B. Multiple Choice

Select the best answer and circle the corresponding letter.

1.   The greatest American military successes of the War of 1812 came
    a.   in the land invasions of Canada.
    b.   in the campaign fought around Washington and Baltimore.
    c.   in the naval battles on the Great Lakes and elsewhere.
    d.   in the defense of Fort Michilimackinac.

2.   Two prominent American military heroes during the War of 1812 were
    a.   Tecumseh and Henry Clay.
    b.   Oliver Hazard Perry and Andrew Jackson.
    c.   Thomas Macdonough and Francis Scott Key.
    d.   Isaac Brock and John Quincy Adams.

3.   The American victory in the Battle of New Orleans proved essentially meaningless because
    a.   General Jackson was unable to pursue the British any further.
    b.   the British continued their attacks on the Mississippi Valley region.
    c.   the peace treaty had been signed several weeks before.
    d.   the British navy retained control of the shipping lanes around New Orleans.

4.   The terms of the Treaty of Ghent ending the War of 1812 provided
    a.   that there would be a buffer Indian state between the United States and Canada.
    b.   that Britain would stop impressment of American sailors.

    c.   that the United States would acquire western Florida in exchange for guaranteeing British control of Canada.

    d.   that the two sides would stop fighting and return to the status quo before the war.

5.   One significant domestic consequence of the War of 1812 was

    a.   a weakening of respect for American naval forces.

    b.   an increased threat from Indians in the West.

    c.   an increase in domestic manufacturing and economic independence.

    d.   a decline of nationalism and a growth of sectionalism.

6.   One significant international consequence of the War of 1812 was

    a.   a growth of good relations between the United States and Britain.

    b.   a growth of Canadian patriotism and nationalism.

    c.   the spread of American ideals of liberty to much of western Europe.

    d.   increased American attention to the threat of attack from European nations.

7.   The Era of Good Feelings was sharply disrupted by

    a.   the bitter political battles over the Tariff of 1816.

    b.   the rise of international tensions with Britain.

    c.   the panic of 1819 and the battle over slavery in Missouri.

    d.   the nasty presidential campaign of 1820.

8.   The new nationalistic feeling right after the War of 1812 was evident in all of the following *except*

    a.   the development of a distinctive national literature.

    b.   an increased emphasis on economic independence.

    c.   the addition of significant new territory to the United States.

    d.   a new pride in the American army and navy.

9.   Besides admitting Missouri as a slave state and Maine as a free state, the Missouri Compromise provided that

    a.   slavery would not be permitted anywhere in the Louisiana Purchase territory north of the southern boundary of Missouri, except in Missouri itself.

    b.   the number of proslavery and antislavery members of the House of Representatives would be kept permanently equal.

    c.   the international slave trade would be permanently ended.

    d.   slavery would be gradually ended in the District of Columbia.

10.   In the case of *McCulloch* v. *Maryland*, Justice John Marshall held that

    a.   the states had the right to regulate commerce within their boundaries.

    b.   the federal Bank of the United States was constitutional, and no state had a right to tax it.

    c.   the Supreme Court had the right to review the decisions of state supreme courts.

    d.   the Supreme Court had the power to determine the constitutionality of federal laws.

11.   The most prominent political figure who shared John Marshall's belief in expanding the power of the federal government at the expense of the states was

    a.   James Monroe.

    b.   John Calhoun.

    c.   Daniel Webster.

    d.   Andrew Jackson.

12.   Andrew Jackson's invasion of Florida led to permanent acquisition of that territory after

    a.   President Monroe ordered him to seize all Spanish military posts in the area.

    b.   the United States declared its rights under the Monroe Doctrine.

    c.   Monroe's cabinet endorsed Jackson's action and told him to purchase Florida from Spain.

    d.   Secretary of State Adams pressured Spain to cede the area to the United States.

13. The original impetus for declaring the Monroe Doctrine came from

    a. a British proposal that America join Britain in guaranteeing the independence of the Latin American republics.
    b. the growing British threat to intervene in Latin America.
    c. the American desire to gain new territory in the Caribbean and Central America.
    d. a Russian plan to expand from Alaska into western Canada and Oregon.

14. As proclaimed by Monroe in his message of 1823, the Monroe Doctrine asserted that

    a. only the United States had a right to intervene to promote democracy in Latin America.
    b. the British and Americans would act together to prevent further Russian expansion on the Pacific coast.
    c. the United States would not tolerate further European intervention or colonization in the Americas.
    d. the United States would support the Greeks in their fight for independence against Turkey.

15. The immediate effect of the Monroe Doctrine at the time it was issued was

    a. a rise in tension between the United States and the major European powers.
    b. very small.
    c. a close alliance between the United States and the Latin American republics.
    d. a series of clashes between the American and British navies.

C. Identification

Supply the correct identification for each numbered description.

1. _____ One of the Great Lakes where Oliver H. Perry captured a large British fleet

2. _____ Stirring patriotic song written by Francis Scott Key

3. _____ Famous American frigate that was larger and heavier than most British ships

4. _____ Gathering of prominent New England Federalists who considered secession

5. _____ Two prominent Washington buildings burned by the British in 1814

6. _____ Intellectual magazine that reflected the post-1815 spirit of American nationalism

7. _____ Henry Clay's ambitious nationalistic proposal for tariffs, internal improvements, and expanded manufacturing

8. _____ Somewhat inappropriate term applied to the Monroe administrations, suggesting that this period lacked major conflicts

9. _____ Once-prominent political party that effectively died by 1820

10. _____ Major water transportation route financed and built by New York State after President Madison vetoed federal funding

11. _____ Line designated as the future boundary between free and slave territories under the Missouri Compromise

12. _____ Supreme Court ruling that defended federal power by denying a state the right to tax a federal bank

13. _____ Supreme Court case in which Daniel Webster successfully argued that a state could not change a legal charter once granted

14. _____ Territory occupied jointly by Britain and the United States under the Treaty of 1818

15. _____ A presidential foreign-policy proclamation that might well have been called the "Adams Doctrine" or the "Self-Defense Doctrine"

D. Matching People, Places, and Events

Match the person, place, or event in the left column with the proper description in the right column by inserting the correct letter on the blank line.

1. ___ Stephen Decatur
2. ___ Treaty of Ghent
3. ___ Rush-Bagot agreement
4. ___ Hartford Convention
5. ___ Henry Clay
6. ___ James Monroe
7. ___ Panic of 1819
8. ___ Missouri Compromise
9. ___ John Marshall
10. ___ John Quincy Adams
11. ___ Florida
12. ___ Andrew Jackson
13. ___ Daniel Webster
14. ___ Latin America
15. ___ Tsar Alexander I

a. Admitted one slave and one free state to the Union, and fixed the boundary between slave and free territories

b. Military commander who exceeded his government's instructions during an invasion of Spanish territory

c. The leading voice promoting nationalism and greater federal power in the United States Senate during the 1820s

d. Aristocratic Federalist jurist whose rulings bolstered national power against the states

e. Eloquent Kentucky spokesman for the "American System" and key architect of the Missouri Compromise in the U.S. Senate

f. Nationalistic secretary of state who promoted American interests against Spain and Britain

g. Area where vulnerable new republics tempted European monarchies to intervene

h. American naval hero of the War of 1812 who said, ". . . our country, right or wrong!"

i. First severe depression since 1790

j. Territory ceded by Spain after Americans invaded and applied diplomatic pressure

k. Gathering of antiwar delegates in New England that ended up being accused of treason

l. President whose personal popularity contributed to the Era of Good Feelings

m. Agreement that simply stopped fighting and left most of the war issues unresolved

n.   1817 agreement that limited American and British naval forces on the Great Lakes

o.   Russian ruler whose mediation proposal led to negotiations ending the War of 1812

E. Putting Things in Order

Put the following events in correct order by numbering them from 1 to 6.

1.   A battle over extending slavery finally results in two new states and an agreement on how to handle slavery in the territories.

2.   A major water route is completed across New York State.

3.   Infant American manufacturers successfully press Congress to raise barriers against foreign imports.

4.   Rather than follow a British diplomatic lead, President Monroe and Secretary Adams announce a bold new policy for the Western Hemisphere.

5.   Spain cedes Florida to the United States.

6.   An unpopular war ends in an ambivalent compromise that settles none of the key contested issues.

F. Matching Cause and Effect

Match the historical cause in the left column with the proper effect in the right column by writing the correct letter on the blank line.

Cause		**Effect**
1. ___	American lack of military preparation and poor strategy	a. Inspired a new sense of Canadian nationalism
2. ___	Oliver H. Perry's and Thomas Macdonough's naval successes	b. Contributed to the death of the Federalist party and the impression that New Englanders were disloyal
3. ___	Tsar Alexander I's mediation proposal	c. Produced a series of badly failed attempts to conquer Canada
4. ___	The Hartford Convention	d. Reduced armaments along the border between the United States and Canada and laid the groundwork for "the longest unfortified boundary in the world"
5. ___	Canadians' successful defense of their homeland in the War of 1812	
6. ___	The Rush-Bagot agreement	e. Caused the economy to collapse in the panic of 1819
7. ___	The rising nationalistic economic spirit after the War of 1812	f. Angered Britain and other European nations but had little effect in Latin America
8. ___	The disappearance of the Federalists and President Monroe's appeals to New England	g. Fueled demands in Congress for transportation improvements and the removal of the Native Americans
9. ___	Overspeculation in western lands	h. Upheld the power of the federal government against the states
10. ___	Cheap land and increasing westward migration	
11. ___	The deadlock between North and South over the future of slavery in Missouri	i. Created a temporary one-party system and an "Era of Good Feelings"
12. ___	The Missouri Compromise	j. Produced the Missouri Compromise, which admitted two states and drew a line between slave and free territories
13. ___	John Marshall's Supreme Court rulings	k. Aroused American and British fears of European intervention in Latin America
14. ___	The rise of European reactionary powers and the loss of Spain's colonial empire	l. Aroused southern fears for the long-term future of slavery
15. ___	The Monroe Doctrine	m. Inspired a new Bank of the United States and the protectionist Tariff of 1816
		n. Eventually led to the beginnings of peace negotiations at Ghent
		o. Reversed a string of American defeats and prevented a British-Canadian invasion from the north

G. Developing Historical Skills

Categorizing Historical Information

Historical events and information are usually presented in chronological order. But it is often useful to organize them into topical or other categories. The central idea of this chapter is the rise of American nationalism in the period 1815–1824. Among the major subdivisions of this general idea would be the following:

a.   Economic nationalism

b.   Political nationalism and unity

c.   Judicial nationalism

d.   Foreign-policy nationalism

Indicate under which of these categories each of the following facts or events from the chapter should be located.

1.   Andrew Jackson's invasion of Florida

2.   *Dartmouth College* v. *Woodward*

3.   The Tariff of 1816

4.   John Quincy Adams's rejection of British Foreign Minister Canning's proposed joint British-American statement

5.   Clay's American System

6.   President Monroe's tour of New England

7.   Daniel Webster's speeches

8.   The election of 1820

H. Map Mastery

Map Discrimination

Using the maps and charts in Chapter 12, answer the following questions:

1. *The Three U. S. Invasions of 1812/Campaigns of 1813*: Near which two Great Lakes were the major battles related to the American invasions of Canada fought?

2. *Presidential Election of 1812*: What were the only two states that voted in part contrary to the general trend of their section (i.e, North vs. South)?

3. *The Missouri Compromise and Slavery, 1820–1821*: After the Missouri Compromise of 1820, only two organized territories of the United States remained eligible to join the Union as slave states. Which were they?

4. *The Missouri Compromise and Slavery, 1820–1821*: As of 1821, how many slave states had been carved out of the territory of the Louisiana Purchase?

5. *The Missouri Compromise and Slavery, 1820–1821*: After Maine was admitted as a free state in 1820, how many *organized* territories were there north of the line 36° 30'—that is, the border between the slave and free territories?

6. *The Missouri Compromise and Slavery, 1820–1821*: As of 1821, which *five* slave states were north of the line of 36° 30' that was intended to be the future northern limit of slavery?

7. *The U.S.-British Boundary Settlement, 1818:* Under the British-American boundary settlement of 1818, which nation gained the most territory (compared with the natural Missouri River watershed boundary)?

8. *The Southeast, 1810–1819*: Which organized American territory lay immediately north of West Florida at this time?

Map Challenge

Using the map on p. 246, write a brief essay explaining how the Missouri Compromise related both to the *existing* territorial status of slavery and to its possible future expansion to the West. (Recall that the Compromise set 36° 30' as the northern boundary of any future slave territory.)

PART III: APPLYING WHAT YOU HAVE LEARNED

1. Why was the American military effort generally unsuccessful, especially the numerous attempts to invade Canada?

2. What were the broad consequences of the War of 1812?

3. What were the most important signs of the new American nationalism that developed in the period 1815–1824?

4. How did the forces of nationalism compete with sectional interests in the economic and judicial struggles of the period?

5. What role did the West play in such crucial issues of the period as the tariff, internal improvements, and the expansion of slavery?

6. Discuss the role of Henry Clay, John C. Calhoun, and Daniel Webster in the events and issues of the period 1815–1824. Is it valid to see Clay as spokesman for the West, Webster for the North, and Calhoun for the South?

7. How did American nationalism display itself in foreign policy, particularly in the Florida crisis and in American policy toward Europe and the Western Hemisphere?

8. Why did the issue of admitting Missouri to the Union precipitate a major national crisis? Why did the North and South each agree to the terms of the Missouri Compromise?

9. Why had the Jeffersonian Republicans, by 1815–1824, adopted many of the principles of "loose construction" once held by Hamiltonian Federalists? (See Chapters 6 and 10.) What kinds of strong federal power did the Republicans use, and what kinds were they still reluctant to employ?

10. Was the Monroe Doctrine fundamentally consistent with the isolationist principles established by George Washington in his Neutrality Proclamation and Farewell Address (see Chapter 10)? Or did it foreshadow America's growing willingness to assert its national power, even at the risk of conflict with European powers?

CHAPTER 13

The Rise of a Mass Democracy, 1824–1840

PART I: REVIEWING THE CHAPTER

A. CHECKLIST OF LEARNING OBJECTIVES

After mastering this chapter, you should be able to

1. describe and explain the growth of "Mass Democracy" in the 1820s.

2. indicate how the "corrupt bargain" of 1824 and Adams' unpopular presidency set the stage for Jackson's election in 1828.

3. analyze the significance of Jackson's victory in 1828 as a triumph of the "New Democracy."

4. describe the political innovations of the 1830s, especially the rise of mass parties, and indicate their significance for American politics and society.

5. describe Jackson's policies of westward expansion and his harsh removal of the southeastern Indian nations on the Trail of Tears.

6. explain Jackson's economic and political motives in the "Bank War," and point out the consequences of Jacksonian economics for his successor Van Buren after the Panic of 1837.

7. describe the different ways that each of the new mass political parties, Democrats and Whigs, promoted the democratic ideals of liberty and equality among their constituencies.

B. GLOSSARY

To build your social science vocabulary, familiarize yourself with the following terms:

1. **deference** The yielding of opinion to the judgment of someone else. "The deference, apathy, and virtually nonexistent party organizations of the Era of Good Feelings yielded to the boisterous democracy. . . ." (p. 256)

2. **puritanical** Extremely or excessively strict in matters of morals or religion. "The only candidate left was the puritanical Adams. . . ." (p. 258)

3. **mudslinging** Malicious, unscrupulous attacks against an opponent. "Mudslinging reached a disgraceful level. . . ."

4. **spoils** Public offices given as a reward for political support. "Under Jackson the spoils system . . . was introduced on a large scale." (p. 262)

5. **denominations** In American religion, the major branches of Christianity, organized into distinct church structures, e.g., Presbyterians, Baptists, Disciples of Christ, etc. ". . . many denominations sent missionaries into Indian villages." (p. 266)

6. **evangelical** In American religion, those believers and groups, usually Protestant, who emphasizes personal salvation, individual conversion experiences, voluntary commitment, and the authority of Scripture. "The Anti-Masons attracted support from many evangelical Protestant groups. . . ." (p. 271)

7.   **hard money** Metal money or coins, as distinguished from paper money. (The term also came to mean reliable or secure money that maintained or increased its purchasing power over time. **Soft money**, or paper money, was assumed to inflate or lose value.) ". . . a decree that required all public lands to be purchased with 'hard' . . . money." (p. 272)

8.   **usurpation** The act of seizing, occupying, or enjoying the place, power, or functions of someone without legal right. "Hatred of Jackson and his 'executive usurpation' was its only apparent cement in its formative days." (p. 272)

9.   **favorite sons** In American politics, presidential candidates who are nominated by their own state, primarily out of local loyalty. "Their long-shot strategy was instead to run several prominent 'favorite sons' . . . and hope to scatter the vote so that no candidate could win a majority." (p. 273)

10. **machine** A hierarchical political organization, often controlled through patronage or spoils, where professional workers deliver large blocs of voters to preferred candidates. "As a machine-made candidate, he incurred the resentment of many Democrats. . . ." (p. 274)

11. **temperance** Campaigns for voluntary commitment to moderation or total abstinence in the consumption of liquor. (Prohibition involved instead forcible legal bans on the production or consumption of alcohol.) ". . . the Arkansas Indians dubbed him 'Big Drunk.' He subsequently took the pledge of temperance." (p. 276)

12. **populist** A political program or style focused on the common people, and attacking perspectives and policies associated with the well-off, well-born, or well-educated. (The Populist Party was a specific third-party organization of the 1890s.) "The first was the triumph of a populist democratic style." (p. 283)

13. **divine right** The belief that government or rulers are directly established by God. ". . . America was now bowing to the divine right of the people." (p. 283)

PART II: CHECKING YOUR PROGRESS

A. True-False

Where the statement is true, circle **T**; where it is false, circle **F**.

1.   T   F   The last election based on the old elitist political system was the four-way presidential campaign of 1824 involving Jackson, Clay, Crawford, and John Quincy Adams.

2.   T   F   Henry Clay disproved the charge of a "corrupt bargain" between himself and President Adams by refusing to accept any favors from the administration.

3.   T   F   President Adams attempted to uphold strong nationalistic principles in a time of growing support for sectionalism and states' rights.

4.   T   F   In his personal lifestyle as well as his policies, Andrew Jackson epitomized the hard-working ordinary frontiersmen in contrast to the wealthy Adams and his supporters.

5.   T   F   The election campaign of 1828 was notable for its focus on the issues of the tariff and democracy rather than on personalities and mudslinging.

6.   T   F   Jackson's victory in 1828 represented the triumph of the West and the common people over the older elitist political system.

7.   T   F   The Jacksonians put into practice their belief that ordinary citizens were capable of holding almost any public office without particular qualifications.

8. T F   One consequence of the spoils system was the building of powerful political machines based on jobs and patronage for political supporters.

9. T F   Opposition to the "Tariff of Abominations" was equally strong in New England and the South.

10. T F   South Carolina's fierce opposition to the tariff reflected anxiety that enhanced federal power might be turned against the institution of slavery.

11. T F   When the Supreme Court attempted to uphold southeastern Indians' rights, Jackson defied the Supreme Court's rulings and ordered them removed to Oklahoma.

12. T F   Jackson used his veto of the bill to recharter the Bank of the United States to politically mobilize the common people of the West against the financial elite of the East.

13. T F   The Whig party was based on a unified ideology of support for states' rights and national expansion into the West.

14. T F   A primary source of tension between settlers in Texas and the Mexican government was Mexico's prohibition of slave importation.

15. T F   William Henry Harrison's authentic background as an ordinary frontiersman born in a log cabin enabled Whigs to appeal to the common man in the campaign of 1840.

B. Multiple Choice

Select the best answer and circle the corresponding letter.

1. The Jacksonian charge of a "corrupt bargain" to gain John Quincy Adams the presidency arose because

    a. William Crawford threw his electoral votes to Adams in exchange for a seat in the Senate.
    b. Adams was charged with having bribed members of the House to vote for him.
    c. Adams ended his previous opposition to Clay's American System.
    d. Clay was named secretary of state after throwing his support to Adams.

2. Which of the following was *not* among the factors that made John Quincy Adams's presidency a political failure?

    a. Adams's anti-western land and Indian policies.
    b. Adams's involvement with correct machine deals and politicians.
    c. Adams's stubborn and prickly personality.
    d. Adams's support for national roads, a national university, and an astronomical observatory.

3. Andrew Jackson's appeal to the common people arose partly because

    a. Americans finally understood the ideas of the Declaration of Independence.
    b. many citizens were tired of the partisan fights between Republicans and Federalists.
    c. he had risen from the masses and reflected many of their prejudices in his personal attitudes and outlook.
    d. farmer and labor organizations aroused populist opposition to elitist politics.

4. One political development that illustrated the new popular voice in politics was

    a. the rise of the caucus system of presidential nominations.
    b. the growth of the spoils system as a basis for large political "machines."
    c. the development of extensive speechmaking tours by presidential candidates.
    d. the hostility to the influence of the Masons in national politics.

5. In the battle over the "Tariff of Abominations,"

    a. New England backed high tariffs while the South demanded lower duties.
    b. both New England and the South opposed the higher tariff rates.

    c.   the South fought for higher tariffs while the West sought lower rates.

    d.   the South backed higher tariffs while New England sought to lower the rates.

6.   Under the surface of the South's strong opposition to the "Tariff of Abominations" was

    a.   a desire to develop its own textile industry.

    b.   competition between southern cotton growers and midwestern grain farmers.

    c.   a strong preference for British manufactured goods over American-produced goods.

    d.   a fear of growing federal power that might interfere with slavery.

7.   Some southeastern Indian tribes like the Cherokees were notable for their

    a.   effectiveness in warfare against encroaching whites.

    b.   development of effective agricultural, educational, and political institutions.

    c.   success in persuading President Jackson to support their cause.

    d.   adherence to traditional Native American cultural and religious values.

8.   In promoting his policy of Indian removal, President Andrew Jackson

    a.   defied rulings of the U.S. Supreme Court that favored the Cherokees.

    b.   admitted that the action would destroy Native American culture and society.

    c.   acted against the advice of his cabinet and his military commanders in the Southeast.

    d.   hoped to split the Cherokees apart from their allies such as the Creeks and Seminoles.

9.   Jackson's veto of the Bank of the United States recharter bill represented

    a.   a bold assertion of presidential power on behalf of western farmers and other debtors.

    b.   an attempt to assure bankers and creditors that the federal government had their interests at heart.

    c.   a concession to Henry Clay and his National Republican followers.

    d.   a gain for sound banking and a financially stable currency system.

10.   One important result of President Jackson's destruction of the Bank of the United States was

    a.   a successful economy that could be handed to his successor, Van Buren.

    b.   a sounder financial system founded upon thousands of locally controlled banks.

    c.   the American banking system's dependence on European investment and control.

    d.   the lack of a stable banking system to finance the era of rapid industrialization.

11.   Among the new political developments that appeared in the election of 1832 were

    a.   political parties and direct popular voting for president.

    b.   newspaper endorsements and public financing of presidential campaigns.

    c.   nomination by congressional caucus and voting by the Electoral College.

    d.   third-party campaigning, national conventions, and party platforms.

12.   In the immediate aftermath of the successful Texas Revolution,

    a.   Texas petitioned to join the United States but was refused admission.

    b.   Texas joined the United States as a slave state.

    c.   Mexico and the United States agreed to a joint protectorate over Texas.

    d.   Britain threatened the United States with war over Texas.

13.   The Panic of 1837 and subsequent depression were caused by

    a.   the stock market collapse and a sharp decline in grain prices.

    b.   a lack of new investment in industry and technology.

    c.   the threat of war with Mexico over Texas.

    d.   over-speculation and Jackson's financial policies.

14.   Prominent leaders of the Whig party included

    a.   Martin Van Buren and John C. Calhoun.

    b.   Henry Clay and Daniel Webster.

    c.   Andrew Jackson and William Henry Harrison.

    d.   Stephen Austin and Sam Houston.

15. In general, the Whig party tended to favor
    a. individual liberty and states' rights.
    b. the protection of slavery and southern interests.
    c. a strong federal role in both economic and moral issues.
    d. the interests of the working people and farmers against the upper classes.

C. Identification

Supply the correct identification for each numbered description.

1. _____ New, circus-like method of nominating presidential candidates that involved wider participation but usually left effective control in the hands of party bosses

2. _____ Small, short-lived third political party that originated a new method of nominating presidential candidates in the election campaign of 1831–1832

3. _____ Contemptuous Jacksonian term for the alleged political deal by which Clay threw his support to Adams in exchange for a high cabinet office

4. _____ Office to which President Adams appointed Henry Clay

5. _____ The popular idea that public offices should be handed out on the basis of political support rather than special qualifications

6. _____ Scornful southern term for the high Tariff of 1828

7. _____ Theory promoted by John C. Calhoun and other South Carolinians that said states had the right to disregard federal laws to which they objected

8. _____ The "moneyed monster" that Clay tried to preserve and that Jackson killed with his veto in 1832

9. _____ Ritualistic secret societies that became the target of a momentarily powerful third party in 1832

10. _____ Religious believers, originally attracted to the Anti-Masonic party and then to the Whigs, who sought to use political power for moral and religious reform

11. _____ Any *two* of the southeastern Indian peoples who were removed to Oklahoma
    _____

12. _____ The sorrowful path along which thousands of southeastern Indians were removed to Oklahoma

13. _____ The nation from which Texas won its independence in 1836

14. _____ Anti-Jackson political party that generally stood for national community and an activist government

15. _____ Popular symbols of the bogus but effective campaign the Whigs used to elect "poor-boy" William Henry Harrison in 1840

D. Matching People, Places, and Events

Match the person, place, or event in the left column with the proper description in the right column by inserting the correct letter on the blank line.

1. ___ John C. Calhoun   a. Cherokee leader who devised an alphabet for his people

2. ___ Henry Clay

3. ___ Nicholas Biddle

4. ___ Sequoyah

5. ___ John Quincy Adams

6. ___ David Crocket

7. ___ Stephen Austin

8. ___ Sam Houston

9. ___ Osceola

10. ___ Santa Anna

11. ___ Martin Van Buren

12. ___ Black Hawk

13. ___ William Henry Harrison

14. ___ Whigs

15. ___ Democrats

b. Political party that generally stressed individual liberty, the rights of the common people, and hostility to privilege

c. Seminole leader whose warriors killed fifteen hundred American soldiers in years of guerrilla warfare

d. Former Tennessee governor whose victory at San Jacinto in 1836 won Texas its independence

e. Mexican general and dictator whose large army failed to defeat the Texans

f. Former vice president, leader of South Carolina nullifiers, and bitter enemy of Andrew Jackson

g. Political party that favored a more activist government, high tariffs, internal improvements, and moral reforms

h. Original leader of American settlers in Texas who obtained a huge land grant from the Mexican government

i. A frontier hero, Tennessee Congressman, and teller of tall tales who died in the Texas War for Independence

j. "Old Tippecanoe," who was portrayed by Whig propagandists as a hard-drinking common man of the frontier

k. Jackson's rival for the presidency in 1832, who failed to save the Bank of the United States

l. The "wizard of Albany," whose economically troubled presidency was served in the shadow of Jackson

m. Talented but high-handed bank president who fought a bitter losing battle with the president of the United States

n. Aloof New England statesman whose elitism made him an unpopular leader in the new era of mass democracy

o. Illinois-Wisconsin area Sauk leader who was defeated by American regulars and militia in 1832

E. Putting Things in Order

Put the following events in correct order by numbering them from 1 to 5.

1. ___ South Carolina threatens "nullification" of federal law and backs down in the face of Andrew Jackson's military threat.

2. ___ A strange four-way election puts an icy New Englander in office amid charges of a "corrupt bargain."

3. ___ A campaign based on hoopla and "log cabins and hard cider slogans" demonstrates that both Whigs and Democrats can effectively play the new mass-party political game.

4. ___ A northern Mexican province successfully revolts and seeks admission to the United States.

5. ___ Despite attempting to follow white patterns of "civilizing," thousands of American Indians are forcibly removed from their homes and driven across the Mississippi River.

F. Matching Cause and Effect

Match the historical cause in the left column with the proper effect in the right column by writing the correct letter on the blank line.

Cause	Effect
1. ___ The growth of American migration into northern Mexico	a. Brought many evangelical Christians into politics and showed that others besides Jackson could stir up popular feelings
2. ___ The demand of many whites to acquire Indian land in Georgia and other states	b. Provoked protests and threats of nullification from South Carolina
3. ___ The Anti-Masonic Party	c. Aroused popular anger and made Jackson's supporters determined to elect him in 1828
4. ___ The failure of any candidate to win an electoral majority in the four-way election of 1824	d. Laid the foundations for the spoils system that fueled the new mass political parties
5. ___ The alleged "corrupt bargain" between Adams and Clay for the presidency in 1824	e. Threw the bitterly contested election into the U.S. House of Representatives
6. ___ President Adams's strong nationalistic policies	f. Laid the basis for a political conflict that resulted in Texas independence
7. ___ The high New England-backed Tariff of 1828	g. Caused widespread human suffering and virtually guaranteed Martin Van Buren's defeat in 1840
8. ___ Andrew Jackson's "war" against Nicholas Biddle and his policies	h. Fueled the political pressures that led Andrew Jackson to forcibly remove the Cherokees and others
9. ___ Jackson's belief that any ordinary American could hold government office	i. Aroused the bitter opposition of
10. ___ The Panic of 1837	

westerners and southerners, who were increasingly sectionalist

j. Got the government out of banking but weakened the American financial system

G. Developing Historical Skills

Interpreting Political Cartoons and Satire

Political cartoons are an important historical source. Even when they are strongly biased one way or another, they can yield information about political conflicts and contemporary attitudes.

The anti-Jackson cartoon on p. 269 reveals a number of things about how his opponents viewed Jackson. Answer the following questions:

1. What is the fundamental point of the cartoon's attack on the Bank of the United States and its supporters?

2. What visual means does the cartoonist use to develop point?

3. In the pro-Jackson cartoon on p. 270, how is Clay's frustration at Jackson's bank veto portrayed? How is Jackson's successful resistance represented?

4. In the satirical bank note mocking pro-Jackson "pet banks," list at least three distinct *visual* symbols that identify the worthless note with Jackson and his policies.

5. List at least three *verbal* terms or phrases that underscore the supposed fraudulency of Jacksonian banking practices.

H. Map Mastery

Map Discrimination

Using the maps and charts in Chapter 13, answer the following questions:

1. *Election of 1824*: In the election of 1824, how many more electoral votes would Jackson have needed to win a majority and prevent the election from going to the House of Representatives?

2. *Presidential Election of 1828*: In the election of 1828, in which states outside New England did John Quincy Adams win electoral votes?

3. *Presidential Election of 1828*: In the election of 1828, which of the eastern "middle states" did Jackson carry *completely*?

4. *Presidential Election of 1828*: Which two states divided their electoral votes?

5. *The Removal of the Southern Tribes to the West*: Of the five southeastern Indian tribes, which *two* were located wholly within the boundaries of a single state? Which tribe was located in four states?

6. *The Texas Revolution, 1835–1836*: A) When Santa Anna's army entered Texas to attack the Alamo, what two major rivers did it cross? B) When Santa Anna's army moved from the site of its greatest victory to the site of its greatest defeat, what direction did it march?

PART III: APPLYING WHAT YOU HAVE LEARNED

1. Why was Andrew Jackson such a *personally* powerful embodiment of the new mass democracy in the 1820s and 1830s? Would mass democracy have developed without a popular hero like Jackson?

2. Why did Calhoun and the South see the Tariff of 1828 as such an "abomination" and raise threats of nullification over it?

3. Discuss the attitudes, policies, and events that led to the "Trail of Tears" Indian removal in 1837.

4. How did Jackson's "Bank War" demonstrate the powerful uses to which the modern mass democratic political machine could be put? Was Biddle's Bank a real threat to the economic welfare of the ordinary citizens to whom Jackson appealed, or was it more important as a symbol of eastern wealth and elitism?

5. How did the Panic of 1837 and the subsequent depression reflect the weaknesses of Jackson's economic and financial policies? Why was Martin Van Buren unable to cope with political opposition as Jackson had?

6. Does Andrew Jackson belong in the pantheon of "great" American presidents? Why or why not?

7. Andrew Jackson was a southerner and a large slaveholder, yet he nearly led the U.S. Army to invade and crush South Carolina when that state attempted to nullify and resist a federal law. Why?

8. Argue for or against: the "Texas Revolution" against Mexico was more about the expansion of American slavery into the West than it was about the rights of settlers in Mexico.

9. What did the two new democratic parties, the Democrats and the Whigs, really stand for? Were they actual ideological opponents, or were their disagreements less important than their shared roots in the new mass democracy?

10. Compare the two-party political system of the 1830s' "New Democracy" with the first two-party system of the early Republic. (See Chapter 10.) In what ways were the two systems similar, and in what ways were they different? Were both parties of the 1830s correct in seeing themselves as heirs of the Jeffersonian Republican tradition rather than the Hamiltonian Federalist tradition?

CHAPTER 14

Forging the National Economy, 1790–1860

PART I: REVIEWING THE CHAPTER

A. CHECKLIST OF LEARNING OBJECTIVES

After mastering this chapter, you should be able to

1. describe the movement and growth of America's population in the early nineteenth century.

2. describe the effects of Irish and German immigration on American society.

3. explain why America was relatively slow to embrace the industrial revolution and the factory.

4. describe the early development of the factory system and Eli Whitney's system of interchangeable parts.

5. outline early industrialism's effects on workers, including women and children.

6. describe the impact of new technology and transportation systems on American business and agriculture.

7. describe the sequence of major transportation and communication systems that developed from 1790 to 1860 and indicate their economic consequences.

8. describe the effects of the market revolution on the American economy, including the new disparities between rich and poor.

B. GLOSSARY

To build your social science vocabulary, familiarize yourself with the following terms:

1. **caste** An exclusive or rigid social distinction based on birth, wealth, occupation, and so forth. "There was freedom from aristocratic caste and state church. . . ." (p. 292)

2. **nativist** One who advocates favoring native-born citizens over aliens or immigrants. "The invasion of this so-called immigrant 'rabble'. . . inflamed the prejudices of American 'nativists.' " (p. 296)

3. **factory** An establishment for the manufacturing of goods, including buildings and substantial machinery. "The factory system gradually spread from England—'the world's workshop'—to other lands." (p. 300)

4. **trademark** A distinguishing symbol or word used by a manufacturer on its goods, usually registered by law to protect against imitators. ". . . unscrupulous Yankee manufacturers . . . learned to stamp their own products with faked English trademarks." (p. 300)

5. **patent** The legal certification of an original invention, product, or process, guaranteeing its holder sole rights to profits from its use or reproduction for a specified period of time. "For the decade ending in 1800, only 306 patents were registered in Washington. . . ." (p. 304)

6. **liability** Legal responsibility for loss or damage. "The principle of limited liability aided the concentration of capital. . . ." (p. 304)

7. **incorporation** The formation of individuals into an organized entity with legally defined privileges and responsibilities. "Laws of 'free incorporation' were first passed in New York in 1848. . . ." (p. 304)

8. **labor union** An organization of workers—usually wage-earning workers—to promote the interests and welfare of its members, often by collective bargaining with employers. "They were forbidden by law to form labor unions. . . ." (p. 304)

9. **strike** An organized work stoppage by employees in order to obtain better wages, working conditions, and so on. "Not surprisingly, only twenty-four recorded strikes occurred before 1835." (p. 304)

10. **capitalist** An individual or group who uses accumulated funds or private property to produce goods for profit in a market. "It made ambitious capitalists out of humble plowmen. . . ." (p. 309)

11. **turnpike** A toll road. "The turnpikes beckoned to the canvas-covered Conestoga wagons. . . ."(p. 310)

12. **posterity** Later descendants or subsequent generations. "He installed a powerful steam engine in a vessel that posterity came to know as the *Clermont*. . . ." (p. 310)

13. **productivity** In economics, the relative capacity to produce goods and services, measured in terms of the number of workers and machines needed to create goods in a certain length of time. "The principle of division of labor . . . spelled productivity and profits. . . ." (p. 317)

14. **barter** The direct exchange of goods and services for one another, without the use of cash or any medium of exchange. "Most families . . . bartered with their neighbors for the few necessities they could not make themselves." (p. 317)

PART II: CHECKING YOUR PROGRESS

A. True-False

Where the statement is true, circle **T**; where it is false, circle **F**.

1. T   F   American frontier life was often plagued by poverty and illness.

2. T   F   The influx of Irish immigrants contributed to America's toleration of ethnic and religious pluralism.

3. T   F   Most early American manufacturing was concentrated in the South.

4. T   F   The principle of "general incorporation" permitted individual businesspeople to apply for limited-liability corporate charters from the state legislatures.

5. T   F   The early industrial revolution greatly benefited workers by opening up well-paying factory jobs.

6. T   F   Early labor unions made very slow progress, partly because the strike weapon was illegal and ineffective.

7. T   F   The steel plow and mechanical reaper helped turn American farmers from subsistence farming to commercial, market-oriented agriculture.

8. T   F   By 1840, overland highways had proved a more effective form of transportation than canals.

9. T   F   The Erie Canal's greatest economic effect was to create strong east-west commercial and industrial links between the Northeast and the West (Midwest).

10. T   F   The railroad gained quick acceptance as a more efficient and flexible alternative to waterbound transportation.

11. T   F   In the sectional division of labor that developed before the Civil War, the South generally provided raw materials to the Northeast in exchange for manufactured goods, transportation, and commercial services.

12. T   F   The growth of a market economy drew most American women off the farms and out of the home into the new factories and mills.

13. T   F   By 1850, permanent telegraph lines had been stretched across both the Atlantic Ocean and the North American continent.

14. T   F   The advances in manufacturing and transportation decreased the gap between rich and poor in America.

15. T   F   In the 1830s new legal and governmental policies prohibiting chartered business monopolies encouraged competition and aided the market economy.

B. Multiple Choice

Select the best answer and circle the corresponding letter.

1.   The experience of frontier life was especially difficult for

   a.   women.
   b.   young people.
   c.   foreign immigrants.
   d.   Roman Catholics.

2.   As late as 1850, over one-half of the American population was

   a.   foreign-born.
   b.   living west of the Mississippi River.
   c.   under the age of thirty.
   d.   living in cities of over 100,000 people.

3.   The primary economic activity in the Rocky Mountain West before the Civil War was

   a.   agriculture.
   b.   fur-trapping.
   c.   mining.
   d.   small business trading.

4.   Americans came to look on their spectacular western wilderness areas especially as

   a.   one of the things that defined and distinguished America as a new nation.
   b.   a source of economic exploitation.
   c.   a potential attraction for tourists from abroad.
   d.   the sacred home of American Indian tribes.

5.   The American painter who developed the idea for a national park system was

   a.   Samuel F. B. Morse.
   b.   Caleb Bingham.
   c.   John James Audubon.
   d.   George Catlin.

6.   The two major sources of European immigration to America in the 1840s and 1850s were

   a.   France and Italy.
   b.   Germany and France.
   c.   Germany and Ireland.
   d.   Ireland and Norway.

7. One consequence of the influx of new immigrants was

    a. a decline in the birthrate of native-born Americans.
    b. an upsurge of anti-Catholicism.
    c. a virtual end to westward migration.
    d. a national decline in wage rates.

8. Industrialization was at first slow to arrive in America because

    a. there was a shortage of labor, capital, and consumers.
    b. low tariff rates invited foreign imports.
    c. the country lacked the educational system necessary to develop technology.
    d. the country lacked a patent system to guarantee investors the profits from new machines.

9. The first industry to be shaped by the new factory system of manufacturing was

    a. textiles.
    b. the telegraph.
    c. agriculture.
    d. iron-making.

10. Wages for most American workers rose in the early nineteenth century, except for the most exploited workers like

    a. immigrants and westerners.
    b. textile and transportation workers.
    c. single men and women.
    d. women and children.

11. A major change affecting the American family in the early nineteenth century was

    a. the rise of an organized feminist movement.
    b. the movement of most women into the work force.
    c. increased conflict between parents and children over moral questions.
    d. a decline in the average number of children per household.

12. The first major improvement in the American transportation system came from

    a. canals and railroads.
    b. railroads and clipper ships.
    c. steamboats and highways.
    d. keelboats and Conestoga wagons.

13. The new regional "division of labor" created by improved transportation meant that

    a. the South specialized in cotton, the West in grain and livestock, and the East in manufacturing.
    b. the South specialized in manufacturing, the West in transportation, and the East in grain and livestock.
    c. the South specialized in cotton, the West in manufacturing, and the East in finance.
    d. the South specialized in grain and livestock, the West in cotton, and the East in transportation.

14. "Limited liability" laws and the Supreme Court's decision prohibiting state governments from granting "irrevocable charters" to corporations greatly aided

    a. private American colleges' ability to compete with state universities.
    b. established businesses with large capital investments.
    c. Americans' ability to compete with cheap British imports.
    d. more entrepreneurial enterprises and greater market competition.

15. One major effect of industrialization was

    a. an increasing economic equality among all citizens.
    b. a strengthening of the family as an economic unit.
    c. an increasingly stable labor force.

d. a rise in the gap between rich and poor.

C. Identification

Supply the correct identification for each numbered description.

1. _____ Nation where a potato famine in the 1840s led to a great migration of its people to America

2. _____ Semisecret Irish organization that became a benevolent society aiding Irish immigrants in America

3. _____ Liberal German refugees who fled failed democratic revolutions and came to America

4. _____ Americans who protested and sometimes rioted against Roman Catholic immigrants

5. _____ The transformation of manufacturing that began in Britain about 1750

6. _____ Whitney's invention that enhanced cotton production and gave new life to black slavery

7. _____ Principle that permitted individual investors to risk no more capital in a business venture than their own share of a corporation's stock

8. _____ Morse's invention that provided instant communication across distance

9. _____ Common source of early factory labor, often underpaid, whipped, and brutally beaten

10. _____ Working people's organizations, often considered illegal under early American law

11. _____ McCormick's invention that vastly increased the productivity of the American grain farmer

12. _____ The only major highway constructed by the federal government before the Civil War

13. _____ Fulton's invention that made river transportation a two-way affair

14. _____ "Clinton's Big Ditch" that transformed transportation and economic life across the Great Lakes region from Buffalo to Chicago

15. _____ Beautiful but short-lived American ships, replaced by "tramp steamers"

D. Matching People, Places, and Events

Match the person, place, or event in the left column with the proper description in the right column by inserting the correct letter on the blank line.

1. ___ Samuel Slater
2. ___ Eli Whitney
3. ___ Elias Howe
4. ___ Samuel F.B. Morse
5. ___ Know-Nothings

a. Inventor of the mechanical reaper that transformed grain growing into a business

b. New York governor who built the Erie Canal

c. Inventor of a machine that revolutionized the ready-made

6. ___   *Commonwealth* v. *Hunt*   clothing industry

7. ___   Cyrus McCormick   d.   Agitators against immigrants and Roman Catholics

8. ___   Robert Fulton

9. ___   Cyrus Field   e.   Wealthy New York manufacturer who laid the first temporary transatlantic cable in 1858

10. ___   Molly Maguires

11. ___   DeWitt Clinton   f.   Immigrant mechanic who initiated American industrialization by setting up his cotton-spinning factory in 1791

                                                g.   Painter turned inventor who developed the first reliable system for instant communication across distance

                                                h.   Developer of a "folly" that made rivers two-way streams of transportation

                                                i.   Radical, secret Irish labor union of the 1860s and 1870s

                                                j.   Yankee mechanical genius who revolutionized cotton production and created the system of interchangeable parts

                                                k.   Pioneering Massachusetts Supreme Court decision that declared labor unions legal

E. Putting Things in Order

Put the following events in correct order by numbering them from 1 to 5.

1. ___   First telegraph message—"What hath God wrought?"—is sent from Baltimore to Washington.

2. ___   Industrial revolution begins in Britain.

3. ___   Telegraph lines are stretched across Atlantic Ocean and North American continent.

4. ___   Major water transportation route connects New York City to Lake Erie and points west.

5. ___   Invention of cotton gin and system of interchangeable parts revolutionized southern agriculture and northern industry.

F. Matching Cause and Effect

Match the historical cause in the left column with the proper effect in the right column by writing the correct letter on the blank line.

Cause		Effect
1. ___ The open, rough-and-	a.	Made the fast-growing United States the

	tumble society of the American West	fourth most populous nation in the Western world
2. ___	Natural population growth and increasing immigration from Ireland and Germany	b. Opened the Great Lakes states to rapid economic growth and spurred the development of major cities
3. ___	The poverty and Roman Catholic faith of most Irish immigrants	c. Encouraged western farmers to specialize in cash-crop agricultural production for eastern and European markets
4. ___	Eli Whitney's invention of the cotton gin	d. Made Americans strongly individualistic and self-reliant
5. ___	The passage of general incorporation and limited-liability laws	e. Aroused nativist hostility and occasional riots
6. ___	The early efforts of labor unions to organize and strike	f. Bound the two northern sections together across the mountains and tended to isolate the South
7. ___	Improved western transportation and the new McCormick reaper	g. Aroused fierce opposition from businesspeople and guardians of law
8. ___	The completion of the Erie Canal in 1825	h. Enabled businesspeople to create more powerful and effective joint-stock capital ventures
9. ___	The development of a strong east-west rail network	i. Transformed southern agriculture and gave new life to slavery
10. ___	The replacement of household production by factory-made, store-bought goods	j. Weakened many women's economic status and pushed them into a separate "sphere" of home and family

G. Developing Historical Skills

Reading a Chart and Bar Graph

Examine the bar graph on p.290 to learn more about the character of the American population from 1790 to 1860.

Answer the following questions:

1. Which decade showed the largest absolute increase in total population?

2. During which decade did the nonwhite population begin to *decrease* as a percentage of the total population?

3. In which census year did the nonwhite population surpass the white population of 1790?

4. Using the bar graph, indicate about how many times larger the total population was in 1860 than it had been in 1820.

H. Map Mastery

Map Discrimination

Using the maps and charts in Chapter 14, answer the following questions:

1. *Cumberland (National) Road and Main Connections*: How many states did the Cumberland Road pass through? (Do not count Missouri.)

2. *Industry and Agriculture, 1860*: Which industry developed near Philadelphia?

3. *Industry and Agriculture, 1860*: If you were a tobacco farmer, in which state would you most likely live?

4. *Principal Canals in 1840*: If you had traveled from Albany, New York, to Evansville, Indiana, which *two* canals and *one* lake would you have traversed?

5. *Principal Canals in 1840*: If you had traveled from Columbia, Pennsylvania, to Cleveland, Ohio, which *two* canals and *one* river would you have traversed?

6. *The Railroad Revolution*: In 1860, how many direct rail lines linked the North and the South west of the Appalachians?

7. *The Railroad Revolution*: Which three Midwestern states had the greatest number of rail lines in 1860?

8. *Main Routes West Before the Civil War*: If you had traveled from Independence, Missouri, to Los Angeles, California, before the Civil War, which major trails would you have traversed?

Map Challenge

Using the maps on pp. 311, 312, and 313, write a brief essay explaining the *economic* importance of the Erie Canal and other canals and railroads for trade between the Northeast and the Northwest.

PART III: APPLYING WHAT YOU HAVE LEARNED

1. How did changes in the size and character of the population affect American social and economic life from 1790 to 1860?

2. How did the existence of a vast western frontier shape Americans' values and society in the period 1790–1860?

3. What were the effects of the new factory and corporate systems of production on early industrial workers, and how did they respond to these conditions?

4. How did the new transportation systems create a commercially linked national economy and a specialized sectional division of labor?

5. What was the impact of the new economic developments on the role of women in society?

6. In America, early industrialization, westward expansion, and growing sectional tension all occurred at the same time. How was the development of the economy before the Civil War related to both the westward movement and increasing sectional conflict?

7. Should the rise of early American industry and the "market revolution" be seen as an *expression* of the American democratic spirit and the rises of mass politics (see Chapter 13), or did emerging market capitalism actually *threaten* American principles of democracy, equality, and liberty?

CHAPTER 15

The Ferment of Reform and Culture, 1790–1860

PART I: REVIEWING THE CHAPTER

A. CHECKLIST OF LEARNING OBJECTIVES

After mastering this chapter, you should be able to

1. describe the changes in American religion and their effects on culture and social reform.

2. describe the cause of the most important American reform movements of the period.

3. explain the origins of American feminism, describe its essential principles, and summarize its early successes and failures.

4. describe the utopian and communitarian experiments of the period.

5. identify the early American achievements in the arts and sciences.

6. analyze the American literary flowering of the early nineteenth century, especially in relation to transcendentalism and other ideas of the time.

B. GLOSSARY

To build your social science vocabulary, familiarize yourself with the following terms:

1. **polygamy** The practice of having two or more spouses at one time. (**Polygyny** refers specifically to two or more wives; **polyandry** to two or more husbands.) "Accusations of polygamy likewise arose and increased in intensity." (p. 323)

2. **theocracy** Literally, rule by God; the term is often applied to a state where religious leaders exercise direct or indirect political authority. ". . . the community became a prosperous frontier theocracy and a cooperative commonwealth." (p. 324)

3. **zealot** One who is carried away by a cause to an extreme or excessive degree. "But less patient zealots came to believe that temptation should be removed by legislation." (p. 330)

4. **utopian** Referring to any place or plan that aims at an ideal social order. "Bolstered by the utopian spirit of the age, various reformers . . . set up more than forty [cooperative] communities. . . ." (p. 333)

5. **communistic** Referring to the theory or practice in which the means of production are owned by the community as a whole. ". . . various reformers . . . set up more than forty communities of a . . . communistic nature." (p. 333)

6. **communitarian** Referring to the belief in or practice of the superiority of community life or values over individual life, but not necessarily the common ownership of material goods. ". . . various reformers . . . set up more than forty communities of a . . . 'communtarian' nature." (p. 333)

7. **free love** The principle or practice of sexual relations unrestricted by law, marriage, or religious constraints. "It practiced free love ('complex marriage'). . . ." (p. 333)

8. **eugenic** Concerning the improvement of the human species through selective breeding or genetic control. "It practiced . . . the eugenic selection of parents to produce superior offspring." (p. 333)

9. **coitus reservatus** The practice of sexual intercourse without the male's release of semen. "It practiced . . . birth control through 'male continence' or *coitus reservatus*." (p. 333)

10. **classical** Concerning the culture of ancient Greece and Rome, or any artistic or cultural values presumed to be based on those enduring ancient principles. "He brought a classical design to his Virginia hilltop home, Monticello. . . ." (p. 338)

11. **mystical** Referring to the belief in the direct apprehension of God or divine mystery, without reliance on reason or human comprehension. "These mystical doctrines of transcendentalism defied precise definition. . . ." (p. 341)

12. **nonconformist** One who refuses to follow established or conventional ideas or habits. "Henry David Thoreau . . . was . . . a poet, a mystic, a transcendentalist, and a nonconformist." (p. 341)

13. **nonviolence** The principle of resolving or engaging in conflict without resort to physical force. "His writings . . . inspired the development of American civil rights leader Martin Luther King, Jr.'s thinking about nonviolence." (p. 341)

14. **urbane** Sophisticated, elegant, cosmopolitan. "Handsome and urbane, he lived a generally serene life. . . ." (p. 342)

15. **providential** Under the care and direction of God or other benevolent natural or supernatural forces. ". . . he lived among cannibals, from whom he providentially escaped uneaten." (p. 344)

PART II: CHECKING YOUR PROGRESS

A. True-False

Where the statement is true, circle **T**; where it is false, circle **F**.

1. T F The Second Great Awakening reversed the trends toward religious indifference and rationalism of the late eighteenth century.

2. T F The religious revivals of the Second Great Awakening broke down regional, denominational, and social-class divisions in favor of a common Christianity.

3. T F The Mormon church migrated to Utah to escape persecution and to establish a tightly organized cooperative social order without persecution.

4. T F The common public schools aimed at the goal of educating all citizens for participation in democracy, without regard to wealth.

5. T F Women achieved equality with men in higher education before the Civil War.

6. T F Many early American reformers were middle-class idealists inspired by evangelical Protestantism.

7. T F The key role of women in American reform movements was undergirded by a growing "feminization" of the churches that spawned many efforts at social improvement.

8. T F A major demand put forward by the more advanced women's-rights advocates was women's suffrage.

9. T F Most early American communal experiments involved attempts to create a perfect society based on brotherly love and communal ownership of property.

10. T   F   Early American science was stronger in biology, botany, and geology than it was in basic theoretical science or medicine.

11. T   F   The first American national literature written by Irving and Cooper appeared in the immediate aftermath of the American Revolution.

12. T   F   Although it rejected most Americans' materialism and focus on practical concerns, transcendentalism strongly reflected American individualism, love of liberty, and hostility to formal institutions and authority.

13. T   F   Ralph Waldo Emerson taught the doctrines of simple living and nonviolence, while his friend Henry David Thoreau emphasized self-improvement and the development of American scholarship.

14. T   F   The works of Walt Whitman, such as *Leaves of Grass*, revealed his love of democracy, the frontier, and the common people.

15. T   F   Most early American imaginative writers and historians came from the Midwest and the South.

B. Multiple Choice

Select the best answer and circle the corresponding letter.

1. The tendency toward rationalism and indifference in religion was reversed about 1800 by
    a.   the rise of Deism and Unitarianism.
    b.   the rise of new groups like the Mormons and Christian Scientists.
    c.   the revivalist movement called the Second Great Awakening.
    d.   the influx of religiously traditional immigrants.
2. Two denominations that especially gained adherents among the common people of the West and South were
    a.   Episcopalians and Unitarians.
    b.   Congregationalists and Mormons.
    c.   Transcendentalists and Adventists.
    d.   Methodists and Baptists.
3. The Second Great Awakening derived its religious strength especially from
    a.   intensely organized "prayer groups" of lay believers.
    b.   the efficient institutional organization of the major American churches.
    c.   the popular preaching of evangelical revivalists in both the West and eastern cities.
    d.   the frontier interest in religious pilgrimages and religious art.
4. Evangelical preachers like Charles Grandison Finney linked personal religious conversion to
    a.   the construction of large church buildings throughout the Midwest.
    b.   the expansion of American political power across the continent.
    c.   the Christian reform of social problems.
    d.   the organization of effective economic development and industrialization.
5. The term "Burned-Over District" refers to
    a.   parts of the West where fires were used to clear the land for farming.
    b.   areas that were fiercely contested by both Baptist and Methodist revivalists.
    c.   the region of western New York State that experienced especially frequent and intense revivals.
    d.   the area of Illinois where the Mormon settlements were attacked and destroyed.
6. The major effect of the growing slavery controversy on the churches was
    a.   a major missionary effort directed at converted African American slaves.

b.   the organization of the churches to lobby for the abolition of slavery.

c.   an agreement to keep political issues out of the religious area.

d.   the split of Baptists, Methodists, and Presbyterians into separate northern and southern churches.

7. Besides their practice of polygamy, the Mormons aroused hostility from many Americans because of

    a.   their cooperative economic practices that ran contrary to American economic individualism.

    b.   their efforts to convert members of other denominations to Mormonism.

    c.   their populous settlement in Utah , which posed the threat of a breakaway republic in the West.

    d.   their practice of baptizing in the name of dead ancestors.

8. The major promoter of an effective tax-supported system of public education for all American children was

    a.   Joseph Smith.

    b.   Horace Mann.

    c.   Noah Webster.

    d.   Susan B. Anthony.

9. Reformer Dorothea Dix worked for the cause of

    a.   women's right to higher education and voting.

    b.   international peace.

    c.   better treatment of the mentally ill.

    d.   temperance.

10. One cause of women's subordination in nineteenth-century America was

    a.   the sharp division of labor that separated women at home from men in the workplace.

    b.   women's attention to causes other than women's rights.

    c.   the higher ratio of females to males in many communities.

    d.   the prohibition against women's participation in religious activities.

11. The Seneca Falls Convention launched the modern women's rights movement with its call for

    a.   equal pay for equal work.

    b.   an equal rights amendment to the Constitution.

    c.   equal rights, including the right to vote.

    d.   access to public education for women.

12. Many of the American utopian experiments of the early nineteenth century focused on

    a.   communal economics and alternative sexual arrangements.

    b.   temperance and diet reforms.

    c.   advanced scientific and technological ways of producing and consuming.

    d.   free-enterprise economics and trade.

13. Two leading female imaginative writers who added to New England's literary prominence were

    a.   Sarah Orne Jewett and Kate Chopin.

    b.   Louisa May Alcott and Emily Dickinson.

    c.   Sarah Grimké and Susan B. Anthony.

    d.   Harriet Beecher Stowe and Abigail Adams.

14. The Knickerbocker Group of American writers included

    a.   Henry David Thoreau, Thomas Jefferson, and Susan B. Anthony.

    b.   George Bancroft, Ralph Waldo Emerson, and Herman Melville.

    c.   Washington Irving, James Fenimore Cooper, and William Cullen Bryant.

    d.   Walt Whitman, Henry Wadsworth Longfellow, and Edgar Allan Poe.

15. The transcendentalist writers such as Emerson, Thoreau, and Fuller stressed the ideas of

    a.   inner truth and individual self-reliance.

b.   political community and economic progress.
c.   personal guilt and fear of death.
d.   love of chivalry and return to the medieval past.

C. Identification

Supply the correct identification for each numbered description.

1. _____ Liberal religious belief, held by many of the Founding Fathers, that stressed rationalism and moral behavior rather than Christian revelation

2. _____ Religious revival that began on the frontier and swept eastward, stirring an evangelical spirit in many areas of American life

3. _____ The *two* religious denominations that benefited from the evangelical revivals of the early nineteenth century

   _____

4. _____ Religious group founded by Joseph Smith that eventually established a cooperative commonwealth in Utah

5. _____ Memorable 1848 meeting in New York where women made an appeal based on the Declaration of Independence

6. _____ Commune established in New Harmony, Indiana by Scottish industrialist Robert Owen

7. _____ Intellectual commune in Massachusetts based on "plain living and high thinking"

8. _____ Thomas Jefferson's stately self-designed home in Virginia that became a model of American architecture

9. _____ New York literary movement that drew on both regional and national themes

10. _____ Philosophical and literary movement, centered in New England, that greatly influenced many American writers of the early nineteenth century

11. _____ The doctrine, promoted by American writer Henry David Thoreau in an essay of the same name, that later influenced Gandhi and Martin Luther King, Jr.

12. _____ Walt Whitman's shocking collection of emotional poems

13. _____ A disturbing New England masterpiece about adultery and guilt in the old Puritan era

14. _____ The great but commercially unsuccessful novel about Captain Ahab's obsessive pursuit of a white whale

15. _____ The masterpiece of New England writer Louisa May Alcott

D. Matching People, Places, and Events

Match the person, place, or event in the left column with the proper description in the right column by inserting the correct letter on the blank line.

1. ___ Dorothea Dix

2. ___ Brigham Young

a.   Leader of a radical New York commune that practiced "complex marriage" and eugenic birth control

3. ___ Elizabeth Cady Stanton

4. ___ Lucretia Mott

5. ___ Emily Dickinson

6. ___ Charles G. Finney

7. ___ Robert Owen

8. ___ John Humphrey Noyes

9. ___ Mary Lyon

10. ___ Louisa May Alcott

11. ___ James Fenimore Cooper

12. ___ Ralph Waldo Emerson

13. ___ Walt Whitman

14. ___ Edgar Allen Poe

15. ___ Herman Melville

b. Bold, unconventional poet who celebrated American democracy

c. The "Mormon Moses" who led persecuted Latter-Day Saints to their promised land in Utah

d. Influential evangelical revivalist of the Second Great Awakening

e. New York writer whose romantic sea tales were more popular than his dark literary masterpiece

f. Pioneering women's educator, founder of Mount Holyoke Seminary in Massachusetts

g. Idealistic Scottish industrialist whose attempt at a communal utopia in America failed

h. Second-rate poet and philosopher, but first-rate promoter of transcendentalist ideals and American culture

i. Eccentric southern-born genius whose tales of mystery, suffering, and the supernatural departed from general American literary trends

j. Quietly determined reformer who substantially improved conditions for the mentally ill

k. Reclusive New England poet who wrote about love, death, and immortality

l. Leading feminist who wrote the "Declaration of Sentiments" in 1848 and pushed for women's suffrage

m. Novelist whose tales of family life helped economically support her own struggling transcendentalist family

n. Path-breaking American novelist who contrasted the natural person of the forest with the values of modern civilization

o. Quaker women's rights advocate who also strongly supported abolition of slavery

E. Putting Things in Order

Put the following events in correct order by numbering them from 1 to 5.

1. ___   A leading New England transcendentalist appeals to American writers and thinkers to turn away from Europe and develop their own literature and culture.

2. ___   A determined reformer appeals to a New England legislature to end the cruel treatment of the insane.

3. ___   A gathering of female reformers in New York declares that the ideas of the Declaration of Independence apply to *both* sexes.

4. ___   Great evangelical religious revival begins in western camp meetings.

5. ___   A visionary New Yorker creates a controversial new religion.

F. Matching Cause and Effect

Match the historical cause in the left column with the proper effect in the right column by writing the correct letter on the blank line.

Cause	**Effect**
1. ___ The Second Great Awakening	a. Created the first literature genuinely native to America
2. ___ The Mormon practice of polygamy	
3. ___ Women abolitionists' anger at being ignored by male reformers	b. Captured in one long poem the exuberant and optimistic spirit of popular American democracy
4. ___ The women's rights movement	c. Caused most utopian experiments to decline or collapse in a few years
5. ___ Unrealistic expectations and conflict within perfectionist communes	
6. ___ The Knickerbocker and transcendentalist use of new American themes in their writing	d. Inspired writers like Ralph Waldo Emerson, Henry David Thoreau, and Margaret Fuller
7. ___ Henry David Thoreau's theory of "civil disobedience"	e. Aroused hostility and scorn in most of the male press and pulpit
8. ___ Walt Whitman's *Leaves of Grass*	f. Made their works little understood in their lifetimes by generally optimistic Americans
	g. Aroused persecution from morally traditionalist Americans and delayed statehood for Utah
9. ___ Herman Melville's and Edgar Allan Poe's concern with evil and suffering	h. Inspired a widespread spirit of evangelical reform in many areas of American life
10. ___ The Transcendentalist movement.	i. Led to expanding the crusade for equal rights to include women
	j. Inspired later practitioners of nonviolence like Gandhi and King

G. Developing Historical Skills

Using Primary-Source Documents

Statements from historical contemporaries often reveal fundamental conflicts over values and demonstrate the shock that occurs when new ideas emerge. The quotations form the London *Saturday Review* and from Walt Whitman (p. 342) illustrate such opposing views.

Answer the following questions:

1. What is the London *Saturday Review*'s primary objection to Whitman's poetry?

2. How does Whitman answer such criticisms?

3. How does Whitman's statement reveal the values of individualism and democracy cherished by the emerging American culture?

4. What does the quotation from *Leaves of Grass* in the text (p. 342) indicate about Whitman's typically American view of Europe?

PART III: APPLYING WHAT YOU HAVE LEARNED

1. What major changes in American religion occurred in the early nineteenth century, and how did they reflect the spirit of American democracy and liberty?

2. What were the successes and failures of the many American reform movements of the early nineteenth century? Was the failure of some of them (e.g., peace reforms) due to entrenched social conservatism, or to weaknesses in the movements themselves?

3. What was the relationship between the evangelical revivals of the "Second Great Awakening" and the spread of American social reform movements and utopian ideas?

4. How did the first American feminists propose altering the condition of women, and what success did they have?

5. Compare the early American achievements in the sciences with those in the arts. Which were the most successful, and why?

6. What were the major concerns of America's greatest imaginative writers in the early nineteenth century? Did those writers fundamentally reflect the deepest values of American culture, or were they at odds with the main currents of American society and politics?

7. In what ways were the movements of American religion, reform, and culture an outgrowth of the American Revolution and American independence, and in what ways did they reflect qualities of American life reaching back to the Puritans?

8. Which American writer or thinker would you select as the most important and insightful figure of the early nineteenth century: Ralph Waldo Emerson, Henry David Thoreau, Elizabeth Cady Stanton, or Herman Melville? Defend your choice by explaining that person's impact on American culture and society.

CHAPTER 16

The South and the Slavery Controversy, 1793–1860

PART I: REVIEWING THE CHAPTER

A. CHECKLIST OF LEARNING OBJECTIVES

After mastering this chapter, you should be able to

1. point out the economic strengths and weaknesses of the "Cotton Kingdom."

2. describe the southern planter aristocracy and identify its strengths and weaknesses.

3. describe the nonslaveholding white majority of the South and explain its relations with both the planter elite and the black slaves.

4. describe the nature of African American life, both free and slave, before the Civil War.

5. describe the effects of the "peculiar institution" of slavery on both blacks and whites.

6. explain why abolitionism was at first unpopular in the North and describe how it gradually gained strength.

7. describe the fierce southern response to abolitionism and the growing defense of slavery as a "positive good."

B. GLOSSARY

To build your social science vocabulary, familiarize yourself with the following terms:

1. **oligarchy** Rule by a small elite. "Before the Civil War, the South was in some respects not so much a democracy as an oligarchy. . . ." (p. 351)

2. **medievalism** Devotion to the social values, customs, or beliefs thought to be characteristic of the European Middle Ages. "Southern aristocrats . . . strove to perpetuate a type of medievalism that had died out in Europe. . . ." (p. 352)

3. **commission** Fee paid to an agent in a transaction, usually as a percentage of the sale. "They were pained by the heavy outward flow of commissions. . . ." (p. 353)

4. **middlemen** In commerce, those who stand between the producer and the retailer or consumer. "[Southern planters] were pained by the heavy outward flow . . . to northern middlemen, bankers, agents, and shippers." (p. 353)

5. **racism** Belief in the superiority of one race over another or behavior reflecting such a belief. "Thus did the logic of economics join with the illogic of racism in buttressing the slave system." (p. 356)

6. **bankruptcy** Legally, the condition of being declared unable to meet legitimate financial obligations or debts, requiring special supervision by the courts. ". . . families were separated with distressing frequency, usually for economic reasons such as bankruptcy. . . ." (p. 359)

7. **overseer** Someone who governs or directs the work of another. ". . . under the watchful eyes and ready whip-hand of a white overseer or black 'driver.' " (p. 359)

8. **sabotage** Intentional destruction or damage of goods, machines, or productive processes. "They sabotaged expensive equipment. . . ." (p. 362)

9. **fratricidal** Literally, concerning the killing of brothers; the term is often applied to the killing of relatives or countrymen in feuds or civil wars. (The killing of sisters is **sororicide**; of fathers **patricide**; and of mothers **matricide**.) ". . . supported a frightfully costly fratricidal war as the price of emancipation." (p. 366)

10. **barbarism (barbarian)** The condition of being crude, uneducated, or uncivilized. "It was good for the Africans, who were lifted from the barbarism of the jungle. . . ." (p. 366)

PART II: CHECKING YOUR PROGRESS

A. True-False

Where the statement is true, circle **T**; where it is false, circle **F**.

1. T   F   After 1800, the prosperity of both North and South became heavily dependent on growing, manufacturing, and exporting cotton.

2. T   F   The southern planter aristocracy was strongly attracted to medieval cultural ideals.

3. T   F   The growing of cotton on large plantations was economically efficient and agriculturally sound.

4. T   F   Most southern slaveowners owned twenty or more slaves.

5. T   F   In 1860, three-fourths of all white southerners owned no slaves at all.

6. T   F   Poor whites supported slavery because it made them feel racially superior and because they hoped someday to be able to buy slaves.

7. T   F   The one group of southern whites who opposed slavery consisted of those who lived in mountain areas far from plantations and from blacks.

8. T   F   Free blacks enjoyed considerable status and wealth in both the North and the South before the Civil War.

9. T   F   Most slaveowners treated their black slaves as a valuable economic investment.

10. T   F   Slavery almost completely destroyed the black family.

11. T   F   American slaves used many small methods of resistance to demonstrate their hatred of slavery and their yearning for freedom.

12. T   F   Abolitionists like William Lloyd Garrison quickly attained great popularity in the North.

13. T   F   The most prominent black abolitionist, Frederick Douglass, supported William Lloyd Garrison's absolutist principles and refusal to engage in politics.

14. T   F   After about 1830, the South no longer tolerated even moderate pro-abolitionist discussion.

15. T   F   Southern whites increasingly argued that their slaves were happier and better off than northern wage earners.

B. Multiple Choice

Select the best answer and circle the corresponding letter.

1. The primary market for southern cotton production was

    a. the North.
    b. France.
    c. Latin America.
    d. Britain.

2. The invention that transformed the southern cotton economy was

    a. the sewing machine.
    b. the mechanical cotton-picker.
    c. the cotton gin.
    d. the steamboat.

3. A large portion of the profits from cotton growing went to

    a. northern traders and European manufacturers.
    b. southern and northern slave traders.
    c. southern textile industrialists.
    d. midwestern farmers and cattlemen.

4. Among the economic consequences of the South's cotton economy was

    a. increasing immigration of laborers from Europe.
    b. a dependence on the North for trade and manufacturing.
    c. a stable system of credit and finance.
    d. a relatively equal distribution of property and wealth.

5. Most southern slaveowners held

    a. over a hundred slaves.
    b. over fifty slaves.
    c. fewer than ten slaves.
    d. only one slave.

6. Even though they owned no slaves, most southern whites supported the slave system because

    a. they were bribed by the planter class.
    b. they enjoyed the economic benefits of slavery.
    c. they felt racially superior to blacks and hoped to be able to buy slaves.
    d. they disliked the northern abolitionists.

7. The only group of white southerners who strongly opposed slavery and the slaveowners were

    a. poor southern whites.
    b. urban merchants and manufacturers.
    c. religious leaders.
    d. Appalachian mountain whites.

8. The condition of the 500,000 or so free blacks was

    a. considerably better in the North than in the South.
    b. notably improving in the decades before the Civil War.
    c. as bad or worse in the North than in the South.
    d. politically threatened but economically secure.

9. Most of the growth in the African American slave population before 1860 came from

    a. the illegal importation of slaves from Africa.
    b. the re-enslavement of formerly free blacks.
    c. natural reproduction.
    d. the incorporation into the United States of new slave territories.

10. Most slaveowners treated their slaves as

    a. objects to be beaten and brutalized as often as possible.
    b. economically profitable investments.
    c. members of their extended family.
    d. potential converts to evangelical Christianity..

11. The African American family under slavery was

    a. generally stable and mutually supportive.
    b. almost nonexistent.
    c. largely female-dominated.
    d. seldom able to raise children to adulthood.

12. Most of the early abolitionists were motivated by

    a. a desire to create an independent black republic in Africa.
    b. anger at the negative economic consequences of slavery.
    c. religious feeling against the "sin" of slavery.
    d. a philosophical commitment to racial integration.

13. Frederick Douglass and some other abolitionists sought to end slavery by

    a. encouraging slave rebellions in the South.
    b. calling on the North to secede from the Union and invade the South.
    c. appealing to the moral consciences of both Northerners and southern slaveowners.
    d. promoting antislavery political movements like the Free Soil and Republican parties..

14. After 1830, most southerners came to look on slavery as

    a. a curse on their region.
    b. a necessary evil.
    c. a positive good.
    d. a threat to their social ideals.

15. By the 1850s, most northerners could be described as

    a. opposed to slavery but also hostile to immediate abolitionists.
    b. fervently in favor of immediate abolition.
    c. sympathetic to white southern arguments in defense of slavery.
    d. eager to let the slaveholding South break apart the Union.

C. Identification

Supply the correct identification for each numbered description.

1. _____   Term for the South that emphasized its economic dependence on a single staple product

2. _____   Prosouthern New England textile owners who were economically tied to the southern "lords of the lash"

3. _____   British novelist whose romantic vision of a feudal society made him highly popular in the South

4. _____   The poor, vulnerable group that was the object of prejudice in the North and despised as a "third race" in the South

5. _____   Theodore Dwight Weld's powerful antislavery book

6. _____   The area of the South where most slaves were held, stretching from South Carolina across to Louisiana

7. _____   Organization founded in 1817 to send blacks back to Africa

8. _____   The group of theology students, led by Theodore Dwight Weld, who were expelled for abolitionist activity and later became leading preachers of the anti-slavery gospel

9. _____   William Lloyd Garrison's fervent abolitionist newspaper that preached an immediate end to slavery

10. _____   Garrisonian abolitionist organization, founded in 1833, that included the eloquent Wendell Phillips among its leaders

11. _____   Strict rule passed by prosouthern Congressmen in 1836 to prohibit all discussion of slavery in the House of Representatives

12. _____   Northern antislavery politicians, like Abraham Lincoln, who rejected radical abolitionism but sought to prohibit the expansion of slavery in the western territories

D. Matching People, Places, and Events

Match the person, place, or event in the left column with the proper description in the right column by inserting the correct letter on the blank line.

1. ___ Sir Walter Scott

2. ___ Harriet Beecher Stowe

3. ___ Nat Turner

4. ___ Liberia

5. ___ Theodore Dwight Weld

6. ___ Lewis Tappan

7. ___ Lane Theological Seminary

8. ___ William Lloyd Garrison

9. ___ David Walker

10. ___ Sojourner Truth

11. ___ Martin Delany

12. ___ Frederick Douglass

13. ___ Virginia legislature

14. ___ John Quincy Adams

15. ___ Elijah Lovejoy

a. Wealthy New York abolitionist merchant whose home was demolished by a mob in 1834

b. Visionary black preacher whose bloody slave rebellion in 1831 tightened the reins of slavery in the South

c. Midwestern institution whose president expelled eighteen students for organizing a debate on slavery

d. New York free black woman who fought for emancipation and women's rights

e. Leading radical abolitionist who burned the Constitution as "a covenant with death and an agreement with hell"

f. Author of an abolitionist novel that portrayed the separation of slave families by auction

g. Site of the last major southern debate over slavery and emancipation, in 1831–1832

h. English novelist whose romantic medievalism encouraged the semifeudal ideals of the southern planter aristocracy

i. Black abolitionist who visited West Africa in 1859 to examine sites where African Americans might relocate

j. Former president who fought for the

right to discuss slavery in Congress

k. Illinois editor whose death at the hands of a mob made him an abolitionist martyr

l. West African republic founded in 1822 by freed blacks from the United States

m. Escaped slave and great black abolitionist who fought to end slavery through political action

n. Black abolitionist writer who called for a bloody end to slavery in an appeal of 1829

o. Leader of the "Lane Rebels" who wrote the powerful antislavery work *American Slavery As It Is*

E. Putting Things in Order

Put the following events in correct order by numbering them from 1 to 5.

1. ___ The last slaves to be legally imported from Africa enter the United States.

2. ___ A radical abolitionist editor is murdered, and so becomes a martyr to the antislavery cause.

3. ___ A radical abolitionist newspaper and a slave rebellion spread fear through the South.

4. ___ A new invention increases the efficiency of cotton production, laying the basis for the vast Cotton Kingdom.

5. ___ A group of seminary students expelled for their abolitionist views spread the antislavery gospel far and wide.

F. Matching Cause and Effect

Match the historical cause in the left column with the proper effect in the right column by writing the correct letter on the blank line.

Cause		Effect
1. ___ Whitney's cotton gin and southern frontier expansionism	a.	Often resulted in the cruel separation of black families
2. ___ Excessive soil cultivation and financial speculation	b.	Kept poor, non-slaveholding whites committed to a system that actually harmed them
3. ___ Belief in white superiority and the hope of owning slaves	c.	Aroused deep fears of rebellion and ended rational discussion of slavery in the South
4. ___ The selling of slaves at auctions	d.	Made abolitionists personally unpopular but convinced many Northerners that slavery was a threat to American freedom
5. ___ The slaves' love of freedom and hatred of their		

	condition	e.	Caused slaves to work slowly, steal from their masters, and frequently run away
6. ___	The religious fervor of the Second Great Awakening	f.	Stirred a fervent abolitionist commitment to fight the "sin" of slavery
7. ___	Politically minded abolitionists like Frederick Douglass	g.	Turned the South into a booming one-crop economy where "cotton was king"
8. ___	Garrison's *Liberator* and Nat Turner's bloody slave rebellion	h.	Opposed Garrison and organized the Liberty party and the Free Soil party
9. ___	White southern defenses of slavery as a "positive good"	i.	Created dangerous weaknesses beneath the surface prosperity of the southern cotton economy
10. ___	The constant abolitionist agitation in the North	j.	Widened the moral and political gap between the white South and the rest of the Western world

G. Developing Historical Skills

Visual Images and Slavery

The bitter controversy over slavery is reflected in the visual images (drawings, prints, photographs) of the "peculiar institution." Some images present slavery from an abolitionist viewpoint, as a moral horror. Others depict it in benign or even favorable terms. Examine eight of the illustrations in this chapter on pp. 351, 352, 357, 358, 359, 360, 363, and 367 answer the following questions:

1. Which four images depict negative features of the slave system? What visual details emphasize the mistreatment of the slaves?

2. Which three images present slavery in relatively positive terms? What visual details show slavery in a favorable light?

3. The photograph on p. 359 seems neither directly "proslavery" nor "antislavery." How might supporters or opponents of slavery each interpret this image of a slave nanny with a white child?

H. Map Mastery

Map Discrimination

Using the maps and charts in Chapter 16, answer the following questions:

1. *Southern Cotton Production, 1860*: Which six states contained nearly all the major cotton-production areas of the South in 1860?

2. *Slaveowning Families, 1850*: Approximately how many slaveowning families owned fifty or more slaves?

3. *Distribution of Slaves, 1820*: Which five states contained a substantial number of slave-majority counties in 1820?

4. *Distribution of Slaves, 1860*: List the six slaveholding states, not counting Texas and Florida, that contained the most counties with less than 10 percent slaves in 1860.

Map Challenge

Using the maps on pp. 354 and 355, write a brief essay explaining the relation between the areas of cotton production and the areas with the heaviest concentration of slaves in 1820 and 1860. Include some discussion of why Virginia and the Carolinas had substantial areas with more than 50 percent slaves but almost no major cotton-production areas.

PART III: APPLYING WHAT YOU HAVE LEARNED

1. Describe the complex structure of southern society. What role did plantation owners, small slaveholders, independent white farmers, poor whites, free blacks, and black slaves each have in the southern social order?

2. Compare the attitudes and practices regarding slavery and race relations in the North and the South. Explain the common statement that southerners liked blacks as individuals but despised the race, while northerners claimed to like blacks as a race but disliked individuals. (p. 357)

3. How did the reliance on cotton production and slavery affect the South economically, socially, and morally, and how did this reliance affect its relations with the North?

4. How did slavery affect the lives of African Americans in both the South and the North?

5. A large majority of Americans, both North and South, strongly rejected radical abolitionism. Why, then, did abolitionism and antislavery come to shape American politics in the 1840s and 1850s?

6. In what ways did slavery make the South a fundamentally different kind of society from the North? Could the South ever have abolished slavery gradually on its own, as the North did after the American Revolution? (See Chapter 9.) Why or why not?

7. If you had been an ordinary northern citizen in the 1830s or 1840s, what would you have proposed to do about the central American problem of slavery, and why? Would either William Lloyd Garrison's radical abolitionism or Frederick Douglass's political abolitionism have appealed to you? Were any other "solutions" seem attractive and plausible?

CHAPTER 17

Manifest Destiny and Its Legacy, 1841–1848

PART I: REVIEWING THE CHAPTER

A. CHECKLIST OF LEARNING OBJECTIVES

After mastering this chapter, you should be able to

1. explain the spirit of "Manifest Destiny" that inspired American expansionism in the 1840s.

2. outline the major conflicts between Britain and the United States over debts, Maine, Canada, Texas, Oregon, and growing British hostility to slavery.

3. explain why the movement to annex Texas gained new momentum and why the issue aroused such controversy.

4. indicate how the issues of Oregon and Texas became central in the election of 1844 and why Polk's victory was seen as a mandate for "Manifest Destiny."

5. describe how the issues of California and the Texas boundary created conflict and war with Mexico.

6. describe how the dramatic American victory in the Mexican War led to the breathtaking territorial acquisition of the whole Southwest.

7. describe the consequences of the Mexican War, especially its effect on the slavery question.

B. GLOSSARY

To build your social science vocabulary, familiarize yourself with the following terms.

1. **caucus** An unofficial organization or consultation of like-minded people to plan a political course or advance their cause, often within some larger body. ". . . the stiff-necked Virginian was formally expelled from his party by a caucus of Whig congressmen. . . ." (p. 372)

2. **royalty** The share of the proceeds from work paid to an inventor, author, composer, and so on. ". . . they were being denied rich royalties by the absence of an American copyright law." (p. 373)

3. **default** To fail to pay a loan or interest due. ". . . several states defaulted on their bonds. . . ." (p. 373)

4. **repudiate** To refuse to accept responsibility for paying a bill or debt. "When . . . several states . . . repudiated [their bonds] openly, honest English citizens assailed Yankee trickery." (p. 373)

5. **protectorate** The relation of a strong nation to a weak one under its control and protection. ". . . Texas was driven to open negotiations . . . in the hope of securing the defensive shield of a protectorate." (p. 374)

6. **colossus** Anything of extraordinary size and power. "Such a republic would check the southward surge of the American colossus. . . ." (p. 374)

7. **resolution** In government, a formal statement of policy or judgment by a legislature, but requiring no legal statute. "He therefore arranged for annexation by a joint resolution." (p. 375)

8.   **intrigue**   A plot or scheme formed by secret, underhanded means. ". . . the Lone Star Republic had become a danger spot, inviting foreign intrigue that menaced the American people." (p. 375)

9.   **parallel**   In geography, the imaginary lines parallel to the earth's equator, marking latitude. (There are 360 degrees of latitude on the globe.) " . . . the United States had sought to divide the vast domain at the forty-ninth parallel." (p. 376)

10.   **deadlock**   To completely block or stop action as a consequence of the mutual pressure of equal and opposed forces. "The Democrats, meeting later in the same city, seemed hopelessly deadlocked." (p. 377)

11.   **dark horse**   In politics, a candidate with little apparent support who unexpectedly wins a nomination or election. "Polk may have been a dark horse, but he was hardly an unknown or decrepit nag." (p. 377)

12.   **mandate**   In politics, the belief that an official has been issued a clear charge by the electorate to pursue some particular policy goal. "Land-hungry Democrats . . . proclaimed that they had received a mandate from the voters to take Texas." (p. 378)

13.   **platform**   The campaign document stating a party's or candidate's position on the issues, and upon which they "stand" for election. "Polk . . . had no intention of insisting on the . . . pledge of his own platform." (p. 379)

14.   **no-man's-land**   A territory to which neither of two disputing parties has clear claim and where they may meet as combatants. ". . . Polk was careful to keep American troops out of virtually all of the explosive no-man's-land between the Nueces and the Rio Grande. . . ." (p. 381)

15.   **indemnity**   A repayment for loss or damage inflicted. "Victors rarely pay an indemnity. . . ." (p. 385)

PART II: CHECKING YOUR PROGRESS

A. True-False

Where the statement is true, circle **T**; where it is false, circle **F**.

1.   T   F   After President Harrison's death, Vice President John Tyler carried on the strong Whig policies of leaders like Clay and Webster.

2.   T   F   By the 1840s, the bitter memories of two Anglo-American wars had disappeared, putting an end to major British-American conflicts.

3.   T   F   The "Aroostook War" over the Maine boundary was settled by a territorial compromise in the Webster-Ashburton Treaty.

4.   T   F   A primary motive driving Americans to annex Texas was fear that the Lone Star Republic would become an ally or protectorate of Britain.

5.   T   F   Because the two-thirds vote necessary for a treaty of annexation could not be obtained in the Senate, Texas was annexed by a simple majority resolution of both houses of Congress.

6.   T   F   In the dispute with Britain over Oregon, the United States repeatedly demanded control of the whole territory as far north as "fifty-four forty."

7.   T   F   In the election of 1844, Clay lost to Polk partly because he tried to straddle the Texas annexation issue and thus lost antislavery support.

8. T F Polk's victory in 1844 was interpreted as a mandate for Manifest Destiny and led directly to the annexation of Texas and a favorable settlement of the Oregon dispute.

9. T F President Polk originally opposed acquiring California because of its large population of Mexican citizens.

10. T F The immediate cause of the Mexican War was an attempt by Mexico to reconquer Texas.

11. T F Polk's primary objective in fighting the Mexican War was to obtain California for the United States.

12. T F The overwhelming American military victory over Mexico led some Americans to call for the United States to take over all of Mexico.

13. T F The Treaty of Guadalupe Hidalgo gave the United States a small slice of present-day southern New Mexico and Arizona.

14. T F The outcome of the Mexican War became a source of continuing bad feeling between the United States and much of Latin America.

15. T F The Wilmot Proviso prohibiting slavery in territory acquired from Mexico helped shove the slavery issue out of sight.

B. Multiple Choice

Select the best answer and circle the corresponding letter.

1. The conflict between President Tyler and Whig leaders like Henry Clay took place over issues of
   a. slavery and expansion.
   b. banking and tariff policy.
   c. foreign policy.
   d. agriculture and transportation policy.

2. Among the major sources of the tension between Britain and the United States in the 1840s was
   a. American involvement in Canadian rebellions and border disputes.
   b. British support for American abolitionists.
   c. American anger at British default on canal and railroad loans.
   d. American intervention in the British West Indies.

3. The "Aroostook War" involved
   a. a battle between American and French fishermen over Newfoundland fishing rights.
   b. a battle between American and Canadian lumberjacks over the northern Maine boundary.
   c. a battle between British and American sailors over impressment.
   d. a battle between Americans and Mexicans over the western boundary of Louisiana.

4. During the early 1840s, Texas maintained its independence by
   a. waging a constant war against Mexico.
   b. refusing to sign treaties with any outside powers.
   c. relying on the military power of the United States.
   d. establishing friendly relations with Britain and other European powers.

5. Which of the following was *not* among the reasons why Britain strongly supported an independent Texas?
   a. Britain was interested in eventually incorporating Texas into the British empire.
   b. British abolitionists hoped to make Texas an antislavery bastion.
   c. British manufacturers looked to Texas as a way to reduce their dependence on American cotton.

    d.   Britain planned to use Texas as a check on American southward expansion.

6.   Texas was finally admitted to the Union in 1844 as a result of

    a.   the Mexican War.
    b.   the Texans' willingness to abandon slavery.
    c.   President Tyler's interpretation of the election of 1844 as a "mandate" to acquire Texas.
    d.   a compromise agreement with Britain.

7.   "Manifest Destiny" represented the widespread American belief that

    a.   Americans were destined to uphold democracy and freedom.
    b.   there would inevitably be a civil war over slavery some time in the future.
    c.   Mexico was destined to be acquired by the United States.
    d.   God had destined the United States to expand across the whole North American continent.

8.   Britain eventually lost out in the contest for the disputed Oregon territory because

    a.   the rapidly growing number of American settlers overwhelmed the small British population.
    b.   the British recognized the greater validity of American legal claims on the territory.
    c.   superior American naval forces made the British position in the region untenable.
    d.   an international arbitration commission ruled in favor of the American claims.

9.   Henry Clay lost the election of 1844 to James Polk because

    a.   his attempt to straddle the Texas annexation issue lost him votes to the antislavery Liberty party in New York.
    b.   his strong stand for expansion in Texas and Oregon raised fears of war with Britain.
    c.   he supported lower tariffs and an independent Treasury system.
    d.   he lacked experience in presidential politics.

10.   The final result of the British-American conflict over the Oregon country in 1844–1846 was

    a.   an American success in winning the goal of a boundary at "fifty-four forty."
    b.   an agreement to continue the joint occupation of Oregon for twenty years more.
    c.   a compromise agreement on a border at the forty-ninth parallel.
    d.   an outbreak of war between the two nations.

11.   The immediate cause of the Mexican War was

    a.   American refusal to pay Mexican claims for damage to its citizens.
    b.   Mexican refusal to sell California and a dispute over the Texas boundary.
    c.   Mexican support for the antislavery movement in Texas.
    d.   American determination to establish democracy in northern Mexico.

12.   The phrase "spot resolutions" refers to

    a.   President Polk's message asking Congress to declare war on Mexico "on the spot."
    b.   the amendment introduced after the Mexican War declaring that not one new spot of land be opened to slavery.
    c.   Congressman Abraham Lincoln's resolution demanding to know the exact spot of American soil where American blood had supposedly been shed.
    d.   the congressional act determining which spots of Mexican land should be ceded to the United States.

13.   The main American military campaign that finally captured Mexico City was commanded by

    a.   General Stephen W. Kearny.
    b.   Captain John C. Frémont.
    c.   General Zachary Taylor.
    d.   General Winfield Scott.

14. The Treaty of Guadalupe Hidalgo ending the Mexican War provided for
    a. a return to the status quo that had existed before the war.
    b. the eventual American acquisition of all of Mexico.
    c. American acquisition of about half of Mexico and payment of several million dollars in compensation.
    d. the acquisition of California and joint U.S.-Mexican control of Arizona and New Mexico.
15. The major domestic consequence of the Mexican War was
    a. the decline of the Democratic party.
    b. a sharp revival of the issue of slavery.
    c. a large influx of Hispanic immigrants into the southern United States.
    d. a significant increase in taxes to pay the costs of the war.

C. Identification

Supply the correct identification for each numbered description.

1. _____ British colony where Americans regularly aided anti-government rebels
2. _____ State where "Aroostook War" was fought over a disputed boundary with Canada
3. _____ Nation that strongly backed independence for Texas, hoping to turn it into an economic asset and antislavery bastion
4. _____ Antislavery Whigs who opposed both the Texas annexation and the Mexican War on moral grounds
5. _____ Act of both houses of Congress by which Texas was annexed
6. _____ Northern boundary of Oregon territory jointly occupied with Britain, advocated by Democratic party and others as the desired line of American expansion
7. _____ Two-thousand-mile-long path along which thousands of Americans journeyed to the Willamette Valley in the 1840s
8. _____ The widespread American belief that God had ordained the United States to occupy all the territory of North America
9. _____ Small antislavery party that took enough votes from Henry Clay to cost him the election of 1844
10. _____ Final compromise line that settled the Oregon boundary dispute in 1846
11. _____ Rich Mexican province that Polk tried to buy and Mexico refused to sell
12. _____ River that Mexico claimed as the Texas-Mexico boundary, crossed by Taylor's troops in 1846
13. _____ Resolution offered by Congressman Abraham Lincoln demanding to know the precise location where Mexicans had allegedly shed American blood on "American" soil
14. _____ Treaty ending Mexican War and granting vast territories to the United States
15. _____ Controversial amendment, which passed the House but not the Senate, stipulating that slavery should be forbidden in territory acquired from Mexico

D. Matching People, Places, and Events

Match the person, place, or event in the left column with the proper description in the right column by inserting the correct letter on the blank line.

1. ____ John Tyler
2. ____ Henry Clay
3. ____ Aroostook War
4. ____ Daniel Webster
5. ____ Texas
6. ____ Oregon
7. ____ James K. Polk
8. ____ John C. Fremont
9. ____ Abraham Lincoln
10. ____ Rio Grande
11. ____ Zachary Taylor
12. ____ Winfield Scott
13. ____ Santa Anna
14. ____ Nicholas Trist
15. ____ David Wilmot

a. Congressional author of the "spot resolutions" criticizing the Mexican War

b. "Old Fuss and Feathers," whose conquest of Mexico City brought U.S. victory in the Mexican War

c. Leader of Senate Whigs and unsuccessful presidential candidate against Polk in 1844

d. Long-winded American diplomat who negotiated the Treaty of Guadalupe Hidalgo

e. Whig leader and secretary who negotiated an end to Maine boundary dispute in 1842

f. Claimed by United States as southern boundary of Texas

g. Dashing explorer/adventurer who led the overthrow of Mexican rule in California after war broke out

h. Clash between Canadians and Americans over disputed timber country

i. Mexican military leader who failed to stop humiliating American invasion of his country

j. Independent nation that was the object of British, Mexican, and French scheming in the early 1840s

k. American military hero who invaded northern Mexico from Texas in 1846–1847

l. Congressional author of resolution forbidding slavery in territory acquired from Mexico

m. Dark-horse presidential winner in 1844 who effectively carried out ambitious expansionist campaign plans

n. Northwestern territory in dispute between Britain and United States, subject of "Manifest Destiny" rhetoric in 1844

o. Leader elected vice president on the Whig ticket who spent most of his presidency in bitter feuds with his fellow Whigs

A.   Putting Things in Order

Put the following events in correct order by numbering them from 1 to 5.

1. ___   United States ends a long courtship by incorporating an independent republic that had once been part of Mexico.

2. ___   The first American president to die in office is succeeded by his controversial vice president.

3. ___   A treaty adding vast territory to the United States is hastily pushed through the Senate.

4. ___   American and Mexican troops clash in disputed border territory, leading to a controversial declaration of war.

5. ___   An ambitious "dark horse" wins an election against an opponent trapped by the Texas annexation issue.

F. Matching Cause and Effect

Match the historical cause in the left column with the proper effect in the right column by writing the correct letter on the blank line.

Cause	**Effect**
1. ___ Tyler's refusal to carry out his own Whig party's policies	a. Thwarted a growing movement calling for the United States to annex all of Mexico
2. ___ Strong American hostility to Britain	b. Enabled the United States to take vast territories in the Treaty of Guadalupe Hidalgo
3. ___ British support for the Texas Republic	c. Helped lead to a controversial confrontation with Mexico along the Texas border
4. ___ Rapidly growing American settlement in Oregon	d. Increased American determination to annex Texas
5. ___ The upsurge of Manifest Destiny in the 1840s	e. Split the Whigs and caused the entire cabinet except Webster to resign
6. ___ Clay's unsuccessful attempts to straddle the Texas issue	f. Heated up the slavery controversy between North and South
7. ___ Polk's frustration at Mexico's refusal to sell California	g. Sparked bitter feuds over Canadian rebels, the boundaries of Maine and Oregon, and other issues
8. ___ The overwhelming American military victory over Mexico	h. Turned antislavery voters to the Liberty party and helped elect the expansionist Polk
9. ___ The rapid Senate ratification of the Treaty of Guadalupe Hidalgo	i. Created widespread popular support for Polk's expansionist policies on Texas, Oregon, and California
10. ___ The Wilmot Proviso	j. Strengthened American claims to the Columbia River country and made Britain more willing to compromise

G. Developing Historical Skills

Reading Maps for Routes

Historical maps often include the routes taken in connection with particular events. The map of the *Major Campaigns of the Mexican War* (p. 382) includes a number of such routes.

Answer the following questions:

1. Near what Mexican port city did both General Taylor and General Scott pass?

2. From which city (and battle site) did American forces move both west to California and south toward Buena Vista?

3. According to the map, where did American naval forces come from? Where did they go during the course of the war? Where were they involved in battles?

4. Across what territories did Kearny and Frémont pass during the war? In which significant battles did each of them take part?

H. Map Mastery

Map Discrimination

Using the maps and charts in Chapter 17, answer the following questions:

1. *Maine Boundary Settlement, 1842*: The Webster-Ashburton Treaty line settled the boundary between the American state of Maine and which two Canadian provinces?

2. *The Oregon Controversy, 1846*: The part of the Oregon Country that was in dispute between the United States and Britain lay between what two boundaries?

3. *The Oregon Controversy, 1846*: How many degrees and minutes (°, ') of latitude were there between the northern and southern boundaries of the *whole* Oregon Country?

4. *Major Campaigns of the Mexican War*: Stephen Kearny's invasion route from Fort Leavenworth to Los Angeles led him across what three rivers?

5. *Major Campaigns of the Mexican War*: Name any three of the cities within present-day Mexico that were occupied by the armies of generals Taylor or Scott.

Map Challenge

Using the map of *Major Campaigns of the Mexican War* on p. 382, write a brief essay explaining the relation between the movement of American military forces during the war and the *political* issues of the Mexican War.

PART III: APPLYING WHAT YOU HAVE LEARNED

1. What led to the rise of the spirit of "Manifest Destiny" in the 1840s, and how did that spirit show itself in the American expansionism of the decade?

2. How did rivalry with Britain affect the American decision to annex Texas, the Oregon dispute, and other lesser controversies of the period?

3. Most Americans believed that expansion across North America was their "destiny." Was expansion actually inevitable? What forces might have stopped it? How would American history have changed if, say, the Mexican War had not occurred?

4. Could the United States have accepted a permanently independent Texas? Why or why not?

5. Why did the crucial election of 1844 come to be fought over expansionism, and how did Polk exercise his "mandate" for expansion in his attempt to obtain California?

6. What were the causes and consequences of the Mexican War?

7. Congressman Abraham Lincoln opposed the Mexican War as an unjust war of aggression against America's neighbor. What arguments would support that view? What arguments might challenge it?

8. How was the "Manifest Destiny" of the 1840s—particularly the expansion into Texas and Mexico—related to the sectional conflict over slavery?

CHAPTER 18

Renewing the Sectional Struggle, 1848–1854

PART I: REVIEWING THE CHAPTER

A. CHECKLIST OF LEARNING OBJECTIVES

After mastering this chapter, you should be able to

1. explain how the issue of slavery in the territories acquired from Mexico disrupted American politics from 1848 to1850.

2. point out the major terms of the Compromise of 1850 and indicate how this agreement attempted to deal with the issue of slavery.

3. indicate how the Whig party disintegrated and disappeared because of its divisions over slavery.

4. describe how the Pierce administration as well as private American adventurers pursued numerous overseas and expansionist ventures primarily designed to expand slavery.

5. describe Americans' first ventures into China and Japan in the 1850s and their diplomatic, economic, cultural, and religious consequences.

6. describe Douglas's Kansas-Nebraska Act and explain why it stirred the sectional controversy to new heights.

B. GLOSSARY

To build your social science vocabulary, familiarize yourself with the following terms:

1. **self-determination** In politics, the right of a people to assert its own national identity or form of government without outside influence. "The public liked it because it accorded with the democratic tradition of self-determination." (p. 391)

2. **homestead** A family home or farm with buildings and land sufficient for survival. ". . . they broadened their appeal . . . by urging free government homesteads for settlers." (p. 391)

3. **vigilante** Concerning groups that claim to punish crime and maintain order without legal authority to do so. ". . . violence was only partly discouraged by rough vigilante justice." (p. 393)

4. **sanctuary** A place of refuge or protection, where people are safe from punishment by the law. ". . . scores of . . . runaway slaves . . . were spirited . . . to the free-soil sanctuary of Canada." (p. 395)

5. **fugitive** A person who flees from danger or prosecution. ". . . southerners were demanding a new and more stringent fugitive-slave law." (p. 395)

6. **topography** The precise surface features and details of a place—for example, rivers, bridges, hills—in relation to one another. "The good Lord had decreed—through climate, topography, and geography—that a plantation economy . . . could not profitably exist in the Mexican Cession territory. . . ." (p. 396)

7.   **mundane**   Belonging to this world, as opposed to the spiritual world. "Seward argued earnestly that Christian legislators must obey God's moral law as well as mundane human law." (p. 397)

8.   **statecraft**   The art of government leadership. "The Whigs . . . missed a splendid opportunity to capitalize on their record in statecraft." (p. 401)

9.   **isthmian (isthmus)**   Concerning a narrow strip of land connecting two larger bodies of land. ". . . neither America nor Britain would fortify or secure exclusive control over any future isthmian water-way." (p. 402)

10.   **filibustering (filibuster)**   Adventurers who conduct a private war against a foreign country. "During 1850–1851 two 'filibustering' expeditions descended upon Cuba." (p. 403) (In a different meaning, the term also refers to deliberately prolonging speechmaking in order to block legislation.)

11.   **mikado**   A title of the Japanese emperor used by foreigners. "The mikado's empire, after some disagreeable experiences with the European world. . . ." (p. 403)

12.   **cloak-and-dagger**   Concerning the activities of spies or undercover agents, especially involving elaborate deceptions. "An incredible cloak-and-dagger episode followed." (p. 404)

13.   **manifesto**   A proclamation or document aggressively asserting a controversial position or advocating a daring course of action. " . . . rose in an outburst of wrath against this 'manifesto of brigands.'" (p. 404)

14.   **booster**   One who promotes a person or enterprise, especially in a highly enthusiastic way. "An ardent booster for the West, he longed to . . . stretch a line of settlements across the continent." (p. 405)

15.   **truce**   A temporary suspension of warfare by agreement of the hostile parties. "This bold step Douglas was prepared to take, even at the risk of shattering the uneasy truce patched up by the Great Compromise of 1850." (p. 406)

PART II: CHECKING YOUR PROGRESS

A. True-False

Where the statement is true, circle **T**; where it is false, circle **F**.

1.   T   F   Democratic politicians and others attempted to avoid the issue of slavery in the territories by saying it should be left to "popular sovereignty."

2.   T   F   The Free Soil party consisted of a small, unified band of radical abolitionists.

3.   T   F   The California gold rush of 1849 diverted the nation's attention from slavery.

4.   T   F   Southerners demanded a more effective fugitive-slave law to stop the "Underground Railroad" from running escaped slaves to Canada.

5.   T   F   In the Senate debate of 1850, Calhoun spoke for compromise, while Clay and Webster each defended his own section's interests.

6.   T   F   In the key provisions of the Compromise of 1850, New Mexico and Utah were admitted as slave states, while California was left open to popular sovereignty.

7.   T   F   The provision of the Compromise of 1850 that aroused the fiercest northern opposition was the Fugitive Slave Law.

8.   T   F   The greatest political winner in the Compromise of 1850 was the South.

9. T   F   The Whig Party disappeared because its northern and southern wings were too deeply split over the Fugitive Slave Law and other sectional issues.

10. T   F   The Pierce administration's expansionist efforts in Central America, Cuba, and the Gadsden Purchase were basically designed to serve southern proslavery interests.

11. T   F   In negotiating the first American treaty with China in 1844, diplomat Caleb Cushing made sure that the United States did not align itself with the imperialistic European great powers in China.

12. T   F   Douglas's Kansas-Nebraska Act was intended to organize western territories so that a transcontinental railroad could be built along a northern route.

13. T   F   Both southerners and northerners alike refused to accept Douglas's plan to repeal the Missouri Compromise.

14. T   F   The Kansas-Nebraska Act wrecked the Compromise of 1850 and created deep divisions within the Democratic Party.

15. T   F   The Republican Party was initially organized as a northern protest against Douglas's Kansas-Nebraska Act.

B. Multiple Choice

Select the best answer and circle the corresponding letter.

1. "Popular sovereignty" was the idea that
    a.   the government of each new territory should be elected by the people.
    b.   the American public should vote on whether to admit states with or without slavery.
    c.   the people of a territory should determine for themselves whether or not to permit slavery.
    d.   the United States should assume popular control of the territory acquired from Mexico.

2. In the election of 1848, the response of the Whig and Democratic parties to the rising controversy over slavery was
    a.   a strong proslavery stance by the Democrats and a strong antislavery stance by the Whigs.
    b.   platforms stressing both parties' clear differences with the antislavery Free Soil party.
    c.   an attempt to ignore the issue.
    d.   to free each individual candidate to take his own stand on the issue.

3. Quick formation of an effective government in California was essential because of
    a.   the desire of antislavery forces to gain a new state for their cause.
    b.   the threat that Mexico would reconquer the territory.
    c.   the need to have a government capable of building a transcontinental railroad.
    d.   the very large and unruly population drawn into the state by the discovery of gold.

4. The proposed admission of California directly into the Union was dangerously controversial because
    a.   the territory was in a condition of complete lawlessness and anarchy.
    b.   the Mexicans were threatening renewed warfare if California joined the Union.
    c.   California's admission as a free state would destroy the equal balance of slave and free states in the U.S. Senate.
    d.   there was a growing movement to declare California an independent nation.

5. The existence of the "Underground railroad" added to southern demands for
    a.   the stationing of armed police and troops along the Ohio River and the Mason-Dixon line to capture runaways.
    b.   the death penalty for abolitionists.
    c.   a stricter federal Fugitive Slave Law.

    d.   the enslavement of free blacks in the South.

6.   Among the notable advocates of compromise in the controversy over slavery in 1850 were

    a.   William Seward and Zachary Taylor.
    b.   Henry Clay and Daniel Webster.
    c.   John C. Calhoun and Abraham Lincoln.
    d.   Stephen Douglas and Harriet Tubman.

7.   During the debate over the Compromise of 1850, northern antislavery forces were particularly outraged by what they considered the "betrayal" of Senator

    a.   Stephen A. Douglas.
    b.   Daniel Webster.
    c.   William Seward.
    d.   John C. Calhoun.

8.   Under the terms of the Compromise of 1850,

    a.   California was admitted to the Union as a free state, and slavery in Utah and New Mexico territories would be left up to popular sovereignty.
    b.   California was admitted as a free state, and Utah and New Mexico as slave states.
    c.   California, Utah, and New Mexico were kept as territories but with slavery prohibited.
    d.   New Mexico and Texas were admitted as slave states and Utah and California as free states.

9.   The final battle to gain passage of the Compromise of 1850 was substantially aided by

    a.   the conversion of William Seward to the idea of compromise.
    b.   the death of President Taylor and the succession of President Fillmore.
    c.   the removal of the proposed Fugitive Slave Law from the compromise bill.
    d.   the agreement to rely on popular sovereignty to resolve the future of slavery in California.

10.   The greatest winner in the Compromise of 1850 was

    a.   the North.
    b.   the South.
    c.   neither the North nor the South.
    d.   the border states.

11.   One of the primary effects of the Fugitive Slave Law passed as part of the Compromise of 1850 was

    a.   an end to slave escapes and the Underground Railroad.
    b.   the extension of the underground railroad into Canada.
    c.   a sharp rise in northern antislavery feeling.
    d.   an increase in violent slave rebellions.

12.   The conflict over slavery after the election of 1852 led shortly to

    a.   the death of the Whig party.
    b.   the death of the Democratic party.
    c.   the death of the Republican party.
    d.   the rise of the Free Soil party.

13.   Southerners seeking to expand the territory of slavery undertook filibustering military expeditions to acquire

    a.   Canada and Alaska.
    b.   Venezuela and Colombia.
    c.   Nicaragua and Cuba.
    d.   Hawaii and Japan.

14.   The primary goal of Commodore Matthew Perry's treaty with Japan in 1854 was

    a.   establishing a balance of power in East Asia.
    b.   opening Japan to American trade.
    c.   guaranteeing the territorial integrity of China.

     d.   establishing American naval bases in Hawaii and Okinawa.

15.   Northerners especially resented Douglas's Kansas-Nebraska Act because

     a.   it aimed to build a transcontinental railroad along the southern route.

     b.   it would make him the leading Democratic candidate for the presidency.

     c.   it repealed the Missouri Compromise prohibiting slavery in northern territories.

     d.   it would bring Kansas into the Union as a slave state.

C. Identification

Supply the correct identification for each numbered description.

1. _____   Hotheaded southern agitators who pushed for southern interests and favored secession from the Union

2. _____   The doctrine that the issue of slavery should be decided by the residents of a territory themselves, not by the federal government

3. _____   The boundary line between slave and free states in the East, originally the southern border of Pennsylvania

4. _____   The informal network that conducted runaway slaves from the South to Canada

5. _____   Senator William Seward's doctrine that slavery should be excluded from the territories as contrary to a divine moral law standing above even the Constitution

6. _____   The provision of the Compromise of 1850 that comforted southern slave-catchers and aroused the wrath of northern abolitionists

7. _____   Third-party entry in the election of 1848 that opposed slavery expansion and prepared the way for the Republican Party

8. _____   A series of agreements between North and South that temporarily dampened the slavery controversy and led to a short-lived era of national good feelings

9. _____   Political party that fell apart and disappeared after losing the election of 1852

10. _____   An agreement between Britain and America concerning any future Central American canal

11. _____   A top-secret dispatch, drawn up by American diplomats in Europe, that detailed a plan for seizing Cuba from Spain

12. _____   Southwestern territory acquired by the Pierce administration to facilitate a southern transcontinental railroad

13. _____   The sectional agreement of 1820, repealed by the Kansas-Nebraska Act

14. _____   The political party that was deeply divided by Douglas's Kansas-Nebraska Act

15. _____   A new political party organized as a protest against the Kansas-Nebraska Act

D. Matching People, Places, and Events

Match the person, place, or event in the left column with the proper description in the right column by inserting the correct letter on the blank line.

1. ___   Lewis Cass   a.   American naval commander who opened Japan to the West in 1854

2. ___   Zachary Taylor

                                         b.   Democratic presidential candidate in 1848,

3. ___	California
4. ___	Caleb Cushing
5. ___	Harriet Tubman
6. ___	Daniel Webster
7. ___	William Seward
8. ___	China
9. ___	Franklin Pierce
10. ___	Winfield Scott
11. ___	Nicaragua
12. ___	Matthew Perry
13. ___	Cuba
14. ___	Tokugawa Shogunate
15. ___	Stephen A. Douglas

a. original proponent of the idea of "popular sovereignty"

c. Weak Democratic president whose pro-southern cabinet pushed aggressive expansionist schemes

d. Famous "conductor" on the Underground Railroad who rescued more than three hundred slaves from bondage

e. Illinois politician who helped smooth over sectional conflict in 1850 but then reignited it in 1854

f. Central American nation desired by proslavery expansionists in the 1850s

g. Military hero of the Mexican War who became the Whigs' last presidential candidate in 1852

h. Whig president who nearly destroyed the Compromise of 1850 before he died in office

i. Rich Spanish colony coveted by American proslavery expansionists in the 1850s

j. American diplomat who negotiated the Treaty of Wanghia with China in 1844

k. The ruling warrior dynasty of Japan with whom Matthew Perry negotiated the Treaty of Kanagawa in 1854

l. New York senator who argued that the expansion of slavery was forbidden by a "higher law"

m. Nation whose 1844 treaty with the United States opened the door to a flood of American missionaries

n. Northern spokesman whose support for the Compromise of 1850 earned him the hatred of abolitionists

o. Acquired from Mexico in 1848 and admitted as a free state in 1850 without ever having been a territory

E. Putting Things in Order

Put the following events in correct order by numbering them from 1 to 5.

1. ___ A series of delicate agreements between the North and South temporarily smoothes over the slavery conflict.

2. ___ A Mexican War hero is elected president, as the issue of how a deal with slavery in the territory acquired from Mexico arouses national controversy.

3. ___   A spectacular growth of settlement in the far West creates demand for admission of a new free state and agitates the slavery controversy.

4. ___   Stephen A. Douglas's scheme to build a transcontinental railroad leads to repeal of the Missouri Compromise, which reopens the slavery controversy and spurs the formation of a new party.

5. ___   The Pierce administration acquires a small Mexican territory to encourage a southern route for the transcontinental railroad.

F. Matching Cause and Effect

Match the historical cause in the left column with the proper effect in the right column by writing the correct letter on the blank line.

Cause	Effect
1. ___ The evasion of the slavery issue by Whigs and Democrats in 1848	a. Was the predecessor of the antislavery Republican Party
	b. Fell apart after the leaking of the Ostend Manifesto
2. ___ The California gold rush	
3. ___ The Underground Railroad	c. Caused a tremendous northern protest and the birth of the Republican party
4. ___ The Free Soil Party	
5. ___ The Compromise of 1850	d. Made the issue of slavery in the Mexican Cession areas more urgent
6. ___ The Fugitive Slave Law	e. Created a short-lived national mood of optimism and reconciliation
7. ___ The Pierce administration's schemes to acquire Cuba	
	f. Heightened competition between southern and northern railroad promoters over the choice of a transcontinental route
8. ___ The Gadsden Purchase	
9. ___ Stephen Douglas's indifference to slavery and desire for a northern railroad route	g. Led to the formation of the new Free-Soil antislavery party
	h. Aroused active northern resistance to legal enforcement and prompted attempts at nullification in Massachusetts
10. ___ The Kansas-Nebraska Act	
	i. Led to the passage of the Kansas-Nebraska Act, without regard for the consequences
	j. Aroused southern demands for an effective fugitive-slave law

G. Developing Historical Skills

Understanding Cause and Effect

It is often crucial to understand how certain historical forces or events cause other historical events or developments. In the pairs of historical events listed below, designated (A) and (B), indicate which was the cause and which was the effect. Then indicate in a brief sentence how the cause led to the effect.

1.   (A) The acquisition of California   (B) The Mexican War

2.   (A) The entry of California into the Union (B) The California gold rush

3.   (A) The death of President Zachary Taylor   (B) The passage of the Compromise of 1850

4.   (A) Northern aid to fugitive slaves (B) The passage of the Fugitive Slave Law

5.   (A) The disappearance of the Whig party   (B) The election of 1852

6.   (A) The Compromise of 1850   (B) Southern "filibuster" ventures

7.   (A) The Gadsden Purchase   (B) The southern plan for a transcontinental railroad

8.   (A) Douglas's plan for a transcontinental railroad   (B) The Kansas-Nebraska Act

9.   (A) The Ostend Manifesto (B) The end of Pierce administration schemes to acquire Cuba

10.   (A) The rise of the Republican party   (B) The Kansas-Nebraska Act

H. Map Mastery

Map Discrimination

Using the maps and charts in Chapter 18, answer the following questions:

1. *Texas and the Disputed Area Before the Compromise of 1850*: A large territory claimed by Texas was taken from it in the Compromise of 1850, and parts of it were later incorporated into *five* other states. Which were they?

2. *Slavery After the Compromise of 1850*: Under the Compromise of 1850, which *free* state was partially located south of the line 36°30' (the southern border of Missouri), which had been established by the Missouri Compromise as the border between slave and free territories?

3. *Slavery After the Compromise of 1850*: Under the Compromise of 1850, which territory located *north* of 36°30' *could* have adopted slavery if it had chosen to do so?

4. *Slavery After the Compromise of 1850*: After 1850, how many organized territories prohibited slavery? Identify them.

5. *Central America c. 1850*: In Central America, British influence extended along the Atlantic coasts of which two nations?

6. *Central America c. 1850*: In the 1850s, the territory of the future Panama Canal was part of which South American country?

7. *The Gadsden Purchase, 1853*: The proposed southern transcontinental railroad was supposed to run through which two Texas cities?

8. *Kansas and Nebraska, 1854*: The proposed *northern* transcontinental railroad was supposed to run through which territory organized by Stephen Douglas's act of 1854?

9. *The Legal Status of Slavery, from the Revolution to the Civil War*: In 1854, what was the status of slavery in the only state that bordered on the Kansas Territory?

10. *The Legal Status of Slavery, from the Revolution to the Civil War*: Under the Kansas-Nebraska Act, how far north could slavery have extended had it been implemented in Nebraska territory?

Map Challenge

Using the map of *The Legal Status of Slavery, from the Revolution to the Civil War*, write a brief essay in which you describe how the Missouri Compromise, the Compromise of 1850, and the Kansas-Nebraska Act each affected the legal status of slavery in various territories.

PART III: APPLYING WHAT YOU HAVE LEARNED

1. What urgent issues created the crisis leading up to the Compromise of 1850?

2. What was the effect of the morally powerful slavery debate on American political parties? What caused the demise of the Whig Party, and the rise of the Free Soil and Republican parties?

3. How did the Compromise of 1850 attempt to deal with the most difficult issues concerning slavery? Was the Compromise a "success?" By what standard?

4. Why were proslavery southerners so eager to push for further expansion in Nicaragua, Cuba, and elsewhere in the 1850s?

5. What fundamentally motivated the new American engagement with China and Japan in the 1840s and 1850s? Were the treaties negotiated by Caleb Cushing and Matthew Perry expressions of the expansionist spirit of "manifest destiny" and general Western imperialism, or were Americans genuinely interested in economic and cultural exchange with East Asia?

6. What were the causes and consequences of the Kansas-Nebraska Act?

7. How similar was the Compromise of 1850 to the Missouri Compromise of 1820? (See Chapter 13.) How did each sectional compromise affect the balance of power between North and South? Why could sectional issues be compromised in 1820 and 1850, but not in 1854?

8. Because Senator Stephen A. Douglas's Kansas-Nebraska Act re-ignited the slavery issue after the Compromise of 1850, should he bear responsibility as an instigator of the Civil War? How and why might Civil War have come even if Douglas's bill had not been enacted?

CHAPTER 19

Drifting Toward Disunion, 1854–1861

PART I: REVIEWING THE CHAPTER

A. CHECKLIST OF LEARNING OBJECTIVES

After mastering this chapter, you should be able to

1. enumerate the sequence of major crises that led from the Kansas-Nebraska Act to secession and explain the significance of each.

2. explain how and why "bleeding Kansas" became a dress rehearsal for the Civil War.

3. trace the growing power of the Republican party in the 1850s and the increasing divisions and helplessness of the Democrats.

4. explain how the *Dred Scott* decision and Brown's Harpers Ferry raid deepened sectional antagonism.

5. trace the rise of Lincoln as the leading exponent of the Republican doctrine of no expansion of slavery.

6. highlight the issues in the election of 1860, the sectional divisions it revealed, and explain why Lincoln won.

7. describe the movement toward secession, the formation of the Confederacy, and the failure of the last compromise effort.

B. GLOSSARY

To build your social science vocabulary, familiarize yourself with the following terms:

1. **puppet government** A government set up and controlled by outside forces. "The slavery supporters triumphed and then set up their own puppet government at Shawnee Mission." (p. 413)

2. **bigoted** Blindly or narrowly intolerant. ". . . the allegation . . . alienated many bigoted Know-Nothings. . . ." (p. 416)

3. **public domain** Land or other things belonging to the whole nation, controlled by the federal government. "Financial distress . . . gave a new vigor to the demand for free farms of 160 acres from the public domain." (p. 419)

4. **bandwagon** In politics, a movement or candidacy that gains rapid momentum because of people's purported desire to join a successful cause. "After mounting the Republican bandwagon, he emerged as one of the foremost politicians and orators of the Northwest." (p. 420)

5. **apportionment** The allotment or distribution of legislative representatives in districts according to population. (**Re-apportionment** occurs after each census according to growth or loss of population.) "Yet thanks to inequitable apportionment, the districts carried by Douglas supporters represented a smaller population. . . ." (p. 422)

6. **splintering** Concerning the small political groups left after a larger group has divided or broken apart. "But Douglas . . . hurt his own chances . . . while further splitting his splintering party." (p. 422)

7. **affidavit** A sworn, written testimony, usually attested to by a notary public or legal officer. "His presumed insanity was supported by affidavits from seventeen friends and relatives. . . ." (p. 422)

8. **martyr** One who is tortured or killed for adherence to a belief. ". . . Ralph Waldo Emerson compared the new martyr-hero with Jesus." (p. 424)

9. **border state** The northernmost slave states contested by North and South; during the Civil War the four border states (Maryland, Delaware, Kentucky, and Missouri) remained within the Union, though they contained many Confederate sympathizers and volunteers. ". . . a man of moderate views from the border state of Kentucky." (p. 425)

10. **vassalage** The service and homage given by a feudal subordinate to an overlord; by extension, any similar arrangement between political figures or entities. ". . . secession [w]as a golden opportunity to cast aside their generations of 'vassalage' to the North." (p. 431)

PART II: CHECKING YOUR PROGRESS

A. True-False

Where the statement is true, circle **T**; where it is false, circle **F**.

1. T F   Harriet Beecher Stowe's *Uncle Tom's Cabin* proved to be the most influential publication in arousing the northern and European publics against the evils of slavery.

2. T F   Prosouthern Kansas pioneers brought numerous slaves with them in order to guarantee that Kansas would not become a free state.

3. T F   The violence in Kansas was provoked by both radical abolitionists and militant pro-slavery forces.

4. T F   By opposing the proslavery Lecompton Constitution in Kansas, Senator Stephen A. Douglas was able to unite the Democratic party.

5. T F   Both South Carolina and Massachusetts defiantly reelected the principal figures in the Brooks-Sumner beating incident.

6. T F   Although the Republican candidate lost to Buchanan, the election of 1856 demonstrated the growing power of the new antislavery party.

7. T F   The *Dred Scott* decision upheld the doctrine of popular sovereignty that the people of each territory should determine whether or not to permit slavery.

8. T F   Republicans considered the Supreme Court's *Dred Scott* decision invalid and vowed to defy it.

9. T F   In the Lincoln-Douglas debates, Lincoln's criticisms forced Douglas to back away from his support for popular sovereignty.

10. T F   John Brown's raid at Harpers Ferry failed to set off a slave uprising but succeeded in inflaming passions in both North and South.

11. T F   Northern Democrats walked out of the Democratic party in 1860 when southerners nominated Stephen A. Douglas for president.

12. T F   The election of 1860 was really two campaigns, Lincoln versus Douglas in the North and Bell versus Breckinridge in the South.

13. T F   The overwhelming support for Lincoln in the North gave him a majority of the total popular vote despite winning almost no votes in the South.

14. T F   Seven states seceded and formed the Confederate States of America during the "lame-duck" period between Lincoln's election and his inauguration.

15. T F   Lincoln made a strong effort to get the South to accept the Crittenden Compromise in order to avoid a civil war.

B. Multiple Choice

Select the best answer and circle the corresponding letter.

1. Harriet Beecher Stowe's *Uncle Tom's Cabin*
    a. greatly strengthened northern antislavery feeling.
    b. argued that nonslaveholding whites suffered the most from slavery.
    c. increased the desire for sectional compromise on the issue of slavery.
    d. was based on Stowe's long personal experience with slavery in the Deep South.

2. Hinton R. Helper's *The Impending Crisis of the South* contended that
    a. slavery violated the essential principles of the U.S. Constitution.
    b. slavery was contrary to the religious values held by most Americans.
    c. slavery did great harm to the poor whites of the South.
    d. slavery violated the human rights of African Americans.

3. The conflict over slavery in Kansas
    a. came about because the first settlers brought substantial numbers of slaves to the territory.
    b. was resolved by the Crittenden Compromise.
    c. was temporarily resolved by the Compromise of 1850.
    d. was greatly escalated by abolitionist-funded settlers and proslavery "border ruffians" from Missouri.

4. As presented to Congress, the Lecompton Constitution provided for
    a. the admission of Kansas as a free state.
    b. a statewide referendum on slavery to be held after Kansas's admission to the Union.
    c. a prohibition against either New England or Missouri involvement in Kansas politics.
    d. the admission of Kansas as a slave state.

5. The fanatical abolitionist John Brown made his first entry into violent antislavery politics by
    a. killing five proslavery settlers at Pottawatomie Creek, Kansas.
    b. organizing a slave rebellion in Missouri.
    c. leading an armed raid on the federal arsenal at Harpers Ferry, Virginia.
    d. organizing an armed militia of blacks and whites to conduct escaped slaves to Canada.

6. The Sumner-Brooks affair revealed
    a. that antislavery northerners were as willing to turn to violence as proslavery southerners.
    b. that violent disagreements about slavery were being felt in the halls of Congress.
    c. that neither northerners nor southerners were yet ready to tolerate political violence over slavery.
    d. how loyalty to section was beginning to supersede loyalty to political party.

7. The election of 1856 was most noteworthy for
    a. the Democrats' surprising loss of the White House.
    b. the support immigrants and Catholics gave to the American Party.
    c. the dramatic rise of the Republican party.

d.   the absence of the slavery issue from the campaign.

8. In the *Dred Scott* decision, the Supreme Court

   a.   avoided controversy by ruling that the slave Dred Scott had no right to sue in federal court.
   b.   ruled that the Kansas-Nebraska Act was unconstitutional.
   c.   ruled that Congress could not prohibit slavery in the territories because slaves were private property.
   d.   ruled that slaves could sue in federal court only if their masters permitted them to do so.

9. The panic of 1857 encouraged the South to believe that

   a.   its economy was fundamentally stronger than that of the North.
   b.   it ought to take new steps to develop its own banking and manufacturing institutions.
   c.   it would be wise to support the Homestead Act.
   d.   its economic future was closely tied to that of the North.

10. A key issue in the Lincoln-Douglas debates was

   a.   whether secession from the Union was legal.
   b.   whether the people of a territory could prohibit slavery in light of the *Dred Scott* decision.
   c.   whether Illinois should continue to prohibit slavery.
   d.   whether Kansas should be admitted to the Union as a slave or a free state.

11. Southerners were particularly enraged by the John Brown affair because

   a.   so many slaves had joined the insurrection.
   b.   they believed Brown's violent abolitionist sentiments were shared by the whole North.
   c.   Brown had expressed his contempt for the southern way of life.
   d.   Brown escaped punishment by pleading insanity.

12. In the campaign of 1860, the Democratic Party

   a.   tried to unite around the compromise "popular sovereignty" views of Stephen A. Douglas.
   b.   campaigned on a platform of restoring the compromises of 1820 and 1850.
   c.   split in two, with each faction nominating its own presidential candidate.
   d.   threatened to support secession if the sectionally-based Republicans won the election.

13. During the campaign of 1860, Abraham Lincoln and the Republican Party

   a.   opposed the expansion of slavery but made no statements threatening to abolish slavery in the South.
   b.   waged a national campaign to win votes in the South as well as the Midwest and the Northeast.
   c.   promised if elected to seek the peaceful abolition of slavery in the South.
   d.   were forced to be cautious about limiting the expansion of slavery because of Stephen A. Douglas's threats to support secession.

14. Within two months after the election of Lincoln,

   a.   Northerners were mobilizing for a civil war.
   b.   seven southern states had seceded and formed the Confederate States of America.
   c.   all the slaveholding states had held conventions and passed secessionist resolutions.
   d.   President Buchanan appealed for troops to put down the secessionist rebellion.

15. Lincoln rejected the proposed Crittenden Compromise because

   a.   it did not address the issue of the future of slavery.
   b.   it permitted the further extension of slavery north of the line of 36° 30'.
   c.   it represented a further extension of Douglas's popular sovereignty idea.
   d.   the Supreme Court would probably have ruled it unconstitutional.

C. Identification

Supply the correct identification for each numbered description.

1. _____ A powerful, personal novel that altered the course of American politics

2. _____ A book by a southern writer that argued that slavery especially oppressed poor whites

3. _____ Rifles paid for by New England abolitionists and brought to Kansas by anti-slavery pioneers

4. _____ Term that described the prairie territory where a small-scale civil war erupted in 1856

5. _____ Tricky proslavery document designed to bring Kansas into the Union but blocked by Stephen A. Douglas

6. _____ Anti-immigrant party headed by former President Fillmore that competed with Republicans and Democrats in the election of 1856

7. _____ Controversial Supreme Court ruling that blacks had no civil or human rights and that Congress could not prohibit slavery in the territories

8. _____ Sharp economic decline that increased northern demands for a high tariff and convinced southerners that the North was economically vulnerable

9. _____ Thoughtful political discussions during an Illinois Senate campaign that sharply defined national issues concerning slavery

10. _____ Newly formed middle-of-the-road party of elderly politicians that sought compromise in 1860, but carried only three border states

11. _____ First state to secede from the Union in December 1860

12. _____ A new nation that proclaimed its independence in Montgomery, Alabama, in 1861

13. _____ A last-ditch plan to save the Union by providing guarantees for slavery in the territories

14. _____ Four-way race for the presidency that resulted in the election of a sectional minority president

15. _____ Period between Lincoln's election and his inauguration, during which the ineffectual President Buchanan remained in office

D. Matching People, Places, and Events

Match the person, place, or event in the left column with the proper description in the right column by inserting the correct letter on the blank line.

1. ___ Harriet Beecher Stowe

2. ___ Hinton R. Helper

3. ___ New England Emigrant Aid Company

4. ___ John Brown

5. ___ James Buchanan

6. ___ Charles Sumner

7. ___ Preston Brooks

a. Southern congressman whose bloody attack on a northern senator fueled sectional hatred

b. Leading northern Democrat whose presidential hopes fell victim to the conflict over slavery

c. Black slave whose unsuccessful attempt to win his freedom deepened the sectional controversy

d. Former United States senator who

8. ___ John C. Frémont

9. ___ Dred Scott

10. ___ Harpers Ferry, Virginia

11. ___ Stephen A. Douglas

12. ___ Pottawatomie Creek, Kansas

13. ___ John C. Breckenridge

14. ___ Montgomery, Alabama

15. ___ Jefferson Davis

in 1861 became the president of what called itself a new nation

e. "The little woman who wrote the book that made this great war" (the Civil War)

f. Fanatical and bloody-minded abolitionist martyr admired in the North and hated in the South

g. Southern-born author whose book attacking slavery's effects on whites aroused northern opinion

h. Scene of militant abolitionist John Brown's massacre of proslavery men in 1856

i. Site where seven seceding states united to declare their independence from the United States

j. Romantic western hero and the first Republican candidate for president

k. Abolitionist senator whose verbal attack on the South provoked a physical assault that severely injured him

l. Site of a federal arsenal where a militant abolitionist attempted to start a slave rebellion

m. Buchanan's vice president, nominated for president by breakaway southern Democrats in 1860

n. Weak Democratic president whose manipulation by proslavery forces divided his own party

o. Abolitionist group that sent settlers and "Beecher's Bibles" to oppose slavery in Kansas

E. Putting Things in Order

Put the following events in correct order by numbering them from 1 to 6.

1. ___ A black slave's attempt to win freedom produces a controversial Supreme Court decision.

2. ___ A newly organized territory becomes a bloody battleground between proslavery and anti-slavery forces.

3. ___   The hanging of a fanatically violent abolitionist makes him a martyr in the North and a hated symbol in the South.

4. ___   A "black Republican" whose minority sectional victory in a presidential election provokes southern secession.

5. ___   The fictional tale of a black slave's vicious treatment by the cruel Simon Legree touches millions of northern hearts and creates stronger opposition to slavery.

6. ___   A group of states calling itself a new southern nation declares its independence and chooses its first president.

F. Matching Cause and Effect

Match the historical cause in the left column with the proper effect in the right column by writing the correct letter on the blank line.

Cause	Effect
1. ___ H. B. Stowe's *Uncle Tom's Cabin*	a. Moved South Carolina to declare immediate secession from the Union
2. ___ The exercise of "popular sovereignty" in Kansas	b. Shattered one of the last links between the sections and almost guaranteed Lincoln's victory in 1860
3. ___ Buchanan's support for the pro-slavery Lecompton Constitution	c. Convinced southerners that the North generally supported murder and slave rebellion
4. ___ The *Dred Scott* case	
5. ___ The 1858 Illinois senate race	d. Made Lincoln a leading national Republican figure and hurt Douglas's presidential chances
6. ___ John Brown's raid on Harpers Ferry	e. Ended the last hopes of a peaceable sectional settlement and an end to secession
7. ___ The splitting of the Democratic party in 1860	f. Paralyzed the North while the southern secessionist movement gained momentum
8. ___ The election of Lincoln as president	
9. ___ The "lame-duck" period and Buchanan's indecisiveness	g. Infuriated Republicans and made them determined to defy the Supreme Court
10. ___ Lincoln's rejection of the Crittenden Compromise	h. Offended Senator Douglas and divided the Democratic party
	i. Persuaded millions of northerners and Europeans that slavery was evil and should be eliminated
	j. Led to a "mini" prairie civil war between proslavery and antislavery factions

G. Developing Historical Skills

Interpreting Primary-Source Documents

In order properly to interpret primary-source documents in history, two skills are essential: first, the ability to read closely and carefully for the intended meaning; and second, the ability to understand the historical context and possible implications of a text or statement.

The small, boxed samples of primary documents in this chapter demonstrate these principles. The questions below will help you practice the skills of textual interpretation by asking you to read the documents very carefully for meaning and to consider some of their implications.

1. Lincoln's statement from the Lincoln-Douglas debate (p. 421).

   a. In what ways does Lincoln claim that blacks are *equal* to whites, and in what ways does he claim that whites are *superior*?

   b. What do the first two sentences tell you about the *reason* Lincoln is making a distinction between equality of natural rights and complete equality of the races?

2. John Brown's letter before his hanging (p. 423).

   a. What does Brown mean when he writes that "I am worth inconceivably more to hang than for any other purpose. . . ."?

   b. What does Brown's statement imply about how abolitionists might make use of Brown's impending death?

3. Greeley's New York *Tribune* editorial (p. 437).

   a. What two arguments does Greeley use for letting the seceding states "go in peace?"

   b. The editorial was written three days after Lincoln's election. What fear is motivating Greeley?

4. Letter of South Carolina Senator Hammond (p. 429).

   a. What does the letter suggest will be the federal government's response to secession?

b.   Why did the attitude reflected in the letter make efforts like the Crittenden Compromise fail?

5.   London *Times* editorial (p. 431).

a.   What is the editorial's view of the relation between the southern states and the United States government?

b.   What position does it appear the London *Times* would advocate the British government take regarding the American Civil War?

6.   Harriet Beecher Stowe's *Uncle Tom's Cabin* (pp. 411 and 412).

a.   What details in Stowe's account of Tom's last morning in the cabin before the sale of his family might especially appeal to female readers?

b.   How does Stowe characterize the black slave Tom and his wife Chloe?

c.   What details in the excerpts in *Examining the Evidence* (p. 411) and on p. 412 show Stowe's explicit appeal to the religious sentiments of her readers?

H. Map Mastery

Map Discrimination

Using the maps and charts in Chapter 19, answer the following questions:

1.   *Presidential Election of 1856*: In the presidential election of 1856, how many electoral votes did Buchanan get from the free states? (See map of *The Legal Status of Slavery*, Chapter 17, for free and slave states.)

2.   *Presidential Election of 1856; Presidential Election of 1860 (electoral vote by state)*: Which four states carried by Democrat Buchanan in 1856 were also carried completely by Republican Lincoln in 1860?

3. *Presidential Election of 1860 (showing popular vote by county)* Using this map of the presidential voting by counties in 1860, indicate which five states gave Douglas his strongest support.

4. *Presidential Election of 1860 (showing popular vote by county)*: In which five states did Bell receive his strongest support?

5. *Presidential Election of 1860 (showing popular vote by county)*: Which Border State was the most closely divided among Douglas, Bell, and Breckenridge?

6. *Presidential Election of 1860 (showing popular vote by county)*: Which state was the only one divided among Lincoln, Douglas, and Breckenridge?

7. *Presidential Election of 1860 (showing vote by county)*: In which six northern states did Lincoln carry every single country?

8. *Southern Opposition to Secession, 1860–1861*: In which four future Confederate states was the *opposition* to secession strongest?

9. *Southern Opposition to Secession, 1860–1861*: In which three states did every single county for which returns are available support secession?

10. *Southern Opposition to Secession, 1860–1861*: In which two states were many county conventions divided about secession?

Map Challenge

Using the electoral maps of *The Presidential Election of 1856* and *The Presidential Election of 1860*, write a brief essay in which you describe what political changes enabled the Republicans to turn defeat in 1856 into victory in 1860.

PART III: APPLYING WHAT YOU HAVE LEARNED

1. How did each of the crisis events of the 1850s help lead toward the Civil War?

2. What role did violence play in increasing the sectional conflict?

3. How did the political developments of the period work to fragment the Democratic party and benefit the Republicans?

4. Explain the crucial role of Stephen A. Douglas in the political events of the 1850s. Why did Douglas's attempts to push the conflict over slavery out of sight fail? What role did Douglas play in the election of 1860?

5. Could the Crittenden Compromise or some other proposal have prevented or at least postponed the Civil War? Why was compromise successful in 1820 and 1850 but not 1860?

6. How did the North and the South each view the various events of the 1850s? Why were their views so different?

7. Abraham Lincoln and the Republicans frequently declared that they sought only to prevent the expansion of slavery, and not to overturn slavery where it existed. Yet immediately after Lincoln's election some southerners pursued secession. Why? Were their fears of Lincoln rational or irrational?

CHAPTER 20

Girding for War: The North and the South, 1861–1865

PART I: REVIEWING THE CHAPTER

A. CHECKLIST OF LEARNING OBJECTIVES

After mastering this chapter, you should be able to

1. explain how the firing on Fort Sumter and Lincoln's call for troops galvanized both sides for war.

2. describe the crucial early struggle for the Border States.

3. indicate the strengths and weaknesses of both sides as they went to war.

4. describe the diplomatic struggle for the sympathies of the European powers.

5. compare Lincoln's and Davis's political leadership during the war.

6. describe the curtailment of civil liberties and the mobilization of military manpower during the war.

7. analyze the economic and social consequences of the war for both sides.

B. GLOSSARY

To build your social science vocabulary, familiarize yourself with the following terms.

1. **balance of power** The distribution of political or military strength among several nations so that no one of them becomes too strong or dangerous. "They could gleefully transplant to America their ancient concept of the balance of power." (p. 435)

2. **moral suasion** The effort to move others to a particular course of action through appeals to moral values and beliefs, without the use of enticements or force. "In dealing with the Border States, President Lincoln did not rely solely on moral suasion. . . ." (p. 437)

3. **martial law** The imposition of military rule above or in place of civil authority during times of war and emergency. "In Maryland he declared martial law where needed. . . ." (p. 437)

4. **ultimatum** A final proposal or demand, as by one nation to another, that if rejected, will likely lead to war. "The London Foreign Office prepared an ultimatum. . . ." (p. 442)

5. **loophole(d)** Characterized by small exceptions or conditions that enable escape from the general rule or principle. "These vessels were not warships within the meaning of the loopholed British law. . . ." (p. 442)

6. **squadron** A special unit of warships assigned to a particular naval task. ". . . they probably would have sunk the blockading squadrons. . . ." (p. 443)

7. **arbitration** The settlement of a dispute by putting the mandatory decision in the hands of a third, neutral party. (**Mediation** is using the services of a third party to promote negotiations and

suggest solutions, but without the power of mandatory decision making.) "It agreed in 1871 to submit the *Alabama* dispute to arbitration. . . ." (p. 443)

8.   **appropriation**   A sum of money or property legally authorized to be spent for a specific purpose. "He directed the secretary of the treasury to advance $2 million without appropriation. . . ." (p. 445)

9.   **habeas corpus**   In law, a judicial order requiring that a prisoner be brought before a court at a specified time and place in order to determine the legality of the imprisonment (literally, "produce the body.") "He suspended the precious privilege of the writ of habeas corpus. . . ." (p. 445)

10.   **arbitrary**   Governed by indeterminate preference or whim rather than by settled principle or law. "Jefferson Davis was less able than Lincoln to exercise arbitrary power. . . ." (p. 445)

11.   **quota**   The proportion or share of a larger number of things that a smaller group is assigned to contribute. ". . . with each state assigned a quota based on population." (p. 445)

12.   **greenback**   United States paper currency, especially that printed before the establishment of the Federal Reserve System. "Greenbacks thus fluctuated with the fortunes of Union arms. . . ." (p. 447)

13.   **bond**   In finance, an interest-bearing certificate issued by a government or business that guarantees repayment to the purchaser on a specified date at a predetermined rate of interest. ". . . the Treasury was forced to market its bonds through the private banking house of Jay Cooke and Company. . . ." (p. 447)

14.   **graft**   The corrupt acquisition of funds, through outright theft or embezzling or through questionably legal methods like kickbacks or insider trading. "But graft was more flagrant in the North than in the South. . . ." (p. 448)

15.   **profiteer**   One who takes advantage of a shortage of supply to charge excessively high prices and thus reap large profits. "One profiteer reluctantly admitted that his profits were 'painfully large.' " (p. 448)

PART II: CHECKING YOUR PROGRESS

A. True-False

Where the statement is true, circle **T**; where it is false, circle **F**.

1.   T   F   Lincoln successfully prevented any more states from seceding after his inauguration.

2.   T   F   In order to appease the Border States, Lincoln first insisted that the North was fighting only to preserve the Union and not to abolish slavery.

3.   T   F   The South's advantage in the Civil War was that it only had to stalemate the war on its own territory, while the North had to fight a war of conquest against a hostile population.

4.   T   F   The North generally had superior military leadership, while the South struggled to find successful commanders for its armies.

5.   T   F   In the long run, Northern economic and population advantages effectively wore down Southern resistance.

6.   T   F   The South's chances for independence when the war began were actually quite good.

7.   T   F   Although officially neutral, Britain sometimes engaged in acts that in effect aided the South.

8.   T   F   Northern pressure forced the British to stop the *Alabama* from raiding Union shipping.

9.   T   F   The Civil War-related crisis in U.S.-British relations threatened to expand into a war over Canada.

10.   T   F   Once the Civil War was over, the threat of U.S. intervention forced Napoleon III of France to withdraw his support of Maximilian in Mexico.

11.   T   F   The Civil War draft reflected the North's commitment to fighting a war based on the principle of equal treatment of citizens from all economic conditions.

12.   T   F   Lincoln's temporary violations of civil liberties were strongly opposed by Congress.

13.   T   F   The North effectively financed its Civil War effort through an income tax, higher tariffs, and the sale of federal government bonds.

14.   T   F   The South in effect used severe inflation as a means of financing its war effort.

15.   T   F   The Northern civilian economy was severely damaged by the war effort.

B. Multiple Choice

Select the best answer and circle the corresponding letter.

1.   Lincoln's plan for the besieged federal forces in Fort Sumter was

    a.   to order the soldiers there to attack the surrounding Confederate army.
    b.   to send about 3,000 soldiers and marines to reinforce the fort.
    c.   to make a symbolic show of support and then withdraw the forces.
    d.   to provision the garrison but not to reinforce it.

2.   The firing on Fort Sumter had the effect of

    a.   pushing ten other states to join South Carolina in seceding from the Union.
    b.   causing Lincoln to declare a war to free the slaves.
    c.   strengthening many Northerners' view that the South should be allowed to secede.
    d.   arousing Northern support for a war to put down the South's "rebellion."

3.   Among the states that joined the Confederacy only after Lincoln's call for troops were

    a.   Florida, Louisiana, and Texas.
    b.   Virginia, Arkansas, and Tennessee.
    c.   Missouri, Maryland, and Delaware.
    d.   South Carolina, North Carolina, and Mississippi.

4.   Lincoln at first declared that the war was being fought

    a.   only to save the Union and not to free the slaves.
    b.   in order to end slavery only in the Border States.
    c.   in order to restore the Missouri Compromise.
    d.   only to punish South Carolina for firing on Fort Sumter.

5.   Which of the following was *not* among the Border States?

    a.   Missouri
    b.   Kentucky
    c.   Oklahoma
    d.   Maryland

6.   The term "Butternut region" refers to

    a.   the mountain areas of the South that remained loyal to the Union.
    b.   the areas of southern Ohio, Indiana, and Illinois that opposed an antislavery war.
    c.   the areas of the upper Midwest that supplied a large portion of the committed Union volunteers.

    d.   the areas of southern Pennsylvania and New York that supported the war but hated the draft.

7.   In the Indian Territory (Oklahoma), most of the "Five Civilized Tribes"

    a.   supported the Confederacy.
    b.   supported a war for the Union but not a war against slavery.
    c.   sent many young warriors to fight for the Union cause.
    d.   tried to stay neutral in the "white man's war."

8.   Among the potential advantages the Confederacy possessed at the beginning of the civil War was

    a.   a stronger and more balanced economy.
    b.   a stronger navy.
    c.   better-trained officers and soldiers.
    d.   a larger reserve of manpower.

9.   Among the potential advantages the Union possessed at the beginning of the Civil War was

    a.   better preparation of its ordinary soldiers for military life.
    b.   a continuing influx of immigrant manpower from Europe.
    c.   more highly educated and experienced generals.
    d.   the ability to fight a primarily defensive war.

10.   The response to the Civil War in Europe was

    a.   almost unanimous support for the North.
    b.   support for the South among the upper classes and for the North among the working classes.
    c.   almost unanimous support for the South.
    d.   support for the South in France and Spain and for the North in Britain and Germany.

11.   The South's weapon of "King Cotton" failed to draw Britain into the war on the side of the Confederacy because

    a.   the British discovered that they could substitute flax and wool for cotton.
    b.   the British were able to grow sufficient cotton in their own land.
    c.   the British found sufficient cotton from previous stockpiles and from other sources like Egypt and India.
    d.   the threat of war with France distracted British attention for several years.

12.   The success of the Confederate raider *Alabama* highlighted the issue of

    a.   Northern inferiority on the high seas.
    b.   Britain's un-neutral policy of allowing Confederate ships to be built in its naval yards.
    c.   the British navy's ability to break the Union blockade of Southern ports.
    d.   the superiority of Confederate ironclad ships over the Union's wooden vessels.

13.   Lincoln argued that his assertion of executive power and suspension of certain civil liberties was justified because

    a.   it was necessary to set aside small provisions of the Constitution in order to save the Union.
    b.   the South had committed even larger violations of the Constitution.
    c.   during wartime a president has unlimited power over the civilian population.
    d.   he had indicated that he would take such steps during his campaign for the presidency.

14.   Many of the new millionaires who emerged in the North during the Civil War

    a.   committed their personal fortunes to the Union cause.
    b.   made their fortunes by providing poorly made "shoddy" goods to the Union armies.
    c.   made their highest profits by selling captured cotton to British textile manufacturers.
    d.   earned public distrust by secretly advocating a negotiated settlement with the Confederacy.

15.   Women made particular advances during the Civil War by

    a.   advocating the right to vote for both African Americans and women.
    b.   entering industrial employment and providing medical aid for soldiers on both sides.
    c.   pushing for women to take up noncombatant roles in the military.
    d.   upholding the feminine ideals of peace and reconciliation.

C. Identification

Supply the correct identification for each numbered description.

1. _____   Four Border States where secession failed but slavery still survived

   _____

   _____

   _____

2. _____   The effective Northern effort to strangle the Southern economy and de-throne "King Cotton"

3. _____   A ship from which two Confederate diplomats were removed, creating a major crisis between London and Washington

4. _____   Vessel built in Britain that wreaked havoc on Northern shipping until it was finally sunk in 1864

5. _____   Ironclad warships that were kept out of Confederate hands by Minister Adams's stern protests to the British government

6. _____   Provision established by Congress in 1863, after volunteers ran out, that provoked violent protests in Northern cities

7. _____   Slippery Northern men who collected fees for enlisting in the Union army and then deserted

8. _____   Medical occupation that gained new status and employment opportunities because of women's Civil War service

9. _____   Financial arrangement set up by the federal government to sell government bonds and stabilize the currency

10. _____   Scornful term for Northern manufacturers who made quick fortunes out of selling cheaply made shoes and other inadequate goods to the U.S. Army

11. _____   Civil liberty that was suspended by Lincoln in defiance of the Constitution and the Supreme Court's chief justice

12. _____   Organization developed to provide medical supplies and assistance to Union armies in the field

D. Matching People, Places, and Events

Match the person, place, or event in the left column with the proper description in the right column by inserting the correct letter on the blank line.

1. ___   Napoleon III

2. ___   Charles Francis Adams

3. ___   Canada

4. ___   Maximilian

5. ___   New York City

6. ___   Britain

7. ___   Abraham Lincoln

a.   American envoy whose shrewd diplomacy helped keep Britain neutral during the Civil War

b.   An Old World aristocrat, manipulated as a puppet in Mexico, who was shot when his puppet-master deserted him

c.   An inexperienced leader in war but a genius at inspiring and directing his nation's cause

8. ___ Jefferson Davis

9. ___ Elizabeth Blackwell

10. ___ Clara Barton

d. Leader whose conflict with states' rights advocates and rigid personality harmed his ability to mobilize and direct his nation's war effort

e. Nation whose upper classes hoped for a Confederate victory, while its working classes sympathized with the antislavery North

f. Slippery French dictator who ignored the Monroe Doctrine by intervening in Mexican politics

g. Site of cross-border raids and plots by Southern agents and anti-British Americans during the Civil War

h. Helped transform nursing into a respected profession during the Civil War

i. Scene of the largest Northern antidraft riot in 1863

j. First woman physician, organizer of the United States Sanitary Commission

E. Putting Things in Order

Put the following events in correct order by numbering them from 1 to 5.

1. ___ Enactment of military draft causes major riot in New York City.

2. ___ Napoleon III's puppet emperor is removed from power in Mexico under threat of American intervention.

3. ___ The firing on Fort Sumter unifies the North and leads to Lincoln's call for troops.

4. ___ The *Alabama* escapes from a British port and begins wreaking havoc on Northern shipping.

5. ___ Charles Francis Adams's successful diplomacy prevents the Confederacy from obtaining two Laird ram warships.

F. Matching Cause and Effect

Match the historical cause in the left column with the proper effect in the right column by writing the correct letter on the blank line.

Cause		Effect
1. ___ South Carolina's assault on Fort Sumter	a.	Split the South in two and opened the way for Sherman's invasion of Georgia
2. ___ Lincoln's first call for troops to suppress the "rebellion"	b.	Enabled Northern generals to wear down Southern armies,

3. ___   Lincoln's careful use of moral suasion, politics, and military force

4. ___   The large Northern human-resources advantage

5. ___   The North's naval blockade and industrial superiority

6. ___   The British aristocracy's sympathy with the South

7. ___   American minister C. F. Adams's diplomacy

8. ___   Grant's victory at Vicksburg

9. ___   The class-biased unfairness of the Civil War draft

10. ___   Lincoln's belief that the Civil War emergency required drastic action

a.   even at the cost of many lives

c.   Unified the North and made it determined to preserve the Union by military force

d.   Eventually gave the Union a crucial economic advantage over the mostly agricultural South

e.   Deterred the British and French from recognizing and aiding the Confederacy

f.   Caused four more Upper South states to secede and join the Confederacy

g.   Kept the Border States in the Union

h.   Led the British government toward actions that aided the Confederacy and angered the Union

i.   Led to riots by underprivileged Northern whites, especially Irish Americans

j.   Led to temporary infringements on civil liberties and Congress's constitutional powers

G. Developing Historical Skills

Interpreting Tables

Tables convey a great deal of data, often numerical, in concise form. Properly interpreted, they can effectively aid historical understanding.

The following questions will help you interpret some of the tables in this chapter.

1.   *Manufacturing by Sections, 1860* (p. 439).

   a.   Compare the *number* of manufacturing establishments in the South and New England. Now compare the amount of invested capital, the number of laborers, and the product value of these same two sections. What do you conclude about the character of the manufacturing establishments in the South and New England?

b.   Approximately how many laborers were employed in the average Southern manufacturing establishment? About how many in the average New England establishment? How many in the average establishment in the middle states?

2.   *Immigration to United States, 1860–1866* (p. 440).

a.   From which country did immigration decline rather sharply at the end as well as at the beginning of the Civil War?

b.   From which country did immigration rise most sharply after the end of the Civil War?

c.   From which country did the coming of the Civil War evidently cause the sharpest decline in immigration?

d.   How was immigration affected by the first year of the Civil War? How was it affected by the second year of war? By the third? How long did it take for immigration from each country to return to its prewar level?

3.   *Number of Men in Uniform at Date Given* (p. 446).

a.   In what period did the absolute difference in military manpower between the two sides increase most dramatically?

b.   What was the approximate manpower ratio of Union to Confederate forces on each of the following dates: July 1861, March 1862, January 1863, January 1865?

c.   What happened to the military manpower ratio in the last two years of the war?

PART III: APPLYING WHAT YOU HAVE LEARNED

1.   How did the Civil War change from a limited war to preserve the Union into a "total war" to abolish slavery?

2. What political factors affected Lincoln's approach to the goals and conduct of the war? Why was he a more successful political leader than Jefferson Davis?

3. Why was Lincoln's skillful handling of the Fort Sumter crisis crucial to arousing the Union's political determination to force the South to stay in the Union?

4. In the spring of 1861, would an objective observer have predicted that the Confederacy would successfully win its independence? Why or why not?

5. Why was the South's confidence in "King Cotton" misplaced? What southern economic weaknesses were exposed by the war?

6. How did careful Union diplomacy manage the Civil War crisis with Britain and end British flirtations with the Confederacy?

7. How did the North and the South each handle their economic and human resources needs? Why were the economic consequences of the war so different for the two sides?

8. What changes did the Civil War bring about in civilian society, North and South? How did it particularly affect women?

9. Some historians have called the Civil War "the Second American Revolution." What was "revolutionary" about the political, social, and economic conduct of the war?

10. Some historians have argued that the North's inherent superiority in manpower and industrial strength made its victory in the Civil War inevitable from the beginning. Would you agree or disagree? Why?

CHAPTER 21

The Furnace of Civil War, 1861–1865

PART I: REVIEWING THE CHAPTER

A. CHECKLIST OF LEARNING OBJECTIVES

After mastering this chapter, you should be able to

1. describe the failure of the North to gain its expected early victory in 1861.

2. explain the significance of Antietam and the Northern turn to a "total war" against slavery.

3. describe the role that African Americans played during the war.

4. describe the military significance of the battles of Gettysburg in the East and Vicksburg in the West.

5. describe the political struggle between Lincoln's "Union party" and the antiwar Copperheads.

6. describe the end of the war and list its final consequences.

B. GLOSSARY

To build your social science vocabulary, familiarize yourself with the following terms:

1. **intelligence** In military affairs or diplomacy, specific information about an adversary's forces, deployments, production, and so on. "He consistently but erroneously believed that the enemy outnumbered him, partly because . . . his intelligence reports were unreliable." (p. 453)

2. **reconnaissance** Operations designed specifically to observe and ferret out pertinent information about an adversary. ". . . 'Jeb' Stuart's cavalry rode completely around his army on reconnaissance." (p. 454)

3. **proclamation** An official announcement or publicly declared order. "Thus, the Emancipation Proclamation was stronger on proclamation than emancipation." (p. 459)

4. **flank** The side of an army, where it is vulnerable to attack. "Lee . . . sent 'Stonewall' Jackson to attack the Union flank." (p. 462)

5. **court-martial** A military court or a trial held in such a court under military law. "Resigning from the army to avoid a court-martial for drunkenness, he failed at various business ventures. . . ." (p. 464)

6. **garrison** A military fortress, or the troops stationed at such a fortress, usually designed for defense or occupation of a territory. "Vicksburg at length surrendered . . . , with the garrison reduced to eating mules and rats." (p. 465)

7. **morale** The condition of courage, confidence, and willingness to endure hardship. "One of his major purposes was . . . to weaken the morale of the men at the front by waging war on their homes." (p. 467)

8. **pillaging** Plundering, looting, destroying property by violence. ". . . his army . . . engaged in an orgy of pillaging." (p. 467)

9.   **tribunal** An agency or institution (sometimes but not necessarily a court) constituted to render judgments and assign punishment. "But he was convicted by a military tribunal in 1863 for treasonable utterances. . . ." (p. 469)

10. **running mate** In American politics, the candidate for the lesser of two offices when they are decided together—for example, the U.S. vice presidency. "Lincoln's running mate was ex-tailor Andrew Johnson. . . ." (p. 469)

PART II: CHECKING YOUR PROGRESS

A. True-False

Where the statement is true, circle **T**; where it is false, circle **F**.

1.   T   F   The First Battle of Bull Run was the turning point of the Civil War because it convinced the South the war would be long and difficult.

2.   T   F   The Emancipation Proclamation was more important for its political effects on the North and Europe than for actually freeing large numbers of slaves.

3.   T   F   The Union's first military breakthroughs came on the eastern front in Maryland and Virginia.

4.   T   F   The Battle of Antietam was a turning point of the war because it prevented British and French recognition of the Confederacy.

5.   T   F   Lincoln's decision to make the war a fight against slavery was widely popular in the North.

6.   T   F   The use of black soldiers in the Union Army proved militarily ineffective.

7.   T   F   Lee's invasion of Pennsylvania in 1863 was intended to encourage the Northern peace movement and promote foreign intervention.

8.   T   F   The Northern victories at Vicksburg and Gettysburg effectively spelled doom for the Confederacy.

9.   T   F   In the final year of the conflict, Grant and Sherman waged a "total war" that was immensely destructive of Southern lives and property.

10. T   F   The Northern Democrats were deeply divided between those who backed the war and those who favored peace negotiations with the South.

11. T   F   The formation of a temporary "Union party" in 1864 was a device used by Lincoln to gain the support of prowar Democrats.

12. T   F   Ulysses Grant's brutal destruction of Union soldiers in frontal military assaults contrasted with Robert E. Lee's care in expending Confederate soldiers' lives through skillful defensive tactics.

13. T   F   The South's last hope was that the victory of a "Peace Democrat" in the election of 1864 would enable it to achieve its political goal of independence.

14. T   F   Most Southerners eventually came to see Lincoln's assassination as a tragedy for them.

15. T   F   The Civil War failed to settle the central issues of slavery, states' rights, and secession that caused the war.

B. Multiple Choice

Select the best answer and circle the corresponding letter.

1. One effect of the first Battle of Bull Run was

    a.   to convince the North that victory would not be difficult.
    b.   to increase the South's already dangerous overconfidence.
    c.   to demonstrate the superiority of Southern volunteer soldiers over Northern draftees.
    d.   to cause a wave of new Southern enlistments in the army.

2. The primary weakness of General George McClellan as a military commander was

    a.   his inability to gain the support of his troops.
    b.   his tendency to rush into battle with inadequate plans and preparation.
    c.   his lack of confidence in his own abilities.
    d.   his excessive caution and reluctance to use his troops in battle.

3. After the unsuccessful Peninsula Campaign, Lincoln and the Union turned to

    a.   a new strategy based on "total war" against the Confederacy.
    b.   a new strategy based on an invasion through the mountains of western Virginia and Tennessee.
    c.   a pattern of defensive warfare designed to protect Washington, D.C.
    d.   a reliance on the navy rather than the army to win the war.

4. The Union blockade of Confederate ports was

    a.   initially leaky but eventually effective.
    b.   challenged by the powerful navies of Britain and France.
    c.   immediately effective in capturing Confederate blockade-running ships.
    d.   largely ineffective in shutting off the sale of Confederate cotton in Europe.

5. Antietam was one of the crucial battles of the Civil War because

    a.   it ended any possibility of Confederate invasion of the North.
    b.   it was the last chance for the Confederates to win a major battle.
    c.   it fundamentally undermined Confederate morale.
    d.   it prevented British and French recognition of the Confederacy.

6. Officially, the Emancipation Proclamation freed only

    a.   slaves who had fled their masters and joined the Union Army.
    b.   slaves under control of the rebellious Confederate states.
    c.   slaves in the Border States and in areas under Union Army control.
    d.   slaves in Washington, D.C.

7. The political effects of the Emancipation Proclamation were

    a.   to bolster public support for the war and the Republican party.
    b.   to strengthen the North's moral cause but weaken the Lincoln administration in the Border States and parts of the North.
    c.   to turn the Democratic party from support of the war toward favoring recognition of the Confederacy.
    d.   to weaken support for the Union among British and French public opinion.

8. The thousands of black soldiers in the Union Army

    a.   added a powerful new weapon to the antislavery dimension of the Union cause.
    b.   were prevented from participating in combat.

    c.   were enlisted primarily to compensate for the military advantage that the South enjoyed because of slavery.

    d.   saw action in the very first days of the war.

9. Lee's goals in invading the North in the summer of 1863 were

   a. to capture major Northern cities like Philadelphia and Pittsburgh.

   b. to deflect attention from "Stonewall" Jackson's movements against Washington.

   c. to strengthen the Northern peace movement and encourage foreign intervention in the war.

   d. to cut off Northern supply lines and damage the Union's economic foundations.

10. Grant's capture of Vicksburg was especially important because

    a. it quelled Northern peace agitation and cut off the Confederate trade route across the Mississippi.

    b. it ended the threat of a Confederate invasion of southern Illinois and Indiana.

    c. it blocked the French army in Mexico from moving to aid the Confederacy.

    d. it destroyed Southern naval power.

11. The "Copperheads" were

    a. Northern Democrats who opposed the Union war effort.

    b. Republicans who opposed the Lincoln administration.

    c. Democrats who backed the Union but opposed a war against slavery.

    d. radical Republicans who advocated a war to destroy slavery and punish the South.

12. Andrew Johnson, Lincoln's vice presidential running mate in 1864, was

    a. a Copperhead.

    b. a War Democrat.

    c. a conservative Republican.

    d. a radical Republican.

13. Lincoln's election victory in 1864 was sealed by Union military successes at

    a. Gettysburg, Antietam, and Vicksburg.

    b. The Wilderness, Lookout Mountain, and Appomattox.

    c. Bull Run, the Peninsula, and Fredericksburg.

    d. Mobile, Atlanta, and the Shenandoah Valley.

14. Sherman's march "from Atlanta to the sea" was especially notable for

    a. its tactical brilliance against Confederate cavalry forces.

    b. its effective use of public relations to turn Southern sympathies against the Confederacy.

    c. its brutal use of "total war" tactics of destruction and pillaging against Southern civilian populations.

    d. its impact in inspiring Northern public opinion to turn against slavery.

15. As the Democratic party nominee in 1864, General George McClellan

    a. denounced Lincoln as a traitor and called for an immediate end to the war.

    b. repudiated the Copperhead platform that called for a negotiated settlement with the Confederacy.

    c. indicated that if elected president he would take personal command of all Union armies.

    d. called for waging a "total war" against the civilian population in the South.

C. Identification

Supply the correct identification for each numbered description.

1. _____ First major battle of the Civil War, in which untrained Northern troops and civilian picnickers fled back to Washington

2. _____ McClellan's disastrously unsuccessful attempt to end the war quickly by a back-door conquest of Richmond

3. _____ Key battle of 1862 that forestalled European intervention to aid the Confederacy and led to the Emancipation Proclamation

4. _____ Document that proclaimed a war against slavery and guaranteed a fight to the finish

5. _____ General U.S. Grant's nickname, taken from his military demand to the enemy at Fort Donelson and elsewhere

6. _____ Crucial Confederate fortress on the Mississippi whose fall to Grant in 1863 cut the South in two

7. _____ Pennsylvania battle that ended Lee's last hopes of achieving victory through an invasion of the North

8. _____ Mississippi site where black soldiers were massacred after their surrender

9. _____ Northern Democrats who opposed the Civil War and sympathized with the South

10. _____ Edward Everett Hale's story of treason and banishment, inspired by the wartime banishing of Copperhead Clement Vallandigham

11. _____ Georgia city captured and burned by Sherman just before the election of 1864

12. _____ The temporary 1864 coalition of Republicans and War Democrats that backed Lincoln's re-election

13. _____ Washington site where Lincoln was assassinated by Booth on April 14, 1865

14. _____ Virginia site where Lee surrendered to Grant in April 1865

15. _____ Romantic name given to the Southern fight for independence, indicating nobility despite defeat

D. Matching People, Places, and Events

Match the person, place, or event in the left column with the proper description in the right column by inserting the correct letter on the blank line.

1. ___ Bull Run

2. ___ George McClellan

3. ___ Robert E. Lee

4. ___ Antietam

5. ___ "Stonewall" Jackson

6. ___ George Pickett

7. ___ Ulysses S. Grant

8. ___ Gettysburg

9. ___ Vicksburg

10. ___ William T. Sherman

11. ___ Clement Vallandigham

12. ___ Salmon P. Chase

13. ___ The Wilderness

14. ___ Andrew Johnson

15. ___ John Wilkes Booth

a. Daring Southern commander killed at the Battle of Chancellorsville

b. Southern officer whose failed charge at Gettysburg marked "the high water mark of the Confederacy"

c. Ruthless Northern general who waged a march through Georgia

d. Fortress whose capture split the Confederacy in two

e. Site where Lee's last major invasion of the North was turned back

f. Gentlemanly top commander of the Confederate army

g. Site of one of Grant's bloody battles with the Confederates near Richmond in 1864

h. Crucial battle in Maryland that staved off European recognition of the Confederacy

i. Ambitious secretary of the treasury who wanted to replace Lincoln as president in 1864

j. Fanatical actor whose act of violence actually harmed the South

k. Union commander who first made his mark with victories in the West

l. Southern War Democrat who ran as Lincoln's "Union party" vice-presidential candidate in 1864

m. Notorious Copperhead, convicted of treason, who ran for governor of Ohio while exiled to Canada

n. Union general who repudiated his party's Copperhead platform and polled 45 percent of the popular vote in 1864

o. Site of Union defeat in very early battle of the war

E. Putting Things in Order

Put the following events in correct order by numbering them from 1 to 5.

1. _____   Within one week, two decisive battles in Mississippi and Pennsylvania almost ensure the Confederacy's eventual defeat.

2. _____   Defeat in a battle near Washington, D.C., ends Union military complacency.

3. _____   A militarily indecisive battle in Maryland enables Lincoln to declare that the Civil War has become a war on slavery.

4. _____   The Civil War ends with the defeated army granted generous terms of surrender.

5. _____   In both Georgia and Virginia, determined Northern generals wage bloody and destructive "total war" against a weakened but still-resisting South.

F. Matching Cause and Effect

Match the historical cause in the left column with the proper effect in the right column by writing the correct letter on the blank line.

Cause	**Effect**
1. ___ Political dissent by Copperheads and jealous Republicans	a. Enabled Lincoln to issue the Emancipation Proclamation and blocked British and French intervention
2. ___ A series of Union military victories in late 1864	
3. ___ The assassination of Lincoln	b. Split the South in two and opened the way for Sherman's invasion of Georgia
4. ___ Grant's Tennessee and Mississippi River campaigns	c. Deprived the nation of experienced leadership during Reconstruction
5. ___ The Battle of Bull Run	d. Made it difficult for Lincoln to prosecute the war effectively
6. ___ The Battle of Antietam	
7. ___ The Battle of Gettysburg	e. Helped lead to the enlistment of black fighting men in the Union Army
8. ___ Grant's final brutal campaign in Virginia	f. Ended the South's effort to win the war by aggressive invasion
9. ___ The Emancipation Proclamation	g. Guaranteed that the South would fight to the end to try to save slavery
10. ___ The growing Union manpower shortage in 1863	h. Forced Lee to surrender at Appomattox
	i. Led some southerners to believe they would win an easy victory
	j. Ensured Lincoln's reelection and ended the South's last hope of achieving independence by political means

G. Developing Historical Skills

Interpreting Painting

Paintings may depict historical subjects and in the process convey information about an artist's interpretation of an event, a problem, or a whole society. Answer these questions about the Winslow Homer painting *Prisoners from the Front.* (p. 474)

1.   Study the clothing carefully. Who is in what kind of uniform, and who is not? What is the artist suggesting about the economic and military condition of the two sides? What is suggested about the condition of civilians in the two sections?

2.   Describe the posture and facial expressions of the five main figures. What kind of attitude does each suggest?

3.   Look at the weapons in the painting, and at the distance between the Northern officer and the Confederates. What does Homer seem to be suggesting about the relations between the sections after the war?

H. Map Mastery

Map Discrimination

Using the maps and charts in Chapter 21, answer the following questions.

1.   *Main Thrusts, 1861–1865*: Which two states of the Southeast saw little of the major fighting of the Civil War?

2.   *Emancipation in the South*: In which four states were the slaves *all* freed by state action—without any federal involvement?

3.   *Emancipation in the South*: Which two states kept slavery until it was finally abolished by the Thirteenth Amendment to the Constitution?

4.   *The Mississippi River and Tennessee, 1862–1863*: On what three rivers were the major Confederate strategic points that Grant successfully assaulted in 1862–1863?

5. *Sherman's March, 1864–1865*: What major secessionist South Carolina city was *not* in the direct path of Sherman's army in 1864–1865?

6. *Grant's Virginia Campaign, 1864–1865*: What major battle of Grant's final campaign was fought very close to the Confederate capital city?

Map Challenge

Using the maps in this chapter, write a brief essay explaining Union military strategy in the Civil War.

PART III: APPLYING WHAT YOU HAVE LEARNED

1. How did the military stalemate of 1861–1862 affect both sides in the Civil War?

2. What were the primary military strategies of each side, and how did each side attempt to carry them out?

3. Why was Lincoln so slow to declare the Civil War as a fight against slavery? Was he wise to move slowly, or could an early Emancipation Proclamation have undermined the Union cause?

4. What role did African Americans, both slave and free, play in the Civil War?

5. What were the key military and political turning points of the war? Why did the South hold onto hopes of winning its goals as late as 1864 and even early 1865?

6. What were the causes and consequences of Sherman's and Grant's turn toward "total war" in the conquest of the South? In what ways is it fair to call the Civil War "the first modern war"?

7. Did the South's best chances for victory lie on the battlefield, or in the hopes of political disillusionment in the North? Was there any chance that Confederate independence could have been won as late as the fall of 1864?

8. Were the costs of the Civil War worth the results to the nation as a whole? What issues were settled by the war, and what new problems were created?

CHAPTER 22

The Ordeal of Reconstruction, 1865–1877

PART I: REVIEWING THE CHAPTER

A. CHECKLIST OF LEARNING OBJECTIVES

After mastering this chapter, you should be able to

1. define the major problems facing the South and the nation after the Civil War.

2. describe the responses of both whites and African Americans to the end of slavery.

3. analyze the differences between the presidential and congressional approaches to Reconstruction.

4. explain how the blunders of President Johnson and the white South opened the door to the radical Reconstruction policies of congressional Republicans.

5. describe the actual effects of congressional Reconstruction in the South.

6. indicate how militant white opposition gradually undermined the Republican attempt to empower Southern blacks.

7. explain why the radical Republicans impeached Johnson but failed to convict him.

8. explain the legacy of Reconstruction, and assess its successes and failures.

B. GLOSSARY

To build your social science vocabulary, familiarize yourself with the following terms:

1. **treason** The crime of betrayal of one's country, involving some overt act violating an oath of allegiance or providing illegal aid to a foreign state. In the United States, treason is the only crime specified in the Constitution. "What should be done with the captured Confederate ringleaders, all of whom were liable to charges of treason?" (p. 477)

2. **civil disabilities** Legally imposed restrictions of a person's civil rights or liberties. "But Congress did not remove all remaining civil disabilities until thirty years later. . . ." (p. 478)

3. **legalistically** In accord with the exact letter of the law, sometimes with the intention of thwarting its broad intent. "Some planters resisted emancipation more legalistically. . . ." (p. 479)

4. **mutual aid societies** Nonprofit organizations designed to provide their members with financial and social benefits, often including medical aid, life insurance, funeral costs, and disaster relief. "These churches . . . gave rise to other benevolent, fraternal, and mutual aid societies." (p. 480)

5. **confiscation (confiscated)** Legal government seizure of private property without compensation. ". . . the bureau was authorized to settle former slaves on forty-acre tracts confiscated from the Confederates. . . ." (p. 481)

6. **pocket veto** The presidential act of blocking a Congressionally passed law not by direct veto but by simply refusing to sign it at the end of a session. (A president can pocket-veto a bill within ten days of a session's end or after.) "Lincoln 'pocket-vetoed' this bill by refusing to sign it after Congress had adjourned." (p. 483)

7. **lease** To enter into a contract by which one party gives another use of land, buildings, or other property for a fixed time and fee. "... some [codes] even barred blacks from renting or leasing land." (p. 484)

8. **chain gang** A group of prisoners chained together while engaged in forced labor. "A black could be punished for 'idleness' by being sentenced to work on a chain gang." (p. 484)

9. **sharecrop** An agricultural system in which a tenant receives land, tools, and seed on credit and pledges in return a share of the crop to the creditor. "... former slaves slipped into the status of sharecropper farmers...." (p. 484)

10. **peonage** A system in which debtors are held in servitude, to labor for their creditors. "Luckless sharecroppers gradually sank into a morass of virtual peonage...." (p. 484)

11. **scalawag** A white Southerner who supported Republican Reconstruction after the Civil War. "The so-called scalawags were Southerners, often former Unionists and Whigs." (p. 492)

12. **carpetbagger** A Northern politician who came south to exploit the unsettled conditions after the Civil War; hence, any politician who relocates for political advantage. "The carpet-baggers, on the other hand, were supposedly sleazy Northerners...." (p. 492)

13. **felony** A major crime for which severe penalties are exacted under the law. "The crimes of the Reconstruction governments were no more outrageous than the scams and felonies being perpetrated in the North at the same time...." (p. 493)

14. **terror (terrorist)** Using violence or the threat of violence in order to create intense fear in the attempt to promote some political policy or objectives. "Such tomfoolery and terror proved partially effective." (p. 493)

15. **president pro tempore** In the United States Senate, the officer who presides in the absence of the vice president. "Under existing law, the president pro tempore of the Senate ... would then become president." (p. 495)

PART II: CHECKING YOUR PROGRESS

A. True-False

Where the statement is true, circle **T**; where it is false, circle **F**.

1. T F The South was economically devastated by the Civil War.

2. T F Military defeat in the Civil War brought white Southerners to accept the reality of Northern political domination.

3. T F The newly freed slaves often used their liberty to travel or seek lost loved ones.

4. T F The focus of black community life after emancipation became the black church.

5. T F Lincoln's "10 percent" Reconstruction plan was designed to return the Southern states to the Union quickly and with few restrictions.

6. T F Southerners at first feared Andrew Johnson because he had been one of the few elite planters who backed Lincoln.

7. T F The cause of black education was greatly advanced by Northern white female teachers who came South after the Civil War.

8. T F The enactment of the Black Codes in the south strengthened those who supported a moderate approach to Reconstruction.

9.   T   F   Congressional Republicans demanded that the Southern states ratify the Fourteenth Amendment in order to be readmitted to the Union.

10.   T   F   Radical Republicans succeeded in their goal of redistributing land to the former slaves.

11.   T   F   During Reconstruction, blacks controlled most of the Southern state legislatures.

12.   T   F   The Republican Reconstruction legislature enacted educational and other reforms in Southern state government.

13.   T   F   The Ku Klux Klan was organized primarily because of white southerners' resentment of growing interracial marriage and corruption among radical black state legislators.

14.   T   F   Johnson's impeachment was essentially an act of political vindictiveness by radical Republicans.

15.   T   F   The moderate Republican plan for Reconstruction might have succeeded if the Ku Klux Klan had been suppressed.

B. Multiple Choice

Select the best answer and circle the corresponding letter.

1. After emancipation, many blacks traveled in order to
   a. return to Africa or the West Indies.
   b. seek a better life in Northern cities.
   c. find lost family members or seek new economic opportunities.
   d. track down and punish cruel overseers.

2. The Freedmen's Bureau was originally established to provide
   a. land and supplies for black farmers.
   b. labor registration.
   c. food, clothes, and education for emancipated slaves.
   d. political training in citizenship for black voters.

3. Lincoln's original plan for Reconstruction in 1863 was that a state could be re-integrated into the Union when
   a. it repealed its original secession act and took its soldiers out of the Confederate Army.
   b. 10 percent of its voters took an oath of allegiance to the Union and pledged to abide by emancipation.
   c. it formally adopted a plan guaranteeing black political and economic rights.
   d. it ratified the Fourteenth and Fifteenth Amendments to the Constitution.

4. The Black Codes passed by many of the Southern state governments in 1865 aimed to
   a. provide economic assistance to get former slaves started as sharecroppers.
   b. ensure a stable and subservient labor force under white control.
   c. permit blacks to vote if they met certain educational or economic standards.
   d. gradually force blacks to leave the South.

5. The congressional elections of 1866 resulted in
   a. a victory for Johnson and his pro-Southern Reconstruction plan.
   b. a further political stalemate between the Republicans in Congress and Johnson.
   c. a decisive defeat for Johnson and a veto-proof Republican Congress.
   d. a gain for Northern Democrats and their moderate compromise plan for Reconstruction.

6. In contrast to radical Republicans, moderate Republicans generally
   a. favored states' rights and opposed direct federal involvement in individuals' lives.
   b. favored the use of federal power to alter the Southern economic system.
   c. favored emancipation but opposed the Fourteenth Amendment.

    d.   favored returning the Southern states to the Union without significant Reconstruction.

7.   Besides putting the South under the rule of federal soldiers, the Military Reconstruction Act of 1867 required that

    a.   Southern states give blacks the vote as a condition of readmittance to the Union.
    b.   blacks and carpetbaggers be given control of Southern legislatures.
    c.   former slaves be given land and education at federal expense.
    d.   former Confederate officials and military officers be tried for treason.

8.   The Fourteenth amendment provided for

    a.   an end to slavery.
    b.   permanent disfranchisement of all Confederate officials.
    c.   full citizenship and civil rights for former slaves.
    d.   voting rights for women.

9.   The Fifteenth Amendment provided for

    a.   readmitting Southern states to the Union.
    b.   full citizenship and civil rights for former slaves.
    c.   voting rights for former slaves.
    d.   voting rights for women.

10.   Women's-rights leaders opposed the Fourteenth and Fifteenth Amendments because

    a.   they objected to racial integration in the women's movement.
    b.   the amendments granted citizenship and voting rights to black and white men but not to women.
    c.   they favored passage of the Equal Rights Amendment first.
    d.   most of them were Democrats who would be hurt by the amendments.

11.   The right to vote encouraged southern black men to

    a.   form a third political party as an alternative to the Democrats and Republicans.
    b.   seek an apology and reparations for slavery.
    c.   organize the Union League as a vehicle for political empowerment and self-defense.
    d.   organize large-scale migrations out of the South to the West.

12.   The radical Reconstruction regimes in the Southern states

    a.   took away white Southerners' civil rights and voting rights.
    b.   consisted almost entirely of blacks.
    c.   included white Northerners, white Southerners, and blacks.
    d.   eliminated the public education systems in most Southern states.

13.   Most of the Northern "carpetbaggers" were actually

    a.   former Union soldiers, businessmen, or professionals.
    b.   undercover agents of the federal government.
    c.   former Southern Whigs and Unionists who had opposed the Confederacy.
    d.   Northern teachers and missionaries who wanted to aid the freedmen.

14.   The radical Republicans' impeachment of President Andrew Johnson resulted in

    a.   Johnson's acceptance of the radicals' Reconstruction plan.
    b.   a failure to convict and remove Johnson by a margin of only one vote.
    c.   Johnson's conviction on the charge of violating the Tenure of Office Act.
    d.   Johnson's resignation and appointment of Ulysses Grant as his successor.

15.   The skeptical public finally accepted Seward's purchase of Alaska because

    a.   there were rumors of extensive oil deposits in the territory.
    b.   it was considered strategically vital to American defense.
    c.   it would provide a new frontier safety valve after the settling of the West.
    d.   Russia had been the only great power friendly to the Union during the Civil War.

C. Identification

Supply the correct identification for each numbered description.

1. _____ Common term for the blacks newly liberated from slavery

2. _____ Federal agency that greatly assisted blacks educationally but failed in other aid efforts

3. _____ The largest African American denomination (church) after slavery

4. _____ Lincoln's 1863 program for a rapid Reconstruction of the South

5. _____ The constitutional amendment freeing all slaves

6. _____ The harsh Southern state laws of 1865 that limited black rights and imposed restrictions to ensure a stable black labor supply

7. _____ The constitutional amendment granting civil rights to freed slaves and barring former Confederates from office

8. _____ Republican Reconstructionists who favored a more rapid restoration of Southern state governments and opposed radical plans for drastic economic transformation of the South

9. _____ Republican Reconstructionists who favored keeping the South out of the federal government until a complete social and economic revolution was accomplished in the region

10. _____ The black political organization that promoted self-help and defense of political rights

11. _____ Supreme Court ruling that military tribunals could not try civilians when the civil courts were open

12. _____ Derogatory term for white Southerners who cooperated with the Republican Reconstruction governments

13. _____ Derogatory term for Northerners who came to the South during Reconstruction and sometimes took part in Republican state governments

14. _____ Constitutional amendment guaranteeing blacks the right to vote

15. _____ "Seward's Folly," acquired in 1867 from Russia

D. Matching People, Places, and Events

Match the person, place, or event in the left column with the proper description in the right column by inserting the correct letter on the blank line.

1. ___ Exodusters
2. ___ Oliver O. Howard
3. ___ Andrew Johnson
4. ___ Abraham Lincoln
5. ___ Civil Rights Bill of 1866
6. ___ Charles Sumner
7. ___ Thaddeus Stevens

a. A constitutionally questionable law whose violation by President Johnson formed the basis for his impeachment

b. The first congressional attempt to guarantee black rights in the South, passed over Johnson's veto

c. Born a poor white southerner, he became the white South's champion against radical Reconstruction

8. ___   Military Reconstruction Act of 1867

9. ___   Hiram Revels

10. ___   Ku Klux Klan

11. ___   Force Acts of 1870 and 1871

12. ___   Tenure of Office Act

13. ___   Union League

14. ___   Benjamin Wade

15. ___   William Seward

d.   Secretary of state who arranged an initially unpopular but valuable land deal in 1867

e.   Laws designed to stamp out Ku Klux Klan terrorism in the South

f.   Black Republican senator from Mississippi during Reconstruction

g.   Secret organization that intimidated blacks and worked to restore white supremacy

h.   Blacks who left the South for Kansas and elsewhere during Reconstruction

i.   Congressional law that imposed military rule on the South and demanded harsh conditions for readmission of the seceded states

j.   Beaten in the Senate chamber before the Civil War, he became the leader of Senate Republican radicals during Reconstruction

k.   Pro-black general who led an agency that tried to assist the freedmen

l.   Leading Black political organization during Reconstruction

m.   Author of the moderate "10 percent" Reconstruction plan that ran into congressional opposition

n.   The president pro tempore of the Senate who hoped to become president of the United States after Johnson's impeachment conviction

o.   Leader of radical Republicans in the House of Representatives

E. Putting Things in Order

Put the following events in correct order by numbering them from 1 to 5.

1. _____   Constitution is amended to guarantee former slaves the right to vote.

2. _____   Lincoln announces a plan to rapidly restore southern states to the Union.

3. _____   Northern troops are finally withdrawn from the South, and Southern state governments are re-constituted without federal constraint.

4. _____   An unpopular antiradical president escapes conviction and removal from office by one vote.

5. _____   Johnson's attempt to restore the South to the Union is overturned because of congressional hostility to ex-Confederates and southern passage of the Black Codes.

F. Matching Cause and Effect

Match the historical cause in the left column with the proper effect in the right column by writing the correct letter on the blank line.

Cause

1. ___ The South's military defeat in the Civil War

2. ___ The Freedmen's Bureau

3. ___ The Black Codes of 1865

4. ___ The election of ex-Confederates to Congress in 1865

5. ___ Johnson's "swing around the circle" in the election of 1866

6. ___ Military Reconstruction and the Fourteenth and Fifteenth Amendments

7. ___ The "radical" Southern state Reconstruction governments

8. ___ The Ku Klux Klan

9. ___ The radical Republicans' hatred of Johnson

10. ___ The whole Reconstruction era

Effect

a. Provoked a politically motivated trial to remove the president from office

b. Intimidated black voters and tried to keep blacks "in their place"

c. Prompted Republicans to refuse to seat Southern delegations in Congress

d. Destroyed the southern economy but strengthened Southern hatred of "yankees"

e. Successfully educated former slaves but failed to provide much other assistance to them

f. Forced all the Southern states to establish governments that upheld black voting and other civil rights

g. Embittered white Southerners while doing little to really help blacks

h. Engaged in some corruption but also enacted many valuable social reforms

i. Weakened support for mild Reconstruction policies and helped elect overwhelming Republican majorities to Congress

j. Imposed slaverylike restrictions on blacks and angered the North

G. Developing Historical Skills

Interpreting Photographs and Drawings

Answer the following questions about the photographs and drawings in this chapter.

1. *The Faculty of a Freedmen's Bureau School near Norfolk, Virginia* (p. 481)

   What is the ratio of black to white teachers on the freedmen's school staff? Who appears to be the principal of the school? Where are the black teachers positioned in the photograph? Might this suggest anything about the relations between white and black teachers in the school?

2. *A Family of Sharecroppers at the End of the Civil War* (photograph, p. 485)

   What physical details suggest the poverty of these former slaves? How would you characterize the attitudes of the people in the photograph?

3. *Freedmen Voting, Richmond, Virginia, 1871* (drawing, p. 482)

   What appears to be the economic status of the new black voters portrayed here? How does their condition differ from that of the voting officials, black and white? What does the drawing suggest about the power of the newly enfranchised freedmen?

PART III: APPLYING WHAT YOU HAVE LEARNED

1. What were the major problems facing the South and the nation after the Civil War? How did Reconstruction address them, or fail to do so?

2. How did freed blacks react to the end of slavery? How did both Southern and Northern whites react?

3. How did the white South's intransigence and President Johnson's political bungling open the way for the congressional Republican program of military Reconstruction?

4. What was the purpose of congressional Reconstruction, and what were its actual effects in the South?

5. What did the attempt at black political empowerment achieve? Why did it finally fail? Could it have succeeded with a stronger Northern political will behind it?

6. How did African Americans take advantage of the political, economic, and social opportunities of Reconstruction, despite their limitations?

7. How effective was the Ku Klux Klan and other white resistance movements in undermining the interracial governments even before the collapse of Reconstruction in 1877?

8. Was the North in general, and the Republican Party in particular, ever really committed to transforming the political, economic, and racial conditions of the South?

9. Why did Reconstruction apparently fail so badly? Was the failure primarily one of immediate political circumstances, or was it more deeply rooted in the history of American sectional and race relations?

10. What was the greatest success of Reconstruction? Would you agree with historians who argue that even if Reconstruction failed at the time, it laid the foundations for the later successes of the civil rights movement?

Answer Key to Volume 1 of the Guidebook

CHAPTER 1

II. A.

1. True

2. False. They walked across a land bridge.

3. False. Their economic foundation was corn (maize).

4. True

5. True

6. False. The Norse (Vikings) had come to North America about A.D. 1000.

7. True

8. False. African slavery had developed before Columbus's voyage.

9. False. He believed that he had encountered the East Indies off the coast of Asia.

10. False. The greatest effect was to decrease the population through disease and warfare.

11. True

12. False. They interacted and intermarried with the native peoples.

13. False. It was settled by Spanish colonists from the South.

14. True

15. True

II. B.

1. a

2. b

3. d

4. a

5. d

6. c

7. c

8. c

9. b

10. b

11. c

12. b

13. b

14. a

15. d

II. C.

1. Great Ice Age

2. corn (maize)

3. Cahokia

4. Portugal

5. Mali

6. Indies

7. horse

8. smallpox, malaria, yellow fever (any one)

9. syphilis

10. Treaty of Tordesillas

11. Tenochtitlán

12. *mestizo*

13. Popé's Rebellion

14. Pueblos

15. Franciscans

II. D.

1. D

2. J

3. L

4. E

5. H

6. A

7. I

8. B

9. C

10. F

11. G

12. K

II. E.

3

2

1

5

4

II. F.

1. D
2. G
3. B
4. J
5. F
6. I
7. A
8. H
9. C
10. E

II. G.

1. Appalachian and Rocky Mountains
2. The melting and retreat of the glaciers *after* the Great Ice Age
3. The melting glaciers raised sea levels, covering the land bridge to Asia.
4. From northwest to south and east

II. H.

1. The founding of Virginia and the end of World War II.

2. c

3. Southwest: Mohave, Yuma, Pima, Papago, Navajo, Hopi, Zuñi, Pueblo (any five)

   Great Plains: Cree, Crow, Mandan, Sioux, Arikara, Pawnee, Arapaho, Iowa, Cheyenne, Missouri, Kansa, Osage, Kiowa, Comanche, Apache, Waco (any five)

   Northeast: Ojibwa, Sauk, Fox, Kickapoo, Illinois, Miami, Potawatomi, Huron, Erie, Iroquois, Massachuset, Pamunkey, Delaware, Susquehanna, Powhatan, Shawnee, Chickahominy, Tuscarora, Catawba (any five)

   Southeast: Wichita, Caddo, Natchez, Tuskegee, Cherokee, Creek, Chickasaw, Choctaw, Alabama, Timukua, Calusa (any five)

4. India

5. Columbus, Balboa, Cortes, Pizarro

6.
   a. Quivira and Mission San Antonio

    b.   About 50 years earlier (51)

7.

    a.   Magellan

    b.   none

CHAPTER 2

II. A.

1.   True

2.   False. The first efforts were total failures.

3.   False. It enabled England to control the Atlantic sea lanes.

4.   True

5.   False. Its original purpose was to make a profit for investors.

6.   True

7.   False. The primary factor was the introduction of disease.

8.   False. It was established for persecuted Roman Catholics.

9.   True

10.   False. The principal export was rice.

11.   False. It sold *Indian* slaves to the West Indies.

12.   True

13.   True

14.   False. It valued it primarily as a military buffer against the Spanish.

15.   True

II. B.

1.   c

2.   d

3.   b

4.   c

5.   d

6.   b

7.   a

8.   d

9.   c

10.   b

11.   c

12. d

13. c

14. a

15. c

II. C.

1. Ireland

2. Roanoke

3. Spanish Armada (Spanish OK)

4. joint-stock company

5. Anglo-Powhatan Wars

6. slave code

7. royal charter

8. indentured servants

9. Iroquois

10. squatters

11. royal colony

12. tobacco

13. South Carolina

14. rice

15. Savannah

II. D.

1. B

2. M

3. I

4. L

5. K

6. A

7. C

8. D

9. H

10. O

11. F

12. E

13. N

14. G
15. J

II. E.

1

3

4

5

2

II. F.

1. B
2. F
3. J
4. A
5. D
6. I
7. C
8. G
9. E
10. H

II. G.

1. In both cases, the English regarded the "natives" as an inferior population to be killed or shoved aside.

2. Both countries had achieved national political and religious unity under popular rulers. Both also experienced greater economic and military strength.

3. The sugar economy depended on large-scale plantations with absentee owners; tobacco could be grown by both small farmers and resident planters.

II. H.

Map Discrimination

1. Norfolk, Suffolk, Essex, Hertfordshire, Kent, Wiltshire, Somerset, Dorset, Devon (any five)

2. Chesapeake Bay

3. Georgia

4. South Carolina

5. Charlestown: South Carolina

Savannah: Georgia

Newbern: North Carolina

Jamestown: Virginia

Map Challenge

1. York River

2. Potomac River

CHAPTER 3

II. A.

1. True

2. False. Most Puritans wanted to stay within the Church of England and purify it; only extreme Puritans, the Separatists, wanted to break away.

3. False. Plymouth was smaller and much less influential than Massachusetts Bay.

4. True

5. False. They were banished for teaching religious and political heresy.

6. True

7. True

8. True

9. False. The war led to further decline in Indian population and morale.

10. False. New York was the most aristocratic and economically unequal of the middle colonies.

11. True

12. False. Penn welcomed people of diverse religious views from the beginning.

13. False. Non-Quakers pushed for harsher Indian policies.

14. True

15. False. The description applies to New England, not the middle colonies, which were socially diverse and full of political conflict.

II. B.

1. b

2. d

3. a

4. a

5. d

6. b

7. a

8. c

9. c

10. d

11. a

12. d

13. c

14. b

15. d

II. C.

1. Protestant Reformation

2. Puritans

3. Separatists

4. Mayflower Compact

5. covenant

6. dismissal of Parliament

7. fishing and shipbuilding

8. antinomianism

9. banishment or exile

10. "praying villages"

11. King Phillip's War

12. Glorious Revolution

13. Hudson

14. test oaths

15. smuggling

II. D.

1. G

2. L

3. M

4. D

5. N

6. J

7. C

8. I

9. A

10. H

11. E

12. O
13. F
14. K
15. B

II. E.

8
2
6
3
1
9
4
7
5
10

II. F.

1. D
2. F
3. J
4. A
5. I
6. H
7. C
8. G
9. E
10. B

II. G.

1. about 25%
2. about 14%

II. H.

1. Connecticut
2. New Hampshire
3. south

4. Massachusetts Bay

5. Plymouth

6. Pennsylvania, Delaware, and West Jersey (New Jersey)

CHAPTER 4

II. A.

1. False. The life expectancy of Chesapeake settlers was under fifty. The statement is true of New Englanders.

2. True

3. True

4. False. The responded by moving westward and planting more acreage.

5. True

6. True

7. False. The rebels were whites only. They attacked and killed Indians as well as wealthy whites.

8. True

9. True

10. False. Between the planters and indentured servants were two other classes: small landowning farmers and landless but free (nonindentured) laborers.

11. True

12. False. New England settlement was carried out in an orderly fashion by town fathers, who obtained charters and distributed land for settlement and town purposes.

13. True

14. False. New England's rich shipping trade was based on fishing, lumber, and other nonagricultural commodities.

15. True

II. B.

1. b

2. a

3. c

4. a

5. c

6. c

7. b

8. c

9. a

10. a

11. d

12. b

13. a

14. d

15. b

II. C.

1. families

2. disease

3. indentured servants

4. headright

5. hanging

6. Rhode Island

7. Royal African Company

8. Gullah

9. slave revolts

10. first families of Virginia (FFVs)

11. early twenties

12. town meeting

13. Half-Way Covenants

14. Salem witch trials

15. farming

II. D.

1. I

2. D

3. N

4. K

5. M

6. E

7. G

8. A

9. F

10. J

11. O

12. L

13. B

14. H

15. C

II. E.

7

8

2

4

9

10

3

6

5

1

II. F.

1. C

2. B

3. J

4. A

5. H

6. F

7. G

8. E

9. I

10. D

II. G.

1. The master seeks a guarantee of the pledged term of service; the servant seeks proper initiation into a craft.

2. The master fears damage, laziness, and moral misbehavior; the servant fears cruel treatment and dishonoring of the terms of the contract.

3. It suggests that he is very young (under the age of consent).

CHAPTER 5

II. A.

1. False. Most of the increase was natural.

2. True

3. False. The colonies were becoming less equal in the eighteenth century.

4. True

5. True

6. False. The ministry was the most honored profession, while doctors and lawyers were not well regarded.

7. True

8. False. American merchants actively pursued trade with non-English markets and evaded British trade restrictions by smuggling.

9. False. Congregationalism was more influential than Anglicanism.

10. True

11. False. Edwards and Whitefield worked to "revive" traditional Calvinist (Puritan) beliefs in new contexts.

12. True

13. True

14. False. Most colonial achievement was in theology and political theory rather than literature and the arts.

15. True

II. B.

1. b

2. d

3. c

4. c

5. b

6. b

7. b

8. c

9. d

10. b

11. a

12. b

13. c

14. a

15. d

II. C.

1.   Pennsylvania Dutch

2.   Scots-Irish

3.   Regulators (Paxton Boys not acceptable)

4.   "jayle birds"

5.   praying towns

6.   lawyers

7.   triangular trade

8.   taverns

9.   established

10. Great Awakening

11. new lights

12. colleges

13. Zenger case

14. council

15. *Poor Richard's Almanack*

II. D.

1.   D

2.   E

3.   K

4.   H

5.   N

6.   I

7.   O

8.   J

9.   A

10. G

11. M

12. B

13. F

14. L

15. C

II. E.

6

1

9

10

2

4

8

7

3

5

II. F.

1.　F

2.　C

3.　E

4.　D

5.　B

6.　J

7.　H

8.　A

9.　I

10.　G

II. G.

1.　very little or not at all

2.　cattle and grain

3.　tobacco, rice, and indigo

4.　Germans

II. H.

1.　New England

2.　Pennsylvania, Virginia, North Carolina, and South Carolina

3.　Pennsylvania

4.　South Carolina

5.　Maryland, Delaware, Virginia, and North Carolina

6.　African Americans

7.

    (1)   lesser tradesmen

    (2)   indentured servants and jailbirds

8.   all of them

9.   fifty-seven

10. five

CHAPTER 6

II. A.

1.   True

2.   False. Its economic foundation was the fur trade.

3.   True

4.   False. The colonies became directly involved in every one of Britain's wars with France.

5.   False. There were only small regular armies in the seventeenth century; most troops were militia.

6.   False. It was a temporary setback that sparked the Seven Years' War (French and Indian War).

7.   True

8.   True

9.   False. Braddock's forces were defeated by the French.

10. False. France lost all its North American possessions. It reacquired Louisiana after the American Revolution.

11. False. The war increased friction between British officers and American colonials.

12. False. Colonists often gave half-hearted support to Britain, and some even worked with the enemy.

13. True

14. True

15. True

II. B.

1.   d

2.   b

3.   b

4.   c

5.   a

6.   b

7.   a

8.   c

9. b

10. b

11. d

12. c

13. b

14. c

15. c

II. C.

1. Huguenots

2. Louis XIV

3. beaver

4. Jesuits

5. *coureurs de bois*

6. ear (Jenkins')

7. Louisbourg

8. Ohio Valley

9. Germany

10. Albany Congress

11. George Washington

12. Quebec

13. militia

14. Indians

15. Seven Years' War

II. D.

1. H

2. N

3. L

4. D

5. J

6. K

7. A

8. G

9. O

10. I

11. M

12. F

13. B

14. E

15. C

II. E.

6

8

1

2

10

4

9

5

7

3

II. F.

1. F

2. G

3. C

4. H

5. J

6. A

7. E

8. I

9. D

10. B

II. G.

1. Quebec controls the mouth of the St. Lawrence River and thus the whole Great Lakes waterway to the Atlantic; Fort Duquesne was on inland rivers that flowed away from the Atlantic.

2. Because if the French retained Louisbourg, they would still have access to the Atlantic and might block or recapture Quebec.

3. They were completely cut off from France and thus unable to get supplies or reinforcements.

II. H.

1. St. Lawrence River

2. Detroit

3. Missouri River

4. twenty-seven

5. Louisbourg

6. Allegheny and Monongahela

7. Montreal

8. Spain

9. Florida

CHAPTER 7

II. A.

1. True

2. True

3. False. European goods could be imported, but they first had to be landed and taxed in Britain.

4. True

5. True

6. False. The colonists accepted the right of Parliament to legislate, but not to tax.

7. False. The colonies did not want representation in Parliament, where they could be outvoted; they wanted to be able to decide their own taxes.

8. True

9. False. The protest was less organized and effective than the Stamp Act protest.

10. False. The Massacre caused outrage even though the British soldiers had been provoked by Boston's citizens.

11. True

12. True

13. False. The Congress only sought an end to Parliamentary taxation and a return to the earlier system, not independence.

14. False. The Americans had almost no stockpiles of weapons or supplies.

15. False. The Americans only needed to fight to a draw; the British had to conquer all of America in order to defeat the Revolution.

II. B.

1. c

2. b

3. b

4. d

5. b

6. b

7. c

8. a

9. b

10. d

11. a

12. d

13. b

14. a

15. c

II. C.

1. mercantilism

2. Navigation Laws

3. enumerated goods

4. admiralty courts

5. virtual representation

6. nonimportation agreements

7. tea

8. committees of correspondence

9. Roman Catholicism

10. Whigs

11. Hessians

12. continentals

13. The Association

14. Minute Men

15. redcoats

II. D.

1. F

2. A

3. B

4. M

5. G

6. K
7. J
8. H
9. O
10. I
11. N
12. C
13. E
14. L
15. D

II. E.

3
9
6
10
5
2
7
4
8
1

II. F.

1. H
2. G
3. B
4. J
5. D
6. I
7. E
8. A
9. C
10. F

II. G.

1. The Bostonians started the fight by attacking the redcoats, and two British soldiers were beaten and knocked down.

2. It shows a British officer with raised sword behind the firing troops, implying that the shooting took place on orders.

3. Several are shown in death throes, with much red blood flowing from heads and elsewhere.

CHAPTER 8

II. A.

1. False. He was chosen more for his personal and political abilities than for his military attributes.

2. False. After Bunker Hill the king proclaimed the colonies in rebellion and slammed the door on reconciliation.

3. True

4. False. Paine's *Common Sense* pushed them to declare independence. They were already in rebellion against the king.

5. True

6. True

7. True

8. False. Only a minority were driven out of the country, and almost none were killed.

9. False. The Patriots were strongest in New England and Virginia; Loyalists were stronger elsewhere in the colonies.

10. True

11. True

12. True

13. False. Yorktown was successful because of French naval aid.

14. False. They gained both political independence and the western territorial concessions they wanted.

15. True

II. B.

1. b

2. c

3. a

4. d

5. b

6. d

7. a

8. c

9. b

10. a

11. d

12. b

13. a

14. c

15. a

II. C.

1. Continental Congress

2. Canada

3. *Common Sense*

4. Declaration of Independence

5. Whigs

6. Loyalists

7. Anglican

8. Hudson Valley

9. armed neutrality

10. South

11. privateers

12. Whigs

13. Mississippi River

14. militia

15. Holland

II. D.

1. J

2. H

3. B

4. M

5. N

6. D

7. I

8. O

9. A

10. E

11. L

12. C

13. G

14. K

15. F

II. E.

5

2

3

6

1

4

II. F.

1. B

2. I

3. E

4. J

5. G

6. H

7. A

8. F

9. D

10. C

II. G.

1. factual: burning of Falmouth. interpretive: King George's proclamation of rebellion. meaning: All hope of reconciliation was gone, and if defeated, the patriot leaders would be hanged as traitors.

2. factual: the death of General Montgomery. interpretive: Tom Paine's *Common Sense*. meaning: Paine's *Common Sense* made the purpose of the war complete independence rather than colonial rights within the Empire.

3. factual: Lee's resolution of July 2, 1776. interpretive: Jefferson's Declaration of Independence. meaning: The purpose of Jefferson's declaration was to indict the British and present the American cause as a fight for universal rights.

II. H.

1. Montreal and Quebec

2.   from Pennsylvania to New Jersey

3.   General Howe

4.   Spain and Holland

5.   any three of the following: Charleston, Wilmington, Charlottesville, Jamestown, and Yorktown.

6.   Ohio

7.   Cahokia, Vincennes, and Kaskaskia

CHAPTER 9

II. A.

1.   True

2.   True

3.   False. Slavery was also abolished in New England.

4.   True

5.   False. The new state governments were more democratic and reflected the interests of western farmers.

6.   True

7.   False. Handling western lands was the greatest success of the national government under the Articles.

8.   True

9.   False. The ordinance set up an orderly process by which territories could become states, with a status equal to that of the original thirteen.

10.   True

11.   False. The delegates' original purpose was to amend the Articles.

12.   False. Nearly all were wealthy, but only some were slaveholders.

13.   True

14.   False. The antifederalists opposed the Constitution because they thought it gave too much power to the whole federal government and not enough to the people.

15.   True

II. B.

1.   c

2.   c

3.   c

4.   b

5.   a

6.   c

7.   b

8. a
9. b
10. c
11. b
12. d
13. d
14. c
15. b

II. C.

1. Protestant Episcopal church
2. republican motherhood
3. Constitutional Convention
4. Articles of Confederation
5. Old Northwest
6. sections
7. territory
8. Shays's Rebellion
9. large-state plan
10. small-state plan
11. Three-fifths Compromise
12. antifederalists
13. *The Federalist*
14. president
15. Bill of Rights

II. D.

1. C
2. E
3. O
4. J
5. G
6. F
7. M
8. B
9. D

10. A

11. L

12. N

13. I

14. K

15. H

II. E.

4

2

1

5

3

II. F.

1. E

2. J

3. C

4. I

5. H

6. A

7. G

8. B

9. F

10. D

II. G.

1. The vote was quite close in all five states. The large states thus contained substantial numbers of opponents as well as supporters of ratification.

2. The vote in three of the smallest states was unanimously for ratification; this supports the theory that most opponents were concentrated in the larger states. New Hampshire and Rhode Island, however, did have close votes—so there were some opponents in smaller states.

3. Only one of the Middle States—New York—ratified after January 1788; only one of the southern states—Georgia—ratified before April 1788. Opinion was most evenly divided in New England.

4. 30 (Pennsylvania: 12 + Massachusetts: 10 + Virginia: 6 + New York: 2)

II. H.

1. Virginia and New York

2. Massachusetts, New York, and Virginia

3. 36

4. Spain

5. two

6. Delaware, New Jersey, Georgia

7. Maryland

8. Pennsylvania, Connecticut, South Carolina, and North Carolina

9. Massachusetts, New Hampshire, Virginia, New York, and Rhode Island

10. three

11. Virginia and Pennsylvania

CHAPTER 10

II. A.

1. True

2. False. It demonstrated the Federalist concession to anti-Federalist fears that a powerful central government would trample individual rights.

3. True

4. True

5. True

6. False. Jefferson favored strict construction and Hamilton favored loose construction.

7. True

8. False. The Federalists opposed the French Revolution, especially in its radical phase.

9. False. Washington was entirely accurate in his assessment that the United States could not compete militarily with the European great powers.

10. False. They vigorously resisted U.S. encroachment, and were overcome only after difficult warfare.

11. True

12. False. The public favored war, and Adams lost popularity by negotiating peace with France.

13. True

14. False. Jeffersonian Republicans believed that common people could be trusted.

15. False. Jeffersonian Republicans sympathized with France, and Hamiltonian Federalists with Britain.

II. B.

1. b

2. a

3. d

4. b

5. c

6. b

7. a

8. a

9. b

10. a

11. b

12. b

13. a

14. c

15. d

II. C.

1. Electoral College

2. vice president

3. secretary of the treasury

4. funding

5. assumption

6. the Bill of Rights

7. political parties

8. French Revolution

9. French-American Alliance

10. Miami Confederacy

11. Jay's Treaty

12. France

13. compact theory

14. nullification

15. Great Britain

II. D.

1. E

2. C

3. M

4. F

5. B

6. H

7. G

8. A

9. O

10. D

11. L

12. J

13. I

14. N

15. K

II. E.

4

5

1

2

3

II. F.

1. C

2. D

3. E

4. B

5. A

6. G

7. I

8. F

9. H

10. J

II. G.

1. The British held frontier posts on American soil. They sold firearms to the Indians. They seized American merchant ships and impressed seamen. (Any two of the above are acceptable.)

2. Adams sent a diplomatic mission to France in 1798. He tried to stop the fighting in the undeclared war by sending a three-man mission in 1800. He negotiated a peace settlement with the French Convention.

    (any two)

3. The Federalists passed (a) the Alien Laws (b) the Sedition Laws. They indicted Jeffersonian editors. They sent Congressman Matthew Lyon to prison.

    (any two)

4. Jefferson secretly wrote the Kentucky Resolution. Madison wrote the Virginia Resolution. The Republicans made the Alien and Sedition Laws major issues in the campaign of 1800.

    (any two)

5. The Jeffersonians advocated small government and little federal spending.

    Jefferson advocated agrarian life and no aid to special interests.

    Jeffersonians were pro-French.

    Federalists advocated strong central government.

    Federalists advocated federal aid to promote private enterprise.

    Federalists were pro-British.

    (any two)

CHAPTER 11

II. A.

1. False. It was a change in political power but not a class revolution.
2. True
3. True
4. False. They tried to impeach Justice Samuel Chase, not Marshall.
5. False. It established judicial review, the right of the Supreme Court to declare legislation unconstitutional.
6. True
7. True
8. False. His deepest doubt was that the purchase might be unconstitutional.
9. True
10. True
11. False. The most explosive issue was the impressment of seamen.
12. True
13. True
14. True
15. False. The war was cause largely by southerner and westerners eager to uphold American rights and seize Canada; New Englanders generally opposed the war.

II. B.

1. c
2. b

3. a
4. b
5. c
6. a
7. c
8. a
9. c
10. b
11. b
12. d
13. b
14. a
15. c

II. C.

1. excise tax
2. pardon
3. midnight judges
4. *Marbury* v. *Madison*
5. judicial review
6. impeachment
7. navy
8. Santo Domingo (Haiti OK)
9. Oregon
10. $15 million
11. *Chesapeake*
12. embargo
13. war hawks
14. Tippecanoe
15. "Mr. Madison's War"

II. D

1. E
2. C
3. O
4. K

5. G

6. L

7. N

8. D

9. M

10. I

11. A

12. H

13. J

14. F

15. B

II. E.

4

1

2

3

5

II. F.

1. E

2. B

3. G

4. J

5. H

6. I

7. A

8. D

9. C

10. F

II. G.

1. 39

2. New York

3. 37

4. Adams: 77; Jefferson: 61. Adams would have been reelected president.

CHAPTER 12

II. A.

1. False. Madison was manipulated by Napoleon.

2. False. They were very concerned about foreign policy.

3. True

4. False. They did not want to acquire Canada at all.

5. False. It was the Navy.

6. False. The strategy was poorly conceived.

7. True

8. False. The victory at New Orleans came after the treaty was signed, and had no effect.

9. False. They were blocked by Republican presidents who had constitutional objections.

10. FalseThe Federalist Pary effectively collapsed and then disappeared during Monroe's presidency.

11. True

12. False. It admitted Missouri as a slave state in exchange for admitting Maine as a free state.

13. True

14. False. Adams acquired Florida but gained only a joint occupation of Oregon.

15. False. It was hardly noticed in Latin America.

II. B.

1. c

2. b

3. c

4. d

5. c

6. b

7. c

8. c

9. a

10. b

11. c

12. d

13. a

14. c

15. b

II. C.

1. Lake Erie
2. "The Star-Spangled Banner"
3. The *Constitution*
4. Hartford Convention
5. White House and Capitol
6. *The North American Review*
7. American Plan
8. Era of Good Feelings
9. Federalists
10. Erie Canal
11. 36° 30′ (Southern boundary of Missouri OK)
12. *McCulloch* v. *Maryland*
13. *Dartmouth College* v. *Woodward*
14. Oregon
15. Monroe Doctrine

II. D.

1. H
2. M
3. N
4. K
5. E
6. L
7. I
8. A
9. D
10. F
11. J
12. B
13. C
14. G
15. O

II. E.

2

5

3

6

4

1

II. F.

1. C

2. O

3. N

4. B

5. A

6. D

7. M

8. I

9. E

10. G

11. J

12. L

13. H

14. K

15. F

II. G.

    a.   Economic nationalism

        The Tariff of 1816

        Clay's American System

    b.   Political nationalism and unity

        President Monroe's tour of New England

        Daniel Webster's speeches

        The election of 1820

    c.   Judicial nationalism

        Dartmouth College v. *Woodward*

    d.   Foreign-policy nationalism

        Andrew Jackson's invasion of Florida

        John Quincy Adam's rejection of Canning's proposed British-American statement

II. H.

1. Lake Erie and Lake Ontario
2. Vermont (north) and Maryland (south)
3. Florida and Arkansas
4. Two: Louisiana and Missouri
5. Only one: Michigan
6. Delaware, Maryland, Virginia, Kentucky, and Missouri
7. The United States
8. Mississippi

CHAPTER 13

II. A.

1. True
2. False. He accepted appointment as secretary of state, fueling charges of a corrupt bargain.
3. True
4. False. Jackson was a wealthy frontier aristocrat, richer than Adams.
5. False. The campaign was marked by mudslinging and personal attacks.
6. True
7. True
8. True
9. False. The opposition was strongest in the South.
10. True
11. True
12. True
13. False. The Whig Party was divided on all these issues.
14. True
15. False. Harrison was an aristocrat, born in luxury in Virgina, not an ordinary frontier farmer.

II. B.

1. d
2. b
3. c
4. b
5. a
6. d

7.   b

8.   a

9.   a

10. d

11. d

12. a

13. d

14. b

15. c

II. C.

1.   conventions

2.   Anti-Masonic Party

3.   "corrupt bargain"

4.   secretary of state

5.   rotation in office (or spoils system)

6.   Tariff of Abominations

7.   nullification

8.   Bank of the United States

9.   masons

10. evangelicals

11. Cherokees, Chickasaws, Choctaws, Creeks, Seminoles (any two)

12. Trail of Tears

13. Mexico

14. Whigs

15. Log cabin and hard cider

II. D.

1.   F

2.   K

3.   M

4.   A

5.   N

6.   I

7.   H

8.   D

9.   C
10. E
11. L
12. O
13. J
14. G
15. B

II. E.

2

1

5

4

3

II. F.

1.   F
2.   H
3.   A
4.   E
5.   C
6.   I
7.   B
8.   J
9.   D
10. G

II. G.

1.   The bank is an overgrown and "sick" monster, served by Nicholas Biddle and Whig politicians.

2.   The enormous "monster" is vomiting up the money it has swallowed. Biddle is trying to help and rescue it while standing astride it. Clay, Webster, and Calhoun are trying to remain distant from the "illness," even while offering advice. Jackson looks on in scorn.

3.   Clay is in effect physically assaulting the innocent Jackson, trying to "shut him up." Jackson is resisting, and it clear that Clay will not succeed.

4.   The hickory leaf, Jackson's top hat, the Democratic donkey, Jackson's face on the coin. (any three)

5. "Humbug Glory" Bank; "Six cents in mint drops or glory"; "In seven months this bank shall be abolished"; The signatures on the currency: "Cunning Reuben" and "Honest Amos." (other answers possible)

II. H.

1. 32 (131 votes needed for majority)

2. New York, New Jersey, Delaware, Maryland

3. Pennsylvania

4. New York and Maine

5. Seminoles and Creeks; Cherokees

6. Rio Grande and Nueces; straight east

CHAPTER 14

II. A.

1. True

2. False. It contributed to the rise of nativism and anti-Catholicism.

3. False. Most manufacturing was concentrated in New England.

4. True.

5. False. Most early factory jobs involved long hours and low wages.

6. True

7. True

8. False. Canals were cheaper and more effective than highways.

9. True

10. False. The early railroads were dangerous and met much opposition, especially from canal interests.

11. True

12. False. Most women remained outside the market economy, in the home.

13. False. The transcontinental and transatlantic telegraphs were not *permanently* laid until after the Civil War.

14. False. There was an increase in the gap between rich and poor as a result of advances in manufacturing and transportation.

15. True

II. B.

1. a

2. c

3. b

4. a

5. d

6. c

7. b

8. a

9. a

10. d

11. d

12. c

13. a

14. d

15. d

II. C.

1. Ireland

2. Ancient Order of Hibernians

3. Forty-Eighters

4. Know-Nothings (nativists OK)

5. industrial revolution

6. cotton gin

7. limited liability

8. telegraph

9. women and children

10. labor unions

11. mechanical reaper

12. National Road (Cumberland Road)

13. steamboat

14. Erie Canal

15. clipper ships

II. D.

1. F

2. J

3. C

4. G

5. D

6. K

7. A

8. H

9. E

10. I

11. B

II. E.

4

1

5

3

2

II. F.

1. D

2. A

3. E

4. I

5. H

6. G

7. C

8. B

9. F

10. J

II. G.

1. 1850–1860

2. 1810–1820

3. 1850

4. over three times larger

II. H.

1. five

2. iron works

3. Virginia or North Carolina

4. Erie Canal, Wabash and Erie Canal, and Lake Erie

5. Pennsylvania Canal, Ohio River, Ohio and Erie Canal

6. none

7. Ohio, Illinois, and Indiana

8. Santa Fe Trail and Spanish Trail

CHAPTER 15

II. A.

1. True

2. False. They tended to increase sectional, denominational, and class division.

3. True

4. True

5. False. Despite women's gains, most of higher education remained in exclusively male hands.

6. True

7. True

8. True

9. True

10. True

11. False. It came in the aftermath of the War of 1812.

12. True

13. False. The reverse is true. Emerson emphasized self-improvement and scholarship; Thoreau emphasized simple living and nonviolence.

14. True

15. False. Most came from New England.

II. B.

1. c

2. d

3. c

4. c

5. c

6. d

7. a

8. b

9. c

10. a

11. c

12. a

13. b

14. c

15. a

II. C.

1. Deism

2. Second Great Awakening

3. Methodists, Baptists

4. Mormons

5. Seneca Falls Convention

6. New Harmony

7. Brook Farm

8. Monticello

9. Knickerbocker group

10. Transcendentalism

11. civil disobedience

12. *Leaves of Grass*

13. *The Scarlet Letter*

14. *Moby Dick*

15. *Little Women*

II. D.

1. J

2. C

3. L

4. O

5. K

6. D

7. G

8. A

9. F

10. M

11. N

12. H

13. B

14. I

15. E

II. E.

3

4

5

1

2

II. F.

1. H
2. G
3. I
4. E
5. C
6. A
7. J
8. B
9. F
10. D

II. G.

1. That it was absurd, obscene, and indecent.

2. That he was expressing his own feelings and not aiming for public popularity.

3. Whitman emphasizes his own individual voice, and looks for approval in the future rather than in past tradition or convention.

4. His view that the new world is superior to the old world of the past, which must be left behind.

CHAPTER 16

II. A.

1. True

2. True

3. False. It was economically inefficient and agriculturally destructive of the soil.

4. False. Most slaveowners owned fewer than ten slaves.

5. True

6. True

7. True

8. False. Free blacks had an extremely vulnerable status and were generally poor.

9. True

10. False. The black family under slavery was generally strong, and most slave children were raised in two-parent homes.

11. True

12. False. Douglass opposed Garrison's moral absolutism, and believed that political organization was the best way to end slavery.

13. True

14. True

15. True

II. B.

1. d
2. c
3. a
4. b
5. c
6. c
7. d
8. c
9. c
10. b
11. a
12. c
13. d
14. c
15. a

II. C.

1. Cotton Kingdom
2. lords of the loom
3. Sir Walter Scott
4. free blacks
5. *American Slavery As It Is*
6. black belt
7. American Colonization Society
8. Lane Rebels

9. *The Liberator*
10. American Anti-Slavery Society
11. gag resolution
12. free-soilers

II. D.

1. H
2. F
3. B
4. L
5. O
6. A
7. C
8. E
9. N
10. D
11. I
12. M
13. G
14. J
15. K

II. E.

2
4
3
1
5

II. F.

1. G
2. I
3. B
4. A
5. E
6. F
7. H

8.   C

9.   J

10. D

II. G.

1.

    a.   Cotton Kingdom on his shoulders

    b.   *The Cruelty of Slavery*: the net and slave collar

    c.   *A Slave Auction*: the whips and harsh faces of the traders; the seated positions of the slaves

    d.   *"Am I Not a Man and a Brother?"*: the chains and kneeling posture of the slaves (other answers possible)

2.

    a.   Harvesting Cotton

    b.   Plantation Kitchen

    c.   A Two-Way Proslavery Cartoon

    d.   the prosperity and fine dress of the slaves

    e.   the pleasantness of the kitchen workplace

    f.   the slave's leisured enjoyment of fishing (other answers possible)

3.   Proslavery advocates might note the closeness of a black nurse and a white child, and the willingness to trust slaves with white children. Antislavery advocates might note the dependence of whites on blacks even for such tasks as child rearing and nursing.

II. H.

1.   Georgia, Alabama, Mississippi, Tennessee, Arkansas, Louisiana

2.   7,900 families

3.   Virginia, South Carolina, Georgia, Mississippi, Louisiana

4.   Missouri, Arkansas, Kentucky, Virginia, North Carolina, Tennessee

CHAPTER 17

II. A.

1.   False. Tyler turned away from the Whig policies of Clay and Webster.

2.   False. Anglo-American hostility remained strong.

3.   True

4.   True

5.   True

6.   True

7.   True

8. True

9. FalsePolk always wanted to acquired California. The Mexican population there was small.

10. False. It was a dispute over the southern boundary of Texas.

11. True

12. True

13. False. It gave the United States very large territorial gains.

14. True

15. False. It forced the slavery controversy to the center of national politics.

II. B.

1. b
2. a
3. b
4. d
5. a
6. c
7. d
8. a
9. a
10. c
11. b
12. c
13. d
14. c
15. b

II. C.

1. Canada
2. Maine
3. Britain
4. "Conscience Whigs"
5. joint resolution
6. 54° 40'
7. Oregon Trail
8. Manifest Destiny
9. Liberty party

10. 49° (49th parallel)

11. California

12. Nueces River

13. "spot resolutions"

14. Treaty of Guadalupe Hidalgo

15. Wilmot Proviso

II. D.

1. O

2. C

3. H

4. E

5. J

6. N

7. M

8. G

9. A

10. F

11. K

12. B

13. I

14. D

15. L

II. E.

3

1

5

4

2

II. F.

1. E

2. G

3. D

4. J

5. I

6. H

7. C

8. B

9. A

10. F

II. G.

1. Matamoros

2. Santa Fe

3. From New Orleans. They went to the east and west coats of Mexico, up to California. They were involved in battles at Matamoros, Vera Cruz, San Diego, Monterey, and San Francisco.

4. Across unorganized Louisiana territory, Texas, and northern Mexico. Kearny fought in the battles of Santa Fe and San Diego; Frémont at Sonoma.

II. H.

1. Quebec and New Brunswick

2. Columbia River and the forty-ninth parallel

3. 12°40′

4. Rio Grande, Gila, and the Colorado

5. three of the following: Matamoros, Monterey, Vera Cruz, and Mexico City

CHAPTER 18

II. A.

1. True

2. False. The Free Soil party consisted of diverse interests that were united only by their opposition to slavery expansion.

3. False. The gold rush forced new attention to the question of slavery in the territory acquired from Mexico.

4. True

5. False. Clay and Webster defended sectional compromise; Calhoun defended sectional (southern) interests.

6. False. California was admitted as a free state. New Mexico and Utah were territories left open to popular sovereignty concerning slavery.

7. True

8. False. The North was the greatest winner.

9. True

10. True

11. False Cushing effectively aligned the United States with European imperialism in China.

12. True

13. False. The southerners voted in favor of the plan and pushed it through Congress.

14. True

15. True

II. B.

1. c

2. c

3. d

4. c

5. c

6. b

7. b

8. a

9. b

10. a

11. c

12. a

13. c

14. b

15. c

II. C.

1. fire-eaters

2. popular sovereignty

3. Mason-Dixon line

4. Underground Railroad

5. higher law

6. Fugitive Slave Law

7. Free Soil party

8. Compromise of 1850

9. Whigs

10. Clayton-Bulwer Treaty

11. Ostend Manifesto

12. Gadsden Purchase

13. Missouri Compromise
14. Democratic party
15. Republican party

II. D.
1. B
2. H
3. O
4. J
5. D
6. N
7. L
8. M
9. C
10. G
11. F
12. A
13. I
14. K
15. E

II. E.
3
1
2
5
4

II. F.
1. G
2. D
3. J
4. A
5. E
6. H
7. B
8. F

9. I

10. C

II. G.

1. cause: Mexican War; effect: Acquisition of California

2. cause: California's gold rush; effect: California's admission to the union

3. cause: death of Taylor; effect: passage of Compromise of 1850

4. cause: northern aid to fugitive slaves; effect: Fugitive Slave Law

5. cause: election of 1852; effect: disappearance of Whig party

6. cause: Compromise of 1850; effect: southern "filibuster" ventures

7. cause: plans for southern railroad; effect: Gadsden Purchase

8. cause: Douglas's railroad plans; effect: Kansas-Nebraska Act

9. cause: Ostend Manifesto; effect: end of Pierce administration's Cuba schemes

10. cause: Kansas-Nebraska Act; effect: rise of Republican party

II. H.

1. Wyoming, New Mexico, Oklahoma, Colorado, and Kansas

2. California

3. Utah

4. two: Oregon and Minnesota

5. Honduras and Nicaragua

6. Colombia (New Granada)

7. El Paso and Houston

8. Nebraska

9. slavery existed in Missouri

10. yes

CHAPTER 19

II. A.

1. True

2. False. Few proslavery people brought slaves with them to Kansas.

3. True

4. False. Douglas's opposition to the Lecompton Constitution divided the Democrats.

5. True

6. True

7. False. The Dred Scott decision held that slavery could not be prohibited in a territory because slaves were property protected by the Constitution.

8. True

9. False. Douglas adhered to popular sovereignty despite Lincoln's criticism.

10. True

11. False. It was southern delegates who walked out when northern Democrats nominated Douglas.

12. True

13. False. Lincoln obtained a only a minority of the popular vote despite his majority in the Electoral College.

14. True

15. False. Lincoln rejected the Crittenden Compromise.

II. B.

1. a
2. c
3. d
4. d
5. a
6. b
7. c
8. c
9. a
10. b
11. b
12. c
13. a
14. b
15. b

II. C.

1. *Uncle Tom's Cabin*
2. *The Impending Crisis of the South*
3. Beecher's Bibles
4. "Bleeding Kansas"
5. Lecompton Constitution
6. Know-Nothing party (American Party OK)
7. Dred Scott case

8. Panic of 1857
9. Lincoln-Douglas debates
10. Constitutional Union party
11. South Carolina
12. Confederate States of America
13. Crittenden Compromise
14. election of 1860
15. "lame-duck" period

II. D.

1. E
2. G
3. O
4. F
5. N
6. K
7. A
8. J
9. C
10. L
11. B
12. H
13. M
14. I
15. D

II. E.

3

2

4

5

1

6

II. F.

1. I
2. J

3.   H

4.   G

5.   D

6.   C

7.   B

8.   A

9.   F

10.   E

II. G.

1.

    a.   Lincoln says that blacks are equal in natural rights of life, liberty, and pursuit of happiness, and in the right to earn their living; he says that whites are superior in moral and intellectual endowment.

    b.   He is refuting a charge by Douglas that he is in favor of complete racial equality.

2.

    a.   Brown means that his cause of abolishing slavery will be advanced by his death.

    b.   Brown knows that the abolitionists will make him a martyr after his execution.

3.

    a.   Greeley admits that a right to secession exists, and he does not think that the republic can be held together only by bayonets.

    b.   Fear of the war that will likely come if the South is not allowed to secede peacefully.

4.

    a.   Hammond suggests that the North is too weak to survive without the South.

    b.   The confidence in southern independence expressed by Hammond leaves no reason to compromise with the North.

5.

    a.   The South is like a colony held by the "empire" of the U.S. government.

    b.   That it recognize southern independence in order to weaken the United States.

6.

    a.   The description of Chloe ironing and folding clothes; the children asleep in their bed.

    b.   Chloe is a caring mother and wife; Tom is gentle and pious, full of warm feelings for his family.

    c.   In the first excerpt, Tom has a New Testament Bible open on his knee; in the second, he declares that his "soul" has been "bought and paid for"—a statement of religious doctrine.

II. H.

1.   fifty-two

2.   Pennsylvania, Indiana, Illinois, and California

3.   Ohio, Indiana, Illinois, Missouri, and California

4.   Maryland, Virginia, Kentucky, Tennessee, and North Carolina

5.   Missouri

6.   California

7.   Maine, Massachusetts, New Hampshire, Vermont, Connecticut, and Rhode Island

8.   Georgia, Alabama, Tennessee, and Virginia

9.   Arkansas, North Carolina, and South Carolina

10.   Georgia and Florida

CHAPTER 20

II. A.

1.   False. Four more states seceded after his inauguration.

2.   True

3.   True

4.   False. The South had superior military leadership, while the North struggled to find commanders.

5.   True

6.   True

7.   True

8.   False. The British permitted the *Alabama* to leave their ports.

9.   True

10.   True

11.   False. The Civil War draft was unfair to poor citizens, who could not afford substitutes.

12.   False. Congress approved Lincoln's acts.

13.   True

14.   True

15.   False. The Northern civilian economy prospered during the war.

II. B.

1.   d

2.   d

3.   b

4.   a

5.   c

6.   b

7.   a

8.   c

9.   b

10. b

11. c

12. b

13. a

14. b

15. b

II. C.

1.   Maryland, Delaware, Kentucky, Missouri (West Virginia also possible)

2.   (naval) blockade

3.   *Trent*

4.   *Alabama*

5.   Laird rams

6.   draft

7.   "bounty jumpers"

8.   nursing

9.   National Banking System

10. "shoddy millionaires"

11. writ of *habeus corpus*

12. United States Sanitary Commission

II. D.

1.   F

2.   A

3.   G

4.   B

5.   I

6.   E

7.   C

8.   D

9.   J

10. H

II. E.

4

5

1

2

3

II. F.

1. C

2. F

3. G

4. B

5. D

6. H

7. E

8. A

9. I

10. J

II. G.

1.

a. The South and New England had about the same number of manufacturers; but New England's businesses were much larger in terms of capital, number of laborers, and product value.

b. South: about five laborers per business; New England: about twenty laborers per business; Middle States: about ten laborers per business.

2.

a. Ireland

b. Germany

c. Germany

d. It remained steady in the first year of the war (1861–1862), rose considerably in the second year (1862–1863), increased slightly in the third year (1863–1864). Britain: 1863; Ireland: 1863; Germany: 1864.

3.

a. From March 1862 to January 1863

b. July 1861: 3:2 (Union to Confederate); March 1862: 3:2; January 1863: 2:1; January 1865: 2:1

c. It remained steady (about 2:1) from January 1863 to January 1865.

CHAPTER 21

II. A.

1. False. The Battle of Bull Run made the *North* expect a longer war.

2. True

3. False. The Union first succeeded in the West.

4. True

5. False. The turn to a war against slavery cost Lincoln popularity.

6. False. Black soldiers were militarily effective.

7. True

8. True

9. True

10. True

11. True

12. False. Lee lost a higher percentage of his soldiers than Grant, and it was he who turned the war into a struggle of bloody attrition.

13. True

14. True

15. False. The war settled all those issues.

II. B.

1. b

2. d

3. a

4. a

5. d

6. b

7. b

8. a

9. c

10. a

11. a

12. b

13. d

14. c

15. b

II. C.

1. First Battle of Bull Run
2. Peninsula campaign
3. Battle of Antietam
4. Emancipation Proclamation
5. "Unconditional Surrender"
6. Vicksburg
7. Gettysburg
8. Fort Pillow
9. Copperheads
10. *The Man Without a Country*
11. Atlanta
12. Union party
13. Ford's Theater
14. Appomattox Court House
15. "The Lost Cause"

II. D.

1. O
2. N
3. F
4. H
5. A
6. B
7. K
8. E
9. D
10. C
11. M
12. I
13. G
14. L
15. J

II. E.

3

1

2

5

4

II. F.

1.   D

2.   J

3.   C

4.   B

5.   I

6.   A

7.   F

8.   H

9.   G

10.   E

II. G.

1.   The Union officer is in a new uniform; the two Confederates are in worn uniforms; the Southern civilians are not in uniform. The North thus seems prosperous and unharmed by the war; the South is suffering from its defeat. Northern civilians are not present, and thus not much affected. The crushed Southern civilians are also under Northern military rule.

2.   The Northern officer is upright—confident and in control. The Southerners are beaten (hands folded or in pockets) but still defiant.

3.   Most of the Southerners are unarmed, with weapons on the ground. The Northerner has sheathed his sword; but one Southerner retains his rifle, suggesting possible future violence. Homer seems to suggest that the two sides are connected, but still hostile and wary of one another.

II. H.

1.   Alabama and Florida

2.   Missouri, Tennessee, West Virginia, Maryland

3.   Kentucky, Delaware

4.   Tennessee, Cumberland, Mississippi

5.   Charleston

6.   Cold Harbor

CHAPTER 22

II. A.

1.   True

2.   False. White Southerners strongly rejected Northern political domination.

3.   True

4.   True

5.   True

6.   False. Johnson had been a poor white who opposed the planter elite.

7.   True

8.   False. It weakened the moderates and strengthened the radicals.

9.   True

10.   False. Redistribution of land was opposed by moderates and never became part of reconstruction policy.

11.   False. Blacks controlled only one house of one state legislature—South Carolina.

12.   True

13.   False. The Klan was organized primarily because of resentment over blacks' growing political power.

14.   True

15.   False. The moderate plan failed to deal with the deeper economic and social aftermath of slavery.

II. B.

1.   c

2.   c

3.   b

4.   b

5.   c

6.   a

7.   a

8.   c

9.   c

10.   b

11.   c

12.   c

13.   a

14.   b

15.   d

II. C.

1.   freedmen

2.   Freedmen's Bureau

3.   Baptist

4.   10 percent plan

5.   Thirteenth Amendment

6.   Black Codes

7.   Fourteenth Amendment

8.   moderates

9.   radicals

10. Union League

11. *Ex parte Milligan*

12. scalawags

13. carpetbaggers

14. Fifteenth Amendment

15. Alaska

II. D.

1.   H

2.   K

3.   C

4.   M

5.   B

6.   J

7.   O

8.   I

9.   F

10. G

11. E

12. A

13. L

14. N

15. D

II. E.

4

1

5

3

2

II. F.

1. D
2. E
3. J
4. C
5. I
6. F
7. H
8. B
9. A
10. G

II. G.

1. Eight whites, three blacks; the white woman seated in the center; they are in the rear and partly hidden, suggesting that they might hold subordinate positions on the staff.

2. The shabby clothes of the boy and young woman; the crude log cabin dwelling. The people seem weary but hopeful: at least three of them have partial smiles.

3. The men in the line appear to be working people—perhaps farmers in their best clothes. The voting officials, black and white, appear more affluent and well-dressed. The drawing shows the new voters as somewhat hesitant and uncertain, perhaps being manipulated by the more politically knowledgeable officials.